A State Within a State

Recent Titles in
Contributions in Labor Studies

The Fictitious Commodity: A Study of the U.S. Labor Market, 1880-1940
Ton Korver

The Re-education of the American Working Class
Steven H. London, Elvira R. Tarr, and Joseph F. Wilson, editors

New Trends in Employment Practices
Walter Galenson

Order Against Chaos: Business Culture and Labor Ideology in America,
1880-1915
Sarah Lyons Watts

The Emancipation of Labor: A History of the First International
Kenryk Katz

The Unsettled Relationship: Labor Migration and Economic Development
Demetrios G. Papademetriou and Philip L. Martin, editors

Workers' Participative Schemes: The Experience of Capitalist and
Plan-based Societies
Helen A. Tsiganou

''Parish-Fed Bastards'': A History of the Politics of the Unemployed in
Britain, 1884-1939
Richard Flanagan

The Social Dimension of 1992: Europe Faces a New EC
Beverly Springer

Farewell to the Self-Employed: Deconstructing a Socioeconomic and
Legal Solipsism
Marc Linder

Trade Unionism and Industrial Relations in the Commonwealth Caribbean:
History, Contemporary Practice and Prospect
Lawrence A. Nurse

Eastern's Armageddon
Martha Dunagin Saunders

A STATE WITHIN A STATE

Industrial Relations In Israel, 1965–1987

Ran Chermesh

Contributions in Labor Studies, Number 43

Greenwood Press
WESTPORT, CONNECTICUT • LONDON

HD
5412.2
A6
C47
1992

Library of Congress Cataloging-in-Publication Data

Chermesh, Ran.
  A state within a state : industrial relations in Israel, 1965-1987
/ Ran Chermesh.
    p. cm.—(Contributions in labor studies, ISSN 0886-8239 ;
no. 43)
  Includes bibliographical references and index.
  ISBN 0-313-28547-0 (alk. paper)
  1. Strikes and lockouts—Israel. 2. Industrial relations—Israel.
3. Histadrut ha-kelalit shel ha-'ovdim be-Erets-Yiśra'el.
I. Title. II. Series.
HD5412.2.A6C47 1993
331'.095694'09045—dc20   92-9264

British Library Cataloguing in Publication Data is available.

Library of Congress Catalog Card Number: 92-9264
ISBN: 0-313-28547-0
ISSN: 0886-8239

First published in 1993

Greenwood Press, 88 Post Road West, Westport, CT 06881
An imprint of Greenwood Publishing Group, Inc.

Printed in the United States of America

The paper used in this book complies with the
Permanent Paper Standard issued by the National
Information Standards Organization (Z39.48-1984).

10 9 8 7 6 5 4 3 2 1

Copyright Acknowledgments

The author and publisher gratefully acknowledge permission to
reprint from the following sources:

The figure on page 231 from *The Impact of Strikes* by N. W.
Chamberlain and J. M. Schilling. Copyright © 1954 by Harper &
Row, Publishers, Inc. Reprinted by permission of HarperCollins
Publishers.

Portions of chapters 6, 7, and 8 from *Israel Social Science Research*,
Ben-Gurion University.

Contents

Tables and Figures   *vii*

Acknowledgements   *xi*

1. General Introduction   1

    Systems and Industrial Relations Systems   4

    The Israeli irs   8

    Israeli irs as an Autonomous irs   15

    Unstated Assumptions of the Israeli irs   16

    Changes in the Functioning of the Israeli irs   18

2. The Israeli irs   31

3. The New Economic Policy and the Autonomy of the Israeli irs   49

4. Strike Management: Norm and Practice   57

    The Workers' Committees Charter   61

5. Strikes in an Action Framework: Israeli Strikes and Their Context   85

    Strike Patterns—A General View   87

    Strikes in Israel since it gained independence (1948 – 1987)   92

    Who Are the Strikers?   97

    The Context—Sector of Ownership and Economic Branch   113

    The Process—What, Why, How, and What For?   120

6. Strikes and irs Autonomy: A Hierarchical Multi-Level Model and Its Demonstration on Israeli Data   141

    The Israeli Situation: Some Structural Characteristics 146

    Israeli Strike Statistics: Some Relevant Data   147

    Methodology   148

    Conclusion   164

7. **Strikes as Social Problems: A Social Problem Matrix Approach** 169

   The Israeli irs 171

   Strikes in Israel 174

   Strikes in Israel—A Social Problem Matrix Analysis 179

   Strikes in Israel—A Macro Social Analysis 186

   Intermediate Conclusions: Strikes in Israel in the Labor
   Dominated Period—The Social Problem Matrix 189

   Strikes in Israel in the Post Labor Dominated Period—A Quasi-
   Social Problem Matrix Analysis 193

8. **Strikes: The Issue of Social Responsibility** 217

   The Model 218

   Method 221

   Results 222

   Strike Damage: Level, Category-specific and Changes over Time 226

9. **Epilogue** 233

   The Three Sub-Periods: Labor, Likud and National Unity
   Governments 236

Appendix: Three-Dimensional Diagrams Corresponding to Tables in
   Chapter 5 243

References 273

Index 279

Tables and Figures

Tables

Chapter 2

2.1: Main actors in the Israeli irs by level and ownership sector. 32
2.2: Hevrat ha'Ovdim: Some economic indicators (1982) (Percentages). 36

Chapter 4

4.1: Strike-related procedures: Their sources and institutional status. 64
4.2: Steps implemented by strike initiators. 66
4.3: Histadrut approval of a meeting sought by level of irs. 67
4.4: Meeting convened with consent of the workers' council. 68
4.5: Percentage of strikes approved by the Histadrut (by secretary general and ruling party). 71
4.6: Percentage of strikes approved by the Histadrut (by secretary general and ruling party) – Analysis of variance. 72
4.7: Labor relations officer notified of planned strike (by secretary general and ruling party). 74
4.8: Reporting of the strike to employer by level of irs. 75
4.9: Reporting of the strike to labor relations officer by level of irs. 76
4.10: Notification of labor relations officer by strike initiator. 77
4.11: Conformity profile by Histadrut approval. 79

Chapter 5

5.1: Strike patterns by the dominant party and the identity of the secretary general of the Histadrut 1965-87. 88
5.2: Israeli strike statistics: Duration of one day or more. 93
5.3: Israeli strike statistics: Duration of two hours or more. 94
5.4: Strike measures and time correlation coefficients for two strike data sources. 95
5.5: Summary strike pattern features for strikers' union and period. 98
5.6: Summary strike pattern features for union type and period. 106

5.7:   Summary strike pattern features for occupation and period.   109

5.8:   Summary strike pattern features for union declaring strike and
        period.   112

5.9:   Strike frequency by economic branch and period.   115

5.10:   Summary strike pattern features for sector and period.   116

5.11:   Number of working-time meetings and warning strikes per 1,000
        days by period and ownership sector.   123

5.12:   Summary strike pattern features for type of strike and period.   125

5.13:   Frequency of strikes by reported cause and period.   127

5.14:   Summary strike pattern features for strike approval and period.   129

5.15:   Summary strike pattern features for collapsed external
        involvement and period.   131

5.16:   Summary strike pattern features for strike outcomes and period.   133

5.17:   Strike frequency by secretary general of the Histadrut and ruling
        party: multiple classification analysis.   136

Chapter 6

6.1:   Number of strikers and the number of salaried workers by
        ownership sector and industrial branch (Israel, 1965-83).   148

6.2:   Strike frequency by Knesset and election-time category.   149

6.3:   Strike frequency and strike frequency per 100 days by election
        period and ruling party.   150

6.4:   Strike activity in Israel: Comparison of various models.   154

6.5:   Israeli strike pattern characteristics by the identity of the secretary
        general of the Histadrut.   158

6.6:   The frequency of strikes and its prediction: economic, political and
        industrial relations variables as predictors by the dominant party
        and the secretary general of the Histadrut.   159

6.7:   A comparison between the determinants of strike frequency
        during the Labor (1965-77), Likud (1977-84), and National
        Unity administrations (1984-87).   161

Chapter 7

7.1:   Degree of authority granted to local managements and local
        unions (self-descriptions).   172

7.2:   Degree of authority imputed to local managements and local
        unions (counterpart descriptions).   172

7.3:   Strike activity levels rank order of 16 countries (Averages
        for 1974-76).   176

7.4   Strikes in Israel by approval status and the degree of success
        (Average for 1974-77).   177

7.5: Strike activity by economic branch (Average for 1974-77). 178

7.6: Attitude toward industrial relations by level and actor. 180

7.7: The social problem matrix strikes in Israel, 1965–77. 190

7.8: The economic branch sensitivity of strikes for government and Histadrut (by dominant party in government). 201

7.9: The sector sensitivity of strikes for government. 201

7.10: Strike approval by ruling party. 201

7.11: Strikes called prior to expiration of contract by dominant party in government. 202

7.12: Follow-up treatment after strike (by dominant party in gov't). 204

7.13: The sector sensitivity of strikes for the Histadrut. 204

7.14: The propensity to call lockouts (by dominant party in gov't). 205

7.15: Causes of strikes (by dominant party in government). 207

7.16: The sector sensitivity of strikes for the private sector (by dominant party in gov't.) 207

7.17: Approval of strikes by an authoritative union (by private sector ranking and dominant party in government). 208

7.18: Was labor relations officer notified about the impending strike (by dominant party in government). 209

7.19: Strikes by their outcomes (by dominant party in government, instrumental strikes only). 211

7.20: Type of strike by dominant party in government. 211

Chapter 8

8.1: Indicators regarding management officials' sensitivity to the damage of a strike in their place of work. 224

8.2: Indicators regarding union representatives' sensitivity to the damage of a strike in their place of work. 225

8.3: Average damage of strikes and strike threats on different categories by interview wave—Management officials' estimates. 227

8.4: Average damage of strikes and strike threats on different categories by interview wave—Labor representatives' estimation. 228

Figures

5.1: Strike pattern characteristics of union types by period. 108

6.1: A hierarchical model of Dunlop's industrial relations system. 144

8.1: A concentric model of strike damage. 219

Acknowledgements

This book sums up a long-term interest in understanding Israeli industrial relations. My interest in the field started with my first research appointment in
the Institute for Economic and Social Research (IESR). I would never have
been able to take this first step without the firm support of Professor Rivka.
Bar-Yossef of the Sociology Department of the Hebrew University of
Jerusalem. Her wit led me to decline any explanation unless supported by
data. Professor Arie Shirom of the Labor Studies Department of Tel-Aviv
University is to be thanked for his collegiality and continuous interest in my
work and in the Labor Studies field. My friends in the IESR were always
available for any need and their data were an essential asset for the current
study. I owe a special thanks to the Chief Labor Officer, Advocate Nachman
Ori, and to the Head of the Institute for the Advancement of Labor Relations,
Dr. Ozer Karmi. Their personal integrity is a safeguard for the promotion of
research in the field.

I thank my friends in the Behavioral Sciences Department of Ben-Gurion
University of the Negev for their interest and goodwill.

This book would have had an altogether different shape without the de-
votion of my editor, Amiel Schotz, also of B.G.U. His critical reading was
invaluable. Camera-ready copy was prepared by "WordByte" of Beer-Sheva.

And finally, my father, wife, and children, have all been keen to see the
results of my work; all have given me encouragement, have played their part
in my efforts, and have their share in the satisfaction of its completion.

A State Within a State

1

General Introduction

Introduction

This book describes and analyses strikes in Israel between the years 1965 and 1987. During these twenty-three years Israel underwent many important developments. First came the Six Day War (1967) which created a larger Israel, extending its control from the Jordan River in the east to the Mediterranean Sea in the west, from the Golan Heights in the north to the Suez Canal in the south. Then came the Yom Kippur War (1973), which demonstrated some of the limitations of the achievements gained during the 1967 war. The territorial buffers that had been established between Israel and its neighbors were not an absolute warranty against a dangerous enemy assault.

In 1977 there was a major development in the political arena. The Labor Alignment lost its position as the leading party group, and the Likud took over the government. This was the single most important internal political event since the declaration of independence in 1948. Following this political upheaval, Anwar Sadat, the Egyptian president, visited Jerusalem. Peace between Israel and its neighbors seemed closer than had ever been imagined.

However, a few years later, in 1982, Israel embarked on a military campaign in Lebanon, a campaign that gave rise to wide internal dissension. At the same time, an economic crisis brought the Israeli economy to the verge of hyper inflation. The failures of the Likud government almost cost it the 1984 general election. A deadlock in the *Knesset*, the Israeli parliament, forced the two major opposing parties to form a "national unity" government, with a rotation agreement for the position of prime minister. Shimon Peres (Labor) served for the first two years, with Yitzhak Shamir (Likud) taking over for the following two years. The impasse in the political sphere was not overcome in the 1988 elections. Perforce, a second national unity government was formed, this time with the Likud somewhat strengthened. However, since the tenure of the second national unity government is beyond the scope of this work, further description is unwarranted.

The developments in the industrial relations (IR) arena during this period are also noteworthy. Since the *Histadrut*, the General Federation of Labor, is the dominant actor in this domain, it will be the focus of this introductory discussion. The Histadrut and the state share many common characteristics. Both are comprehensive democratic entities. In both, elections are held every four years. Both have adopted a relative, party list system of elections. Most

Israeli parties take part in both state and Histadrut elections. A high percentage of voters in general elections vote in Histadrut elections, although individual voting decisions are not necessarily the same—not all voters act the same in these two arenas. This explains why the Likud formed the state coalition in 1977, while Labor managed to hold onto its majority in the Histadrut. This brief survey is given in an expanded form later in this chapter, but is provided here for the sake of clarity.

Four different secretary generals held this position in the Histadrut during the period under discussion. First was Aharon Becker (1962-69), a veteran functionary in the trade union field and a devoted member of the Labor Party. His last five years in office, those covered by the present work, were years of uneasiness in the Histadrut. First came the introduction of a new grading system for positions in the public sector (1965-66). This reform, which was long overdue, followed the recommendations of a public committee headed by David Hurowits, the Chancellor of the Bank of Israel. The implementation of the recommendations led to a record number of strikes.

Then came an economic recession (1966-67). This half-planned half–self-inflicted crisis brought the Israeli economy to its lowest point since the early 1950s. The Six Day War (1967) then turned the Israeli economy around. Heavy investments were made in defense, and a large reservoir of unskilled workers became available from the occupied territories. The West Bank and the Gaza Strip became a natural market for Israeli products. The feelings of military self-confidence and material affluence served as fertile ground for raising standards of living. A sense of the need for change in the Histadrut was in the air.

In 1969, the Labor Party, searching for an agent of change, selected Yitzhak Ben-Aharon, a kibbutz member, pronounced ideologue, eloquent speaker, and an independent public figure, as its candidate for the post of secretary general of the Histadrut. Ben-Aharon served one turbulent term (1969-73). These years were fertile in ideas, but meager in accomplishments. His inspiration surpassed reality. The democratic rhetoric worried both Histadrut functionaries and party leaders. Ben-Aharon tried to nourish authentic grass-roots leaders, and to bypass formal Histadrut bureaucracy. No wonder, that he gained the support of many local union leaders, but was completely isolated both in his own party and in the Histadrut.

When his first term ended the Labor Party entered elections without committing itself to a specified candidate for the next secretary general. Ben-Aharon gained a modest victory while receiving only lip service and perfunctory help from his own party, and failed to convince it that he was indispensable. The party looked for an attractive substitute. Yeruham Meshel, the head of the Trade Union Division in Becker's time, the main opponent of Ben-Aharon[1] and the strong man of the Histadrut establishment, finally took office (1972).

Meshel, an experienced trade unionist subsequently headed the Histadrut for a lengthy eleven-year period. The Histadrut of his days lacked the rhetoric of Ben-Aharon's period, but managed to cope with uniquely hard times. Meshel was the first secretary general of the Histadrut to face an adversary government. He was confronted with the necessity of making an unprecedented decision, whether to cooperate with his own party or with the legal government of Israel. The fact that he served under a Likud-dominated government opened new paths for the Histadrut, leading to a major leap towards an autonomous industrial relations system (irs).[2] The Histadrut was no longer expected to serve as the standard-bearer of a national liberation movement. A redefinition of its identity as a General Federation of Labor was necessary.

The next secretary general was Israel Kessar of the Labor Alignment (1984). Kessar, a witty, veteran Histadrut functionary, a Yemenite and with a master's degree in Labor Studies from Tel-Aviv University, was chosen by Meshel as his successor. He gained, however, the support of both Becker and Ben-Aharon. For a short period before elections were held, Kessar served as secretary general under the approval of Histadrut convention. Shortly afterwards he ran for office in a Histadrut general election. He preferred to carry out a personal-style election campaign. This way he gained office with little commitments to his party. The Meshel period both consolidated the status of the Histadrut and brought it into stagnation. The new secretary general promised to be an agent of change. However, the political and economic situation described above limited progress in this direction. After a few weeks in office he faced the first non-war-time national unity government in Israeli history.[3]

This government initiated an emergency economic policy, in order to combat both a frightening three digit rate of inflation and a deteriorating balance of payments. A priority target for action was the labor market. The plan included both a national wage freeze and large-scale layoffs in the public sector. Because of past experiences, when similar programs had failed at their implementation stage, the plan included a legislated provision. Kessar, while ready to negotiate major concessions in order to stabilize the economic situation, challenged the idea that the IR sphere should be controlled through legislation. He regarded this principle as a *casus belli* for the Histadrut. The fact that his opponent in the dispute was Prime Minister Peres, the leader of his own party, did not make the situation easier for him. After a vociferous crusade, Kessar managed to achieve his goals. The Histadrut found itself back as a partner of equal status in the economic sphere, instead of remaining a subordinate factor in it.

As we approach the end of the studied period, we find that the relationships between the Israeli irs and its political environment have radically changed. In Becker's day Histadrut leadership was an *undifferentiated* part of the leading elite. Its relative position in it was, however, inferior. The first in rank were party officials who served in key positions in the government. In the Likud's day, the Histadrut was kept out of the political arena. The rejection by the government and the miserable state of the Labor Alignment, put the Histadrut into an independent position. At the end of the period, following the tough negotiations on the implementation of the new economic policy, the Histadrut regained its position in the political sphere. This readmittance, however, increased its involvement in state affairs and decreased its ability to disregard its environment. It was again part of the Israeli elite. Its claim to sovereignty in the IR domain was substantiated. As a result, although it could afford to abandon its traditional modus operandum in the party backrooms, and to negotiate in the open political air, its involvement in political affairs made it once again vulnerable to political and economic exposure.

The twenty-three year period covered by this work is therefore a very volatile era. I do not plan to deal with chronological details. My real interest is with the unraveling of its systemic features. I hope to show that *the Israeli IR sphere gained the characteristics of an autonomous industrial relations system.* The systemic features of this domain make any effort to explain it in political or economic terms a futile endeavor. In order to be able to adopt the system approach, a short conceptual discussion is needed. First, I will briefly explain the essential features of the term "system," and then, in greater detail, present the elements of an industrial relations system.

Systems and Industrial Relations Systems

A system is a conceptual construct. When we look for the systemic characteristics of a given object, we make assumptions on its nature. We assume that: 1) it is composed of a limited number of elements, 2) these elements are interrelated, and 3) they are relatively detached from their environment. What do these three assumptions specifically imply?

In order to draw a map of a system, we ought to be able to identify its components. The human blood-vascular system includes the heart, arteries, veins and capillaries. The transportation system includes vehicles, roads and luggage. The school system includes schools, personnel and students. Only when we make up a list of elements can we start conceptualizing a system.

Such elements by themselves are not a system. A system is more than the sum of its parts. It includes an understanding of the ways elements are related to one another. The heart pumps blood through the arteries, not through the veins. Cars carry luggage, and run on roads, not the other way round. When cars run over luggage or human beings, it is a case of malfunction, not of ordinary operation.

School systems include students, but usually exclude parents. Pupils, however, do not cease to be the offspring of their parents because the latter are excluded from the educational system. Parents are still part of the environment of the educational system. The relationships between teachers and students are more intense than those between teachers and parents. When a parent enters a class room and insists on the right to tell a son or daughter what to do during school hours, the functioning of the school system is interrupted. The parent may threaten to take the child out of school, but it is up to the school to decide how to approach such a threat. The school system builds walls and gates in order to control the coming and going of visitors, pupils and personnel. It is defended by state and city ordinances. This way, a school can function as a system.

Still, interrelatedness and detachment remain relative terms. Some systems have a more condensed network of relationships than others. The elements of all systems, as a set, are more interrelated to one another than they are to their environment, but although all systems are detached from their environments, some are more detached than others. Some systems are thus more systematic than others.

When we apply a system approach to an object we claim it has system characteristics. The proof of this claim is entirely empirical. If we fail to enumerate the elements of a system, if we identify no orderly relationships among them, or if we distinguish no discernible environment for the object, then we fail to substantiate our system claim. If we do, however, pass all three tests, then we substantiate our understanding of the object in a systemic way.

Treating the IR sphere as a system implies an assertion that all three prerequisites hold for this domain. Dunlop, in his book "Industrial Relations Systems" (1958) was the first to approach the IR domain as a system. His book suggested a conceptual paradigm of a three element system with three environmental contexts. An irs, following Dunlop, is a set of actors, rules and ideology. It is constrained by economic (market or budgetary), political (power context) and technological systems.

THE ELEMENTS OF AN IRS

The elements of Dunlop's scheme are, as noted the actors, the rules and the ideology.

Actors

The actors of an irs are defined as "1) a hierarchy of managers and their representatives in supervision, 2) a hierarchy of (non-managerial) workers and any spokesmen, and 3) specialized governmental agencies (and specialized private agencies created by the first two actors) concerned with workers, enterprises, and their relationships" (Dunlop, 1958, p. 7).

Rules

The network of rules "consists of procedures for establishing rules, the substantive rules, and the procedures for deciding their application to particular situations." (Ibid., p. 13)

Ideology

The ideology of an irs is a "set of ideas and beliefs commonly held by the actors that helps to bind or to integrate the system together as an entity"(ibid., p. 16).

THE ENVIRONMENTAL CONTEXTS OF AN IRS

The Economic Context

The actors in an industrial relations system confront given product-market or budgetary constraints and labor market characteristics. A number of features of the market or budgetary context are to be distinguished: (1) competitive position or budgetary control, (2) the scope of the market or budget, (3) market or budget homogeneity among enterprises, (4) the size of the enterprise, (5) secular expansion or contraction, (6) the characteristics of the labor force, (7) labor market stringency, and (8) the ratio of labor costs to total costs. (Ibid., p. 93)

The Political Constraint

The environment of the actors in an industrial relations system consists also of the power context of the larger society and the derived status of the managerial hierarchy, workers and their organization, and governmental agencies... The status of these actors in any industrial relations system is defined in terms of their prescribed functions and the full network of interrelations among them and with rival organizations of workers and managers. (Ibid., p. 127)

The Technological Constraint

The technological context defines the type of work place and the operations and functions of workers and managers... The following facets of technical contexts were particularly distinguished: (1) fixed or variable work place, (2) relation of work place to residence, (3) stable or variable work force and operations, (4) size of the work group, (5) job content, (6) relation to machines or customers, and (7) the scheduled hours and shifts of the work place." (Ibid., p. 61)

DUNLOP'S IRS—SUMMARY AND EVALUATION

It is apparent that Dunlop has presented a detailed catalogue of items and considerations. The scheme is undoubtedly useful for descriptive purposes. Whenever any of us enters an enterprise, studies an industry, or reports on a country, we know what to look at. The descriptive tool is, however hardly satisfactory when we approach the same sites from the point of view of a system approach. Dunlop does not dwell much on the way the elements on his list interact. He states a set of environmental constraints, but he does not discuss to what degree these external factors shape the way the irs functions. Therefore, his contribution is both a step forward and a hindrance to the understanding of the way IR processes take place.

As stated above, the most important features of a system theory are the premises of interconnectedness and detachment. A simple example may help clarify these terms. An employer in a highly competitive market hires workers to work for him. After interviewing candidates, he assigns them to given ranks and allocates them to appropriate jobs. Each employee works independently, seldom encountering any of the others. The employer replaces workers on the basis of market needs. Whenever he gains orders, he looks for workers. Whenever the demand for his products slackens, he lays them off.

Is this organization a system? Let us apply Dunlop's paradigm to it. The organization has a set of actors, an employer and his employees. It has a set of rules that specifies the ranking of employees and describes the requirements of positions. The members of the organization act as though they have an ideology. Both the employer and his employees try to maximize their returns, the employer of his investment and the workers, of their efforts. They seem to believe that this is the way business should act. Does this organization have economic, political or technological constraints? The changes in demand for the products of the organization show the impact of economic considerations. The structure of positions reflects the need for specialization and division of labor. Both features indicate the influence of technology. The fact that the employer has the right to select his workers and to fix their terms of employment indicates the weight of political factors. Nevertheless, in approaching this organization as a system, all we gain is a synonym of the term organization.

When does the use of the term "system" add to our understanding of this organization? Only when we find out if and how its various elements its actors, rules and ideology, adhere to system characteristics. The workers, for example, may come to oppose the fact that their employment depends on the demand for their product. If they agree among themselves to adjust their working hours so as to secure permanent employment, their behavior reflects both interconnectedness and detachment. If this offer meets the opposition (or the enthusiasm) of their employer, then that is another indication of connectedness. The actors shape their ideology and their rules. They do not succumb to the dictates of the economy. They search for preferred strategies to deal with it. Actors, rules and ideology become interconnected. The organization builds a buffer between internal processes and external influences.

Let us leave our hypothetical organization and turn to the main topic of this book, the issue of strikes. Many politicians assume that legislation can regulate strikes. What do they mean by regulation? They expect industrial conflicts to be subordinated to political control. This expectation makes an unstated assumption that strikes are directly controllable by political means. This assumption is a clear rejection of the notion of an irs. If the IR domain acts as a system, and strikes are an essential process of within this system, then legislation is no more than an environmental threat. A system does not react to such a stimulus with automatic compliance. It digests the message and acts accordingly. Internal considerations, such as ideology or power, raise alternative scenarios and influence final selections. Most econometric studies of strike activity fall into this same pitfall. They look for the economic determinants of strikes. They believe that the level of unemployment or the level of price change does shape the degree of industrial conflict. But, *if economic factors do have the ability to determine the volume of strikes, strikes are themselves an integral element of the economic system.*

THE IRS AS A COLLECTIVISTIC ENTITY

The industrial relations system is a set of interrelated elements that interact in determining the terms of employment. This concept gains importance in modern industrial society. Here, terms of employment are shaped in a collective context. Many workers gain their living under the same, or at least very similar, conditions. Many people earn their living working in organizations, while many employers are either members of employers' associations or become depersonalized by incorporation. Both employees and employers apply for assistance to the labor court, to mediators and arbitrators. None of these functionaries acts as an individual. They occupy roles and interact with their counterparts on the basis of these roles. The actors of a modern irs, therefore, act as *sets* of individuals. Thus, their interactions are not cases of individual-level behavior. They have a very pronounced collectivistic nature.

Neither are the norms that regulate the terms of employment in a modern irs the product of individual-level negotiations. Legally binding contracts cover a wide range of circumstances. In many cases, before we approach individuals, we assign contractual terms to classes of people. As such, managers, union officials, judges, mediators, and arbitrators can deal with them. When a disagreement arises, relating it to a set of generalizations can indicate which party to the dispute has the better case.

Neither acts nor regulations have justification merely by existing. We, the actors, assign to them a meaning. This meaning, which can be either shared by actors or disputed, stems from an ideology. An ideology defines the goals of a system and the position of the various actors in it. It creates the difference between the dead word of the law book and the regulating norm.

It is a major thesis of this book that the Israeli IR domain gained a remarkable level of interrelatedness and detachment. This feature makes the Israeli case an interesting setting for general theoretic purposes besides its interest for an Israeli audience.

The Israeli irs

MAIN FEATURES OF ISRAELI IRS

The Israeli irs is unique since it has an exceptional set of actors and a particular ideology. These two elements have shaped a distinctive set of rules. In the following discussion I will describe the various elements of the Israeli irs. The term "cell" will serve as a synonym for the term "element," that reflects a graphic representation of the system.

Main irs Cells

Actors

Three different categories of actors make up the actors cell: workers and their representatives, employers and their associations and third parties. Given the highly collectivistic nature of the Israeli irs I will limit myself to a presentation of workers' *representation*, ignoring, as it were, the workers themselves.

Labor Representation

The most significant feature of the actors cells of the Israeli irs is the Histadrut. Both the strengths of the system and its deficiencies stem from the functioning of the Histadrut. In 1920, when it was established, it served more a vision of the future than a set of existent needs. The founders of the Histadrut hoped to establish a society of Jewish work[4] on a neglected piece of land. They envisioned an influx of hundreds of thousands of Zionist new-comers. The Histadrut was the tool they designed to promote the Jewish national revival movement. As such, it is a multi-goal organization. It served a variety of purposes, the creation of an economy, the resurrection of a culture, the formation of a welfare service and, last but not least, the formation of a comprehensive trade union.

This multipurpose conception made the Histadrut into a nationwide union, a large-scale employer and a significant supplier of economic and social services. This peculiar combination shaped it as a unique organization. Therefore, the Histadrut is not a conventional trade union. It so happens that among other components, it incorporates a very large trade union element. The Histadrut is a social movement that underwent a process of institution-alization. With its national vision, it preceded all other actors of the irs. It was not the first union. Unions and employers' associations did exist in Israel[5] prior to the establishment of the Histadrut, but their scope, impact and vision were much more limited.

The Histadrut developed the way it did *in spite* of the vision that inspired its founders and not *because* of it. The expected early influx of immigrants did not materialize. The Jews of the early 1920s were not ready to leave their countries of origin and immigrate to Palestine. The incoming pioneers were mostly young and without capital. Therefore, national capital became a dominant factor in the process of colonization. Control over this resource became a political issue, and the Histadrut, with its nationwide organization and interest, managed to establish such control. Almost ten years after establishing the Histadrut, the Labor Party[6] (Mapai), the leading party in the Histadrut, gained control of the political organizations of the *Yishuv*.[7] From then until 1977 Labor was the dominant factor in *Eretz Israel*. To a very significant degree this long period shaped the structure and functioning of the Israeli irs.

The Histadrut fulfills simultaneously all three primary roles of an irs. On the management side, the Histadrut is the sole owner of *Hevrat ha-Ovdim*, a holding company of all Histadrut-owned enterprises. This sector is an important part of the economy. It employs as much as a fifth of the total labor force. It produces close to a quarter of the total national product. On the union side, the Histadrut represents nine out of every ten Israeli employees. On the third party standing, the Histadrut fulfills both formal and informal functions. Formally, its Trade Union Division is the final arbiter for Hevrat ha-Ovdim. It has the authority to impose its decisions both on the managers of the Histadrut sector and on the representative unions of its employees. On the informal level, Histadrut figures have served both as mediators and as arbitrators in many public and private sector disputes. They served in these capacities in many cases in past. Contrary to popular belief, statistical data show that this involvement is on the increase.

The Histadrut takes part in IR affairs on all conceivable levels. Branches of the Histadrut function on the national level (Trade Union Division), on the craft and industry levels (National Unions), on the national employer's level (National Committees), on the local level (Workers' Councils), and on the organization and plant levels (Workers' Committees).

Employers

The structure of employers' organization follows a primarily sectorial arrangement. Since the Israeli economy has three major ownership sectors, private, public and Histadrut. I will adopt this dimension in the following description.

The government has its own representative structure. It includes the Commissioner of State Service, the director of wages and salaries in the Ministry of Finance, and the State Enterprises Authority. Public employers outside the state framework, such as local government, have their own parallel arrangements.

In the private sector, a set of employers' associations function on the industry level. The Coordinating Bureau of Economic Organizations functions on the national level. Individual employers retain wide discretion on the terms of employment in the enterprises when it comes to plant level issues.

The managements of the Histadrut's large concerns (Solel Boneh, Koor, Tnuva, etc.) and a national-level secretariat serve the same function on behalf of their sector.

Third parties

The state supplies two major third-party functions through the IR Commissioner[8] and the Labor Court. These two agencies serve different publics in different ways. The Labor Relations Officer has narrowed his activity to disputes of a smaller scale, while the Labor Court is called in to deal with larger disputes. Still, Histadrut officials and other mediators and arbitrators fulfill a much more pervasive role, even though it is seldom noticed by the public.

Rules

When we employ terms such as rules, contract and agreement, a very formal construct comes to mind, but Israeli IR rules are much less formal than the terms imply. Even though collective agreements and labor laws cover most employment aspects throughout the labor market, the written word is not sanctified. Precedence and common knowledge are not of lesser importance.

A law is a rule enacted through a legal procedure by a legal authority. Here, once again the words imply a one-sided process. The legislature enacts and the subordinate citizens obey. As far as labor laws are concerned, this is not the case. All major laws are more an adoption of common practice than an effort to change it. Legislation in most cases makes an impact in the following ways. First, it serves as a symbolic exposition of institutionalization. Second, it serves as a way of incorporating marginal segments of the labor force within the main core of collective agreements. It thus defends the center from competition from non-unionized settings. The issue of legislation has a political-ideological flavor. The Labor Party regarded it as a safeguard for the achievements of the labor movement. The Likud Party, on the other hand, saw it as a lever for change, as a way to liberalize the Israeli economy. In spite of this ideological disparity, even Likud dominated governments have been very hesitant to introduce any major legislative initiative. Legislation both of a Trade Union Law and of obligatory arbitration were on its platform. However, neither have been implemented.

The various versions of collective agreements are the cornerstone of the Israeli irs rules cell. They are the first layer in the historic-sociological sense, and a second layer, in the legal sense. They include nationwide or industry-wide general collective agreements, employer or specific local collective agreements, a state employment code and codes for local government and Histadrut employees. The common feature of all these forms of rules is their bilateral authorship. Even where the codes are formally the exclusive product of management, the facade usually conceals a collaborative venture. On the periphery of the economy, however, unorganized labor is a common phenomenon. This occurs both in some of the most technologically advanced segments and in the small employment sites of service and rural segments. The influx of Arab workers from the occupied areas made this type of employment the rule in construction, agriculture, services and in some industrial domains.

Ideology

Ideology is a conception of reality. It is a conception of the *ideal* reality. As such, it is an important feature of all irs's. The IR domain has long been monopolized by the legal profession, leading to an overemphasis of the formal aspects of IR rules. To this field economics have added a flavor of a market and a set of abstract competing actors. Even the institutional school of economics has not passed the stage of treating the union as an indispensable actor in the labor market. Sociologists and anthropologists, on the other hand, treat the ideological element of the irs as a facet of primary importance. Sociological research into this aspect of the IR field is rather new, therefore, it is much more difficult to present the ideology of the Israeli irs.

Some theoreticians conceive of the ideology of a system as the *shared* conception of the good. But, not all conceptions of the good are shared. Some may be highly disputed. By stressing the consentual aspect of ideology they have caused a neglect of its adversary aspect. Sociologists of the consensus school would argue that no system can persist without a significant degree of ideological overlap. Other sociologists, those belonging to the Marxist tradition for example, agree that ideology is shared. They argue, however, that this sharing stems from coercion and indoctrination, not from voluntary agreement. Since the sharing of the ideology is partial, there is some truth in the claims of both schools. We should, therefore, distinguish between the shared parts and unshared parts of the ideology. I regard the former as the ideology *of the system,* and the latter as the ideology of *a specific actor in the system.* Thus, for example, management and union can agree on the benefits of adopting a specific set of rules, may disagree on the issue of security versus profit as the ultimate goal of the system, and be indifferent to the way each party elects or nominates its higher ranking officials. In the following paragraph I will dwell on the ideology *of* the system. The ideological inclinations of the actors will be dealt later.

The ideology of the Israeli irs has been transition during the last decades. The following description fits the earlier period (1960s) more than it does the later one (1980s). The most important features of the ideological element are the following:

First, unions and management, in this order, are the major legitimate actors of the irs. This turns insiders like the Labor Court or the IR Commissioner, and outsiders like the government, into figures of lesser ideological desirability. Managers are important, but the "real" producers are the workers. A place of work is an economic unit, but economic considerations are not its primary criteria. Job security and workers' welfare are of higher importance. If layoffs, for example, are a compelling must, a LIFO (Last in, First Out) view is almost sanctified.

Second, the individual worker is subordinate to the collective dictate of the collective. In most cases, whenever there is a contradiction between collective and individual benefits, the former take precedence. An employee cannot waive any of his privileges, since such an act may harm his comrades.

Third, unionization is preferred to a free market. Society at large is expected to do anything possible to defend its unionized segment from "unfair" competition. Non-unionized enterprises may enhance their competitive strength by avoiding granting wage increases, so government should have the power to equalize their costs. This ideological tenet has led to the idea of extension regulations *(Tsavei Harhava),* which enforce terms of employment in the unionized part of the economy on its non-unionized counterpart.

Levels of the irs

A unitary approach to the concept of an irs hides an important aspect of modern industrial relations, its multiplicity of levels. irs's come in many forms; the simpler ones have fewer levels than the more developed. A simplified model of an underdeveloped irs includes a set of many small systems, each of them functioning in parallel to the others. In such an irs, the managements of existent enterprises directly negotiate with the represen- tatives of their own employees. No national union exists. Neither does a higher-level employers' association. This segmental model approximates the situation in the Yishuv prior to World War I. Unions, wherever they existed, tended to be local, or at the most regional. Employers' associations hardly existed at all. The Second World War brought a major change. Israel was then under British mandate. Above all, the British Mandate administration was interested in promoting peaceful labor relations, as an important prerequisite of a functioning wartime economy. This political factor encouraged a struc- tural change in the labor market. The centers of both unions and employers' associations gained importance.

The establishment of a Department of Trade Union (to be later replaced by a *Division* of Trade Union) in Tel-Aviv was indicative of this trend. From then on, an additional level of irs gained importance. The creation of the new center did not lead to the disappearance of the former Histadrut bodies which continued to function. The change was in the structure of the system, which become more elaborate. It is this structural elaboration that I refer to as the issue of levels. At this introductory stage, I a comprehensive description of the cells of the Israeli irs and their three contextual environments would be both redundant and difficult. Of the three irs cells, actors, rules and ideology, I will focus on the first. The actors' cell is both easier and more essential to present than the other two cells. While a short, classified actors' listing is sufficient for the reader at this stage, any discussion of the others must be more elaborate. For this reason I will pass over any reference to the external contexts of the system, the economy, the polity and the technological system.

National Level

On the national level of the Israeli irs, we look for three groups of actors, management, union and third parties. Even a cursory look can show that the structure is unbalanced. On the labor side we find one huge body, the Trade Union Division of the Histadrut, while on the employers' side the structure is much more complicated, following the sectorial demarcation. The Coor- dinating Bureau of Economic Organizations (CBEO) represents the *private* sector employers, but in the *public* sector we find more than one official address. The Civil Service Commissioner, the Wages Deputy in the Ministry of Finance, the Authority of State Enterprises, the Center of Local Government and other public bodies, all occupy employers' positions in this sector. The secretariat of Hevrat ha-Ovdim represents the management of the Histadrut sector.

Putting the third parties aside for a minute, the split among the employers is in complete contrast to the solidified labor front, although split is on the decrease. This division developed through the following two processes: first, the private sector Coordinating Bureau is relatively new. The more experienced its leaders become, the more they understand their strategic importance. The CBEO gains its importance from the need of the center, both government and Histadrut, for a partner in national-level policy negotiations. Since the crisis of the Israeli economy is continuous, there is a constant need for establishing national agreements. As a result, a representative body of the employers is an important political asset. The more the CBEO participates in tripartite agreements, the more its status is institutionalized.

A second factor facilitates the rise in status of the private sector representative body to the national level. The reluctance of the political leadership to allow an involvement of public sector management in policy formulation leaves the stage open for the representatives of the private sector. Therefore, the Trade Union Division is less preponderant than it seems.

The third-party cast of actors includes the State Labor Court and the Principal Labor Relations Officer. Third party officials are secondary on the national level, since neither the main actors nor the political elite allows it substantial prominence.

Industrial-Sectoral-Occupational Level

A large variety of organizations take part in IR affairs on this second level of the irs. On the union side, many industrial, craft and sector specific national unions handle their daily affairs, and some scores of employers' associations serve as their counterparts. Since the public sector, which includes state, local government and Histadrut affiliated organs has not established a coordinated front on the national level, these organizations assume the actors' role at this intermediate level as well. On this tier we can find representatives of non-Histadrut unions such as physicians, high school teachers, etc. acting beside Histadrut affiliated unions. The extra-Histadrut union organizations doubly gain from their choice of a restricted domain. On the one hand they do not enter into conflict with the huge national union. On the other hand, they gain implicit support from the legitimacy established by the Histadrut.

The Principal Labor Relations Officer and State Labor Court are not as active on this level as they are on the lower one. Political considerations and involvement of the Trade Union Division limit the demand for their services.

Organization

The organizational tier of the Israeli irs confronts the most dynamic union side actors, the workers' committees with their counterparts, the managers. Workers' committees, and in particular, leaders of national committees, increased their level of militancy during the 1970s and the 1980s. Their activity was most pronounced in public sector enterprises. In private sector organizations, on the other hand, they tend to avoid the use of strikes as a tool of negotiation.

While strikes are customarily an outcome of disagreements between the disputants, this is not always the case in the public sector. Organization-level managements and unions share a common goal for enhanced organizational autonomy. They believe that they would do better if only they had wider discretion to make decisions. This belief manifests itself in a variety of forms. Managers, for instance, protest against political nominations. Local unions in the more successful enterprises, for their part, raise demands to link their economic remuneration to profitability.

Israeli irs as an Autonomous irs

Social differentiation constrains the level of irs autonomy. In an undifferentiated society, such as the pre-independence Jewish Yishuv, all social settings are interwoven. during that period the Histadrut served as the promoter of most social functions. It acted as the headquarters for topics ranging from defense and foreign policy through health, insurance and education to economic and trade union affairs. With such a wide range of topics, no domain can act independently. This situation has undergone a process of change. First came the state, appropriating many of the above-mentioned functions from the Histadrut. Defence has been the exclusive provenance of the state since its establishment. David Ben-Gurion, the first prime minister of Israel, imposed this policy both on his political allies[9] and his opponents.[10] Education followed a few years later (1952). The labor movement agreed to dissolve its primary schooling system even though such an accord was not adopted by the religious parties.

The transfer of control of the labor exchange and part of the social insurance services was a further curtailment of the services supplied by the Histadrut. Then came the political upheaval of 1977, which freed the Histadrut from the control of the Labor Party's representatives in the government. Intra-party mechanisms, which dealt with the coordination between the government and the Histadrut ceased to function. The Histadrut could allow IR considerations to shape IR decisions, and economic decisions to shape economic activities. All these development enhanced the shift from an irs hardly discernible from the political and economic systems to a model of system autonomy.

Political developments, however, did not stop with the Likud coming to power in 1977. The delicate balance which eventually emerged between the two Israeli major party groups, the Labor Alignment and the Likud, led to the forming of a national unity government in 1984. During this period the Histadrut increased its extra-IR activities. These political actions forced the Histadrut to increase its level of differentiation. While the Federation, led by Secretary General Israel Kessar, acted as an undifferentiated social movement, the trade union division on the one hand and Hevrat ha'Ovdim on the other hand, established their own autonomy inside the organization. This made the Histadrut a more complicated system, structured to deal with an increasingly complicated environment.

Unstated Assumptions of the Israeli irs

Unstated assumptions are ideas that people impute to an object. As such, they are difficult to refute. We look for unstated assumptions to explain a phenomenon that seems illogical or meaningless. An acceptable explanation must stand up to two sets of criteria: the event under consideration must be geared to a context, and it has to satisfy our judgment. Therefore, some myths become generally accepted, while others do not.

Two unstated assumptions are commonly accepted *vis-à-vis* the functioning of the Israeli irs: 1) centralization and 2) loyalty to fundamental societal needs and goals.

CENTRALIZATION

Since World War II, the IR domain has been dominated by the national elites of the workers, the employers and the ruling political leadership. As described above, the structure of the national level of the irs is relatively simple. A single dominant General Federation of Labor assumes authority for almost all unions. The political elite, represented by the government, is also easily identifiable. The only underorganized leg of the tripod is that of the employers. This deficiency has now been almost overcome. The CBEO, even though a latecomer, is taking a respected place at the summit. This triadic structure is a potential source for the creation of such a society. The government gains voluntary compliance, while its partners gain status and consideration of their primary interests. The concept of centralization implies the existence of a regulated society. In such a situation, tripartite negotiations are the model solution to labor problems. Package deals are the natural outcomes.

Some may wonder if this is not an accurate description of the actual system. To some degree it is. Any tabular description of the actors' cell on the national level attests to the validity of this description. This model, however, if it ever was accurate, is certainly not a realistic model of the contemporary Israeli situation. The widespread *belief* in it, however, is an important normative resource for the way the actors in the system do behave. Since there is a belief that the Histadrut has the capacity to control the stage, its leaders are blamed for many cases of labor unrest. Since the Histadrut is regarded as the big brother of Israeli unions, the power of these unions is seldom put to the test. The secretary generals of the Histadrut have been aware of the imputed omnipotence attributed to their organization. Some have tried to act on the basis of this idea and call deviant union leaders to order. Becker (1962-69) probably fits this conception. Others, Ben-Aharon (1969-73) for example, hoped to recover waning dominance by developing and encouraging popular support to the Histadrut. Meshel (1973-84) was the first to acknowledge the limits of Histadrut authority. Since his party, the Labor Party, had lost a general election, he could not ignore the new political reality. The Histadrut tried to mobilize its members to strike and demonstrate against the government. but failed to mobilize public support. Therefore, he realized the limits of his organization's power. Nevertheless, Meshel still continued to maintain the facade of a key national figure. Each month, following the publication of the most recent consumers' price index (CPI), he used to appear on Israeli television. In this ritualistic interview he would condemn the government for its failure to control the economy.

Kessar (1984–), took office in the midst of a national crisis. This crisis made him, temporarily, a key national figure. The new economic policy of Prime Minister Peres had to be implemented by a national unity government. It was obvious that an emergency economic plan must be agreed upon by all major institutional centers. This understanding allowed Kessar to gain one of his finest hours. As an equal with the prime minister, he negotiated the terms of the economic measure to be taken. When the emergency situation dissipated, however, he returned to a much less dominant status.

The reader may question why it is important to regard centralization as an unstated assumption. The findings of the following chapters of this book provide the answer. Contrary to common belief, macro-political and economic factors do not shape the frequency of strikes. Political, technological or economic factors do not explain the differences in strike propensity between various sites. The features of the irs in the lower level of the system, on the other hand, do explain it. The national level of the irs serves as an umbrella for the lower participants. They, however, make the real decisions as to its functioning.

LOYALTY TO FUNDAMENTAL SOCIETAL NEEDS AND GOALS

Each society has its own elements. The legitimacy of an element, be it an organization, a role, or a system, stems from an imputed functionality. The status of the Israeli army is high so long as people believe that it satisfies Israeli need for defense. So long as people believe that the irs supports the ideology of the state, they grant it legitimacy . As long as the Labor Party ruled in both the government and the Histadrut this belief could not be disputed. The center of the social network included both the leaders of the state and those of the Histadrut. People of similar public image held, interchangeably, both Histadrut and government positions.

Americans use the slogan, 'General Motors is the US.' An Israeli parallel is the expression "the good of the Histadrut and the good of the state are the same." After all, the membership overlap between the two is almost total! This fact assigns to the Histadrut the status of guardian of the general welfare. Any external effort to reshape the Histadrut has, until recently, been regarded as an unpatriotic act. Interestingly enough, in the framework of the existing institutional setting this is a valid claim. When the various parts of the

Histadrut suffer, it is the Israeli people that pays the price. An economic crisis in the Histadrut-owned sector can give rise to the serious threat of widespread unemployment. A crisis in *Kupat Cholim*, the Histadrut-owned health service, is a disastrous obstacle to public health. A delay in the negotiations for a general wage or cost of living agreement brings the economy almost to a standstill. Therefore, *in the context of the contemporary social fabric*, the identity between the Histadrut and the state is a fact of life. The unsubstantiated aspect of this claim arises from the fact that it is rooted in a transient situation. A departure from this state may create conditions in which this congruence will not hold as at present. The Histadrut may, therefore, become a very critical obstacle to needed change, just because it is so much identified with the contemporary structure.

Changes in the Functioning of the Israeli irs

The present work covers a period of twenty three years (1965-87). On the one hand, this is a short period of less than three decades. On the other hand, much has happened in that time. A long-established dominant party, the Labor Party, lost its control over the government. The state experienced three wars, the Six Day War (1967), the Yom Kippur War (1973) and the Lebanon War (1982-4). Four elected officials occupied the position of Histadrut secretary general. A national unity government headed by a rotatory prime minister replaced Likud governments headed by two party leaders. This is a substantial list of major events for a relatively short period of time.

Our attention is focused less on political development at state level than on the IR sphere. Has it changed? Was the change internal, that is, a modification in the structure of the irs. Was it external, meaning an alteration in the relationships between the irs and its external context?

Internal changes in an irs can take place in any of the cells of the system (actors, rules, ideology) or in the relationship among them. On the surface, there was little change in the actors' cell. The list of actors stayed the same for the entire period. A reform in the Trade Union Division took place in 1977, but it was hardly a radical change. In the rules cell, hardly anything happened. Legislation of new labor laws was not a prominent feature of this period, although a somewhat greater measure of legal power to counter strike action in the public sector was enacted. As to ideology, there was less rhetoric on the mission of the Histadrut at the end of the period than at its start. Still, even this was merely a minor change.

LABOR PARTY DOMINATION (1977)

The Labor Party domination of Israeli society started, as I noted above, in the early 1930s. This was a period of intensive collectivization and political activity in which the labor movement was the major agent. The outcome of all this huge human effort brought about the establishment of the State of Israel (1948). For the next twenty-nine years the Labor Party led the country.

These three decades were not identical. In very rough terms, the first decade of the new state dealt with the immediate absorption of a huge wave of immigration. A small Jewish community of less than 800,000 absorbed an influx of Jews from all over the world, mostly from the survivors of the holocaust in Europe and from countries of Islamic heritage. The first years were characterized by a clear distinction between the veterans, who managed the system, and the newcomers, who filled subordinate positions. Two main events dominated the second decade, a recession in the middle of the period and the Six Day War. The impressive victory of the 1967 war transformed Israeli society. Attention focussed on an increase in the standard of living and on social problems stemming from the immense process of population growth. The Labor Party, which had never managed to gain an absolute majority in the Knesset started losing public support.

The problematic Yom Kippur War in 1973 helped to prolong Labor Party rule, but four years later, in 1977, it lost the general election. A concatenation of two groups brought about this change. On one side were white-collar workers and intellectuals. They formed a new party, *Dash* (Democrats for Change), and hoped to become a lever for renewal of the stagnant state. Most Dash supporters were former Labor Party voters. They hoped to join a Labor dominated coalition, and to turn it towards modernization and further democratization. The U.S.A. served as their model. On the other side stood the Likud Party group. Excluding a short term in an emergency government (1967-71) the leading element of this group, Herut, had always been in opposition. The Likud gained the support of many Jews who had emigrated from Moslem countries. A coalition of three blocks, the Likud Party, Dash and the religious parties, which had until then been coalition partners with Labor, made an end to the rule of the socialist-democratic Labor Party.

The Early Period

There is no clear-cut way to divide the Labor dominated years into sub-periods. Still, even though the change was gradual, I will make a distinction between the early and the later years. The first stage precedes the years covered by this investigation. I will, therefore, describe it in schematic terms. My purpose is more to draw a baseline model, than to supply a detailed historic report.

Government and Histadrut Led by the Same Party

During the early period, almost all senior- and middle-level socialist leaders had come from East Europe, not later than the mid-1920s. This situation corresponded to an undifferentiated social system, where leaders could be at the same time ideologists, politicians, and economic entrepreneurs. They had come a long way together and formed established intra-group mechanisms for ruling the country. The industrial relations realm was no exception to this rule. If at all, it was the prototype of intra-party processes of dispute management and policy shaping. Most of the leaders of the Labor

Party were active in the Histadrut at one time or another. Many of them occupied important positions in the Histadrut hierarchy. Therefore, they tended to consider this field as a domain of shared expertise. The formulation of general wage policy, which is usually a core issue of the irs actors in more differentiated countries, was carried out in party committees and by informal consultations. Histadrut and non-Histadrut functionaries took part in the process. Whenever disagreements arose, they were either referred to wider forums or to the conclusive decision of senior party leaders. Thus, we hear of discussions which took place in "the committee of the nine" or the "committee of the eleven." The official policy of the Histadrut is formally decided in its central bodies. In fact, however, such approval is more ritualistic than real.

The monolithic character of the system did not stop in its higher echelons. The party had its cadre of activists spread over all spheres and levels of society. In the IR realm, this phenomenon found its expression in widespread membership of local workers' committees. Part of it was formal. Workers chose their candidates from a set of party-recommended lists. Each Histadrut affiliated party had the right to submit its list. The individual worker had no choice of individual candidates. His only choice was between parties. This rigid party line system could maintain itself so long as party structure served a dominant function. In the early period this was the case. Since party dominated organizations supplied most subsistence needs, housing, health, and employment, the dependence of the public on the establishment was enormously high. The lack of personal connections, social skills and resources of the new immigrants was an essential ingredient in this state of dependency.

The Later Period

The later phase of the Labor period is characterized by a progressive decline in the state of dependence. This process stemmed partly from objective factors and partly from the achievements of the new Jewish state. Objectively, the longer people stay in a country, the more they gain resources. The immigrants learnt the new language, accumulated economic savings, and established new networks of friendship and support. Therefore, as time passed, dependence became less and less accepted. The fact that the state was run as a welfare state was also an important source of change.The supply of services, appreciated at the beginning, in time became part of the routine. There is no gratitude for privileges taken for granted. Moreover, the development of the state created a need for workers with higher qualifications. The modern educational system and compulsory service in the army shaped a new generation. This younger generation looked for its place in the social fabric. Neither the more qualified older workers, nor the persons who joined the labor market later on were ready to accept the rigid party-sponsored system as a given.

The first clues of coming change arose in the periphery. In the early days, Israel was a centralized society. All major and minor decisions were made in Tel Aviv or in Jerusalem, most of them being taken in a few major organizations. The periphery, therefore, had two levels. Workers' councils (*Moatsot ha-Poalim*) were the gateway to upward mobility on the local level. Entry into them was the first step the new immigrants managed to take. At the same time, unsatisfied workers formed their own operation committees, many of which gained the support of workers in general. They called strikes and demonstrations, trying to push for better working conditions and higher pay. It was only a matter of time until they either replaced the formal institution of workers' committees or gained control of them. The Histadrut managed to avoid the former option by relaxing party-list elections to workers' committees. Authentic representatives of the workers started to occupy the strategic position of the immediate representatives of the public.

In the later years of the Labor period we meet an ever increasing number of committee members uncommitted to the party. This independence led them to be less restrained in trade union activities. They were less reluctant to defy Histadrut orders. The Histadrut, however, had no real way to discipline these newly emerging leaders. It did not dare to dismiss them from their elected position. Officially, according the bylaws of the Histadrut, it has the authority to do so. Still, what can be more embarrassing than the re-election of a formerly dismissed candidate. The support of the public supplied such officials with an essential resource. The Histadrut, therefore, proceeded with an ever-increasing but unstated policy of loosening its control. A smaller percentage of the strikes remained unofficial, and workers' committees negotiated and reached collective agreements with merely ritualistic participation of the Histadrut. A division of labor has been established, where the Histadrut negotiates national baseline agreements, while the workers' committees add their important imprint to daily terms of employment.

Strategies Adopted by Histadrut Leadership to Deal with Tension

The Israeli irs developed into a multilevel system. The designers of Histadrut bylaws had had such a structure in mind, but they had not, or perhaps could not, have envisioned its complexity. The Histadrut is an outcome of political negotiations between political parties. The reality of the early 1920s imposed on these parties a need for coordination, but it did not go so far as to lead to their merger. As a result, a semi-state structure was adopted. In this structure, the political involvement of the individual member of Histadrut is limited to a once-in four-years vote casting act. At this celebrated event he votes for a party list. After leaving the election booth, the Histadrut member assumes the status of an observer. The first object he may observe is the convention, which takes place right after the elections. It has an enormous number of delegates (1,501), turning it into a ceremonial event. As such, it is very important. The convention gains its authority directly from the elections. Therefore, it has the highest authority of all its subordinate derivations. It meets once or twice in four years. Therefore, it is usually a well-organized show.

The next forum in line is the Histadrut council. It is three times smaller than the convention (501), but still too big to be functionally operative. That leaves us with the Executive Committee, an assembly of 151 members. The Executive Committee is similar in size to most parliaments, and here some legislative work can be done. At no time, however, has there been a possibility of a successful no confidence vote in the Executive Committee. The Labor Party has managed to keep a steady majority in the Histadrut since the early days of its establishment. Therefore, while this structure may serve political needs, it cannot raise involvement and enthusiasm among the Histadrut members. Workers' committees are the mirror image of Histadrut political hierarchy. They supply a framework which is elected each two years by the total community of workers it claims authority to represent.

The concept of total community must be emphasized. Not only Histadrut members elect their representatives in the committee. Even unorganized employees have the right to do so. That may be less far-reaching than it appears, since in a country where most workers are members of the Histadrut, only a small minority of voters may be non-Histadrut members. This fact has symbolic meaning. It is *us*, the workers of a given plant or office, that the workers' committee represents. It is not the established Histadrut. The members of the committee stand for elections each two years. Therefore, whenever a problem arises, they are either not long after an election campaign, or are expecting a new one. Thus their motivation to benefit their constituency may be higher than that of a party-dependent functionary, elected once in four years.

As long as the Histadrut was in its growth stage and the members of the workers' committees identified ideologically with it, the potential structural tension between the Histadrut and the workers' committees did not materialize. This period lasted longer than might have been expected. In the first years of the state, most plant-level leadership posts were held by veteran Zionists. The influx of both young and new immigrants to these positions let the potential tension manifest itself. The challenge of chaining workers' committee members to the policies of the Histadrut was a real issue for all secretary generals from the 1960s on. Their strategies, however, differed.

The first secretary general for the period covered by this study is Aharon Becker. Becker came to office in 1962 bringing with him ideological commitment to Zionism, socialist ideology and many years of experience in union affairs. His term was characterized by many strikes and efforts to curb them. A long awaited reform in work grades in the public sector instigated a long wave of industrial unrest. The new system followed the recommendations of a highly respected committee, of which the chancellor of the Bank of Israel served as chairperson. The committee followed the theoretical approach of one of Israel's most distinguished social scientists, Prof. Louis Guttman. Guttman's theoretical model envisioned a universal employment ranking ordered on one single dimension. The committee recommended that all public sector positions be ranked on the basis of a single set of criteria. The recommended ranking was of positions, not of employees.

In reality, however, positions are held by people. Since salaries were to be based on the ranking of the position the worker held, a theoretical job classification venture turned into a wage negotiation. The committee recommended that job description be based—admittedly only in part—on self-description. This made each and every employee involved in the evaluation process. As can be expected in a highly unionized society, the task of ranking was given to bipartite committees. Given the wide scope of the project, most committees included members of the local workers' committees. This situation was an ideal recipe for labor disputes. A wide involvement of both rank-and-file and local leaders, the fundamental issue of earnings, a feeling that a system is established for the long term, a set of criteria which allowed comparison to *any* position *anywhere* in the country—all these were inherent in the plan. An all-time high number of strikes was the inevitable outcome.

The ports were a second source of labor unrest in Becker's time. While ports are a source of high levels of industrial conflict all over the world, they are not so to such an extent in Israel. The main Israeli port for many years was at Haifa. Haifa was a city with a peculiar irs. The workers' council of the town was dominant. The social structure of the city included overlapping networks of people, all of whom followed the lead of the key leaders. In particular, two people come to mind: Aba Choushi, the eventual mayor of Haifa and Yossef Almogi, the Secretary of the Workers' Council and the eventual Minister of Labor. They were capable of mobilizing the network to act in a coordinated way. Therefore, whenever a strike was called, support and sympathy were readily available. When an agreement was undersigned, however, everybody honored it, including port employees. A change came through the establishment of a new port in Ashdod. This project required the closing of a small, but emotionally important, port in Tel Aviv, the transfer of some of its workers to Ashdod, the construction of a port and the establishing of a workers' community in the newly-formed developing town. All these factors were potential sources of conflict. The major source of tension, however, was the emergence of a new kind of leadership in Ashdod.

The leader of the port workers was Yehoshua Peretz. He was a charismatic Moroccan-born Jew, whose commitment to the Histadrut and its extensions was short-lived. The base of his authority was more related to the community than to his status as a foreman in the port. The workers' committee of the stevedores disregarded the authority of the Histadrut. A number of repeatedly defiant acts, followed by unwillingness on the side of Peretz to honor his own promises, raised a distasteful challenge to the secretary general. Government and public opinion expected him to bring the ports to a manageable state. Becker opted for disciplinary action. Peretz and his colleagues were summoned by the Histadrut to an internal judicial tribunal, but they taught the Histadrut a lesson on the limits of legal actions The courtroom was flooded by port workers; the defendants turned prosecutors, and the trial ended with no effective results. The vulnerability of the Histadrut was clearly shown.

Becker's last four years in office, the years for which detailed statistical data are available, were a sequence of peak economic activity and of deep recession. These years demonstrated a typical feature of the Israeli irs—its lack of responsiveness to economic processes. The final stages of the classification of the public services took place in the middle of a clear recession. Although low economic activity is generally associated with a decrease in the number of strikes, particularly wage improvements strikes, the situation in which Becker had to function was different. On the one hand, wage increases were called for in hundreds of strikes, most which took place in the public sector. On the other hand, workers who faced layoffs and delays in paying their salaries also went out on strike. One group seemed unrelated to the other. The largest sector in the Israeli economy acted purely in terms of irs-related logic. Economic constraints were shown to be irrelevant in this context.

The flamboyant Yitzhak Ben-Aharon was the antithesis of Becker. While Becker grew up in the trade union lines, Ben-Aharon was a man of many kinds of experience. He was a kibbutz member and, at one time or another, had been a secretary of the Tel-Aviv Workers' Council, a volunteer in the British army, a prisoner of war in World War II, and a minister in the Israeli government. He was well known for independent views. In a world of party officials he was a unique personality. His nomination as the Labor Party candidate for the post of secretary general of the Histadrut was something of a gamble, and the party accepted it with ambivalent feelings. When Ben-Aharon took office he called for a radical change in Israeli society. Neither the Histadrut nor Israeli society were ready for this moral challenge. Ben-Aharon believed in the wisdom of the people. He expected local union leaders to be the most appropriate leaders of the trade union movement. He was, however, not naive. He acknowledged the fact that inexperienced popular leaders may be expensive. He believed that such a cost was worthwhile. So, the new secretary general called for incorporating authentic representatives of the workers in all Histadrut spheres. He contemplated a trade union division highly influenced by delegates democratically elected by the workers in the plant or the office.

He accepted the doctrine that the Histadrut is an organization led by representatives of parties, but he called for widening the discretion of these representatives. The party should formulate a platform, a general policy, said Ben-Aharon. Party representatives in the Histadrut should have the authority to act within the framework of guidelines, rather than in response to specific instructions. During the whole period of his administration, Ben-Aaron was a lonely person in the senior office. The establishment of the Histadrut regarded him as an alien. To say it held no loyalty to him is an understatement. His power base was the people. This base was sufficient to bring him back to office when he resigned, but it was not strong enough to make him the secretary general for a second term.

Ben-Aharon preferred to join forces with the uprising from below, while his predecessor hoped to solve it by discipline. Nevertheless, this policy didn't mean relaxing control. The Histadrut was no more liable to approve strikes during Ben-Aharon's term than before. Either the secretary general did not have enough authority to bring about a *de-facto* change in policy, or he still believed that calling strikes should be a serious matter, not to be granted off hand. Both Becker and Ben-Aharon made a clear distinction as to who should be granted approval to strike and who should not. Strikes in the private sector are approvable. Strikes in the governmental sector are not. Strikes in the Histadrut sector should almost never be approved. Strikes in agriculture or industry are affordable. Strikes in the public services must be avoided. Strikes of essential services, electricity and water, should never be approved. So, while the rhetoric had changed, in practice the change in style did not bring about a change in action.

Yeruham Meshel, the third secretary general, was the antithesis of Ben-Aharon. A behind-the-scenes leader, he grew up in the Trade Union Division and knew the IR field in all its depth. The second in ranking in Becker's time, he had aspired to be his successor. The Histadrut, however, lacked an agent of change. Meshel was not that type of official. He was a member of the establishment, trusted by the leaders of the party and by the officials of the Histadrut. No one could imagine that he would head the Histadrut in its most volatile period. Meshel started his administration during the last year of the Labor Party reign. His first period, while serving with a Labor dominated government, was peaceful. The number of strikes was reduced from its recent apex. While Becker's period brought a record of 486 strikes per 1,000 days of administration, and Ben-Aharon—333, Meshel's first part had only 262. Meshel's administration tended to avoid strikes as much as possible. This was achieved both by behind-the-scenes negotiations, mediations and arbitration, and by an increased reluctance to approve strikes. No more than 81 strikes per 1,000 days were approved in this first period. This strike approval figure is the record lowest for any secretary general of the Histadrut under the ruling coalition.

Strikes in Meshel's Labor Party coalition period had one more important feature. They were responsible strikes. No research has been carried out on this topic on the earlier or later periods. The only research—on which I will report in more detail in a later chapter—was conducted on this period. One finding of this research shows that both unions and managements tended to avoid strikes in sensitive sites. The higher the damage the actors thought a strike in their place of work would incur, the less did they tend to call strikes. When the enthusiasm and overstatements of a crisis situation passed, actors regarded a strike that did take place in their place as having minimal negative consequences.

LIKUD DOMINATION (1977-84)

In May 1977 the Labor Party lost its dominant position in the Knesset. This defeat was a traumatic experience for Israeli society. A country in which a government without the Labor Party was unthinkable suddenly woke up to a new situation. One obvious question was how would the Histadrut—the only stronghold left for Labor—act. Politicians expected that the antagonism between the two major parties would spill over into the IR sphere. On the face of it, this was a sound prediction. The approaches of the two parties to industrial relations were completely polar. The Likud supports a distinction between union and management functions. The Histadrut is both a union and an economic entrepreneur. Labor rejected vehemently any thought of compulsory arbitration. The Likud promised to put it into legislation. Labor treated labor law legislation as a final step, following a process of autonomous negotiations and agreements. The Likud Party regarded the legislative procedure as a preferred method of state building.

Both vested interests and ideology threw the two major parties into polarization. The newly victorious Likud wanted to change the status quo. The party reigning in the Histadrut regarded maintaining the status quo as both preferred ideologically and important as a tactic.

The political change brought all traditional Histadrut claims to a test. Is it a political tool in the hands of a party, or is it a general federation of labor, as its official title indicates. After a short period of indecisiveness a clear choice was made. The General Federation of Labor quit party lines action and preferred to act as a mature union. The same is true for the government. Ideological considerations were much more prominent on the party platform than on the agenda of the government. No real effort to adopt compulsory arbitration, or to legislate a Union Law took place. So, while the political upheaval was an important turning point for the Israeli irs, it was not as cardinal as we could be easily tempted to think.

While the frequency of strikes and the its breakdown to approval status did not change significantly during the transition to the Likud era, a very pronounced change did take place along another dimension of the strike pattern—its average breadth. Strikes ceased to be actions mobilizing hundreds of workers. Their average size grew to the thousands. This is surely an important change. Although the Histadrut continued to disapprove small or medium strikes, it condoned larger ones.

The Histadrut's tendency to approve strike requests of larger, rather than smaller groups of workers, did not start with the political upheaval. Ben-Aharon was the first secretary general in whose time approved strikes were usually bigger in scale than unapproved strikes. For Ben-Aharon, this policy seemed like a probable derivation of his populist inclination. Meshel rejected this approach. He preferred union operations to run along conventional lines. Nevertheless, even during Meshel's Labor period approved strikes were double the size of unapproved ones. However, during the Likud period they reached a factor of 6.77![11] An average approved strike in Meshel's Likud time mobilized 6,835 workers, while the average size of an unapproved strike totalled 1,009. As the data show, this tendency to approve bigger strikes and to keep under control smaller ones was not spread throughout the economy. The stronger unions, those in the public services branch and in the public and governmental sector, were able to take advantage of it.

The Histadrut refused to serve as the gate keeper under the new regime. Those who had the power to raise and promote their demands encountered no opposition from the higher echelons of the union movement. This phenomenon may indicate that the Histadrut did tend to use its power against the Likud government. Still, this use is more a case of action by default than centrally-implemented policy. Moreover, as I will show in the following chapters, the government as employer and not the government as the ruler was the actual target.

The Likud government, as noted above, failed to initiate much new labor law legislation. It did, however, use the existing legal arsenal to its fullest capacity. An interesting example is the use of *"tsavei rituk"* (back-to-work orders). These have been part of the legal code since 1948. Labor governments, however, had an ideological repulsion to using them. What's more, the professional advice which the Labor government relied on warned against overusing this means. Both of these barriers disappeared when the Likud gained control of the industrial relations arena. State control of IR affairs had been traditionally supported by the Revisionist movement, which was the predecessor of the Likud. The academic consultants of the Labor governments came usually from Labor adjacent spheres. The Likud government hardly used their services. As a result, the average number of applications of *tsavei rituk* per year of Likud governments (1978-81) was twenty times higher than their average number during Labor's reign (1948-76).[12]

Beyond the increase in the size of strikes during the Likud era, radicalization of IR found its expression in the symbolic gestures of industrial conflict. Threats became more explicit. Instead of calling a workers meeting during work hour time, unions opted for warning strikes. This change is at its clearest in the public services.

THE NATIONAL UNITY ERA

The 1984 national elections brought the Israeli political system to a clear impasse. Even though the Labor Party had a significant lead in the public opinion polls, it failed to substantiate this lead in the voting booth. Neither the Likud nor Labor could establish a majority backed government. The only option left was to establish a national unity government with rotating prime ministers. The new government inherited an economy accelerating towards hyperinflation. Moreover, the country was involved in a highly disputed and clearly unsuccessful war in Lebanon. With such formidable problems, the situation was ripe for a dynamic government. Prime Minister Shimon Peres (Labor), who held the first half of the prime ministership, served for two years. Prime Minister Shamir occupied the second half-term. With so many developments in the political arena, the analysis of strike statistics is almost impossible. A distinction should be made between the interim period, until an agreement to form a unity government was reached, the Labor dominated two years and the Likud dominated period. Our data for this period covers only forty four months.

A further complication is the nomination of Israel Kessar, a new type of secretary general for the Histadrut. Unlike his East European predecessors, he is a Yemenite Jew, who earned a master's degree in Labor Studies at Tel-Aviv University. He served under his predecessor, Meshel, who recommended him for office. He was hailed by both living former secretary generals, Becker and Ben-Aharon. He ran an American style election campaign, focusing on his personal virtues and underplaying party considerations. His period shows a culmination of the processes which started prior to his inauguration. Kessar regards himself as the leader of a labor movement and not of a union. He prefers to let his second-in-command, the head of the Trade Union Division, Hayim Haberfeld, handle union affairs. He regards his main task as the safeguarding of the Histadrut institutional setting. He did not have to wait long for challenges to this setting.

The new economic policy, as planned by the leader of his own party, Prime Minister Peres, called for emergency legislation in the labor market. Such a legal act has never been enacted in Israel. Kessar believed that its implementation could hamper free negotiations in the foreseeable future. Therefore, instead of arguing against substantive proposals, like freezing of wages or wide scale lay-offs, Kessar chose another target. The campaign against compulsory legislation of terms of employment forced the government to negotiate. The Histadrut acted on a par with the government and gained its objectives. The compulsory legislation has never been implemented.

Kessar brought the policy—which I prefer to call an umbrella policy—to perfection. The Histadrut no longer tries to control industrial conflict by either disciplinary or administrative means. It is highly involved in the daily functioning of the irs, but its involvement has taken a new form. On the one hand, we see a clear interest in supplying an institutional patronage to the IR field. Whoever acts in this field or tries to influence its activity should be aware of its autonomous identity. At the functional level, on the other hand, Histadrut lower-level functionaries, mostly elected by their immediate constituencies, are the carriers of the daily routines of the domain. Neither the institutional sponsorship nor the decentralization of tasks are assured. Contemporary political and economic developments are not promising. The prediction of future developments is, however, beyond the scope of this introductory chapter.

Notes to Chapter 1

1. Meshel was officially the vice-secretary general in Ben-Aharon's term of office. This nomination exemplifies Ben-Aharon's peculiar isolation, rather than having any collaborative connotations.
2. The term "industrial relations system" refers traditionally both to the specific elements if the industrial relations arena (actors, ideology, rules) and to these elements together with its economic, political and technological constraints. In the present manuscript, the first, more specific meaning , will be denoted as "UOA". The term unit of analysis (UOA) emphasizes my present stress on the hierarchical mature of industrial relations processes.
3. The only previous National Unity government to be formed in Israel was in 1967. It was imposed on prime minister Levi Eshkol by sweeping public opinion and the preference explicitly expressed by senior officers reflecting the mood of the army.
4. This term, "society of Jewish work," is a quotation from the Histadrut founding charter. It focuses attention on the unique character of Zionist ideology. The Zionist movement did not limit itself to the formidable tasks of return to an ancient homeland and gaining independence. It also envisioned a complete transformation of the Jewish nation from communities mostly involved with commerce, to a "normal" nation engaged in manual work. Return to the land by means of agricultural work was regarded as the highest fulfillment of the Zionist dream.
5. The term "Israel" is used throughout in an ahistorical fashion, The territory of contemporary Israel is referred to as Israel even if it was under Turkish or British mandate rule at the relevant period.
6. The term "Labor Party" will be used for any of the ancestral formations preceding the establishment of the present Labor Party.
7. The term "Yishuv" (settlement) was used to identify the Jewish Zionist community in Palestine under the British mandate. It had its own autonomous political establishment, closely connected to the World Zionist Organization and the Jewish establishment in the diaspora.
8. The terms "IR Commissioner" and "labor officer" are used interchangeably throughout the text.
9. The disbanding of the Palmach (fighting companies), a military unit of the underground Haganah (defence organization), was not easily accepted by the left wing of the labor movement.
10. The use of military force was needed to convince the Irgun underground movement (a radical rival of the Palmach), headed by Menachem Begin, that no fractional armies would be allowed in the newly declared state.
11. All following figures refer to Histadrut affiliated strikes. Other stoppages are excluded from the computations.
12. Since the change in ruling parties occurred in the middle (May) of 1977, the data for this year were dropped.

2

The Israeli irs

Introduction

THE MAIN ACTORS

As noted in the introductory chapter, following Dunlop (1958), it is customary to divide the actors of an industrial relations system (irs) into three categories: 1) employers and employers' associations; 2) workers and their trade unions, and 3) third parties. Each of these three types of actor may be differentiated at the various levels of the economy, national, industrial, local, or plant level. A far reaching characteristic of Israeli society can be discerned by reference to the major types of ownership, private, public, or Histadrut-owned. Table 2.1 presents the main actors of the Israeli irs by their category, level and sector of ownership.

With even a cursory glace at Table 2.l, two main features of the Israeli irs force themselves on us: 1) the omnipresence of the Histadrut and 2) the lack of unity of the employers. The Histadrut appears both on the headings of a column, as the major union in all three ownership sectors and on both levels of negotiation, and on the heading of a row, as a distinct ownership sector. What's more, its extension on the local level (Local Labor Council), and its national Trade Union Division serve as third parties at both national and plant levels of the Histadrut sector. This structural feature of the Israeli irs assigns the Histadrut a central function, leaving its partners with a somewhat more peripheral status. This characteristic gives the Histadrut a widely based perspective, allowing the other actors to pursue their more particularistic concerns.

Employers' Associations

The simplest meaning of the term employers' association is

> the organization of employers, who are free to enter negotiations and to take contractual obligations, with the intervention of neither of government nor a trade union, in their autonomy and decisions. It is an association of employers whose considerations stem from their status as owners of capital invested in profitable target. (Dror and Shirom, 1983, p. 5)

This looks like a counter-definition to that of a trade union. It stresses both voluntarism and personal membership. Notwithstanding its intuitive attractiveness, this definition cannot suffice to represent the counterparts of Israeli unions on the employers' side. No one single entity in the management column of Table 2.1 fits this definition. The Coordinating Bureau of Economic Associations is a fragmented organization of associations and not of individual people. The Civil Service Commissioner is a statutory position, and the commissioner is a state employee, while *Hevrat ha'Ovdim* is a holding company and all its shares are owned by the Histadrut. Employers' associations are to be identified, therefore, by their function in the irs and not by their motivating power or ideology.

Table 2.1: Main actors in the Israeli irs by level and ownership sector.

Level and Ownership Sector	Industrial Relations Actor Classification		
	Management	Union	Third Party
NATIONAL Private	Coordinating Bureau Labor Court, of Economic Organizations	Trade Union Division	Histadrut – Department of Labor Relations
Public	Civil Service Commission	Histadrut – Trade Union Division	Labor Court
Histadrut	Histadrut – Hevrat Ha'Ovdim	Histadrut – Trade Union Division	Histadrut – Trade Union Division
LOCAL Private	Local Management	Workers' Committee	Labor Court, Department of Labor Relations
Public	Local Management	Workers' Committee	Histadrut – Local Labor Council
Histadrut	Local Management	Workers' Committee	Trade Union Division

Private Sector Employers' Associations

Israeli private sector employers' associations started as trade associations. The Manufacturers' Association was formally established in 1920 (but started to operate only in 1923), the Farmer's Association was founded in 1927, and the Diamond Manufacturers' Association in 1939. At their inception, all these associations were more interested in issues like price control, marketing, political lobbying etc., than in collective bargaining. Right from the start, they faced a dominant trade union, the Histadrut. This situation eventually made them enter the rabor relations arena, with political and economic conditions as facilitating factors (Shirom, 1984). Dror and Shirom (1983) present a listing of eighteen employers' associations, but caution us that

> any effort to specify the names of an associations that represent employers must be defined to a specific point in time. Once in a while new associations come into being, others split or unite, seldom some association even cease to operate or even disintegrate formally. (1981, p. 37)

Therefore, a detailed description of these bodies is not essential for our purposes. A presentation of the most important single association, the Manufacturers' Association of Israel (MAI) and the central body of the private sector employers, the Coordinating Bureau of Economic Associations (CBEA), will suffice. In the years preceding World War II, industry had a low priority both for the British mandate administration and the Zionist movement. The virtual blockade causes by the war and the interest of the British in assuring a stable supply of products to the Allied Forces in the Middle East established Jewish industry as an asset to be maintained in as smooth a running order as possible for the Mandate administration. When wartime inflation threatened to upset labor relations in Palestine, the government preferred to channel its efforts at conciliation through a limited number of outlets. The Association of Industrialists, as it was called then, seemed like a suitable partner.

Under the auspices of the administration, a first co-agreement was signed with the Histadrut. By this method, industrial peace was sought. (In addition, a law was introduced that prohibited strikes and imposed obligatory arbitration.) This agreement brought the Association to the fore. The establishment of the State of Israel gave further impetus to the organization. The labor dominated coalition government, which ruled Israel until 1977, believed in a mixed economy and tried to promote industrialization. Private sector industrialists were regarded both as entrepreneurs and as attractive partners for foreign investors. Thus, their association received support, and its staff started to grow in the early 1960s. At present, MAI's professional staff includes economists, engineers, and lawyers. An important step in the development of the association was taken in 1965, when its strike insurance fund was established. At the beginning, membership in the fund was optional, but since 1977, joining the fund has been a requirement of MAI members. At present, affiliation with the fund is not limited exclusively to MAI members. The fund, which is managed professionally, adheres to a solid and conservative ideology and has contributed to the formation of a responsible irs in Israeli industry.

The Coordinating Bureau of Economic Associations is a recent actor in the Israeli irs. It was established in 1965 as an interim arrangement towards a desired federation of employers' associations. The CBEA's finest hour came in the early 1970s, when an era of tripartite national level package agreements started. Various price-wage-tax regulation contracts brought the national representation of the private sector employers to the fore. Israeli Employers' associations supported an ideology of free enterprise, opposing any government intervention in wage determination or the fixing by legislation of employment conditions. This negation of central legislation in labor relations brought them quite naturally to the negotiating table with the Histadrut (Dror and Shirom, 1983, p. 18).

The tripartite package agreements were, in a way, a culmination of this non-intervention ideology. The government, or to phrase it differently, even the government, must negotiate in order to promote its economic policies. This zealous belief in the idea of an autonomous irs is a cornerstone of the ideology of the CBEA. A recent example for this thesis was the CBEA's staunch rejection of any minimum wage legislation, an issue that has been approached quite hesitantly, and with meager results, through contract negotiations. Wide political support eventually led to the enactment of a minimum wage act (1984), forced on a resistant government because it feared a collapse of wage stability. In a very exceptional mood, the Histadrut, which usually argues against imposed legislation, preferred this time to support the initiative favoring substance over procedure in this case. The CBEA opposed both substance and procedure.

The CBEA is led by a five-member committee composed of the presidents of the industrialists', farmers', building contractors', merchants', and artisans' associations. The president of the CBEA is the president of the MAI, and the offices of the CBEA are in the headquarters of the MAI. Therefore, the Coordinating Bureau is clearly dominated by the industrial sector, although the maintenance of solidarity and discipline is a major challenge for it. A norm of consensus has so far kept the fragile organization from an enduring threat of disintegration.

The Structure of Public Sector Employership

Approximately a quarter of the salaried workers in Israel are employed by a public (non-Histadrut) employer. This sector includes civil service, public associations, local government, institutions of higher learning, and defense and government owned companies. The government controls, or at least tries to shape industrial relations in this sector by various means and methods. The Civil Service Commissioner (CSC) used to be the sole authorized office holder to negotiate with the various unions on behalf of the government as the direct employer of civil service employees. Recently, a new position of wage controller has gained priority in contract negotiations. The publicly-owned associations (National Insurance, Employment Service, Ports Authority, Civil Aviation Authority, etc.) are run by semi-autonomous officials who are expected to follow Civil Service policy, with "needed adjustments."

These adjustments are vaguely defined. Their vague definition is, however, not unintentional. It allows these enterprises somewhat more flexible arrangements than those customary for the civil service. Still, the conditions of employment as practiced by the civil service act as a frame of reference, whether as a positive frame and a object for adoption, or as a negative frame, leading to conscious rejection. Somewhat further apart from the CSC stand local government, universities and colleges. These units are simultaneously independent organs and heavily supported by government budgets. By controlling the financial resources, the government tries, with some degree of success, to adjust wages and salaries in this subsector to the norms of the civil service.

The lesson that economic solvency consolidates independence has been learned by government-owned industry. Companies owned by the government are managed through a board of directors, the members of which assume a difficult task. On the one hand they serve as the representatives of government and are expected to abide by its policy. On the other hand, they are required by the Government Companies Law to put the economic interests of their company as their primary consideration (unless explicitly ordered to act differently by an authorization committee). The burden of political pressure feels much lighter when a firm can show economic success. Therefore, the impact of the CSC fades with an increase in profitability.

The terms of employment of almost all public sector employees are determined through collective bargaining. The Civil Service Code provides a detailed specification of wages, salaries and conditions of employment, stemming from a complicated web of collective agreements. Public sector employment is under budgetary constraints, but the institutionalization of the budget, in its sociological rather than the legal meaning, has never been high. Deviations from the budget are a frequent phenomenon, and updating of allocations and tolerance of over-spending are the common. Under these conditions, industrial relations issues are raised, negotiated, and agreed in the framework of the collective bargaining logic, with minimal sensitivity to budgetary constraints. So, once again, public employers tend to acknowledge the autonomy of the industrial relations sphere and to abide by its norms.

The Structure of the Histadrut Sector (Hevrat ha'Ovdim)

Being a member in the Histadrut has three elements: first, it is a political process, whereby the rank-and-file can vote and be elected to various legislative and executive positions. Second, it is an economic act, by which a member becomes a shareholder in an enormous economic enterprise, Hevrat ha'Ovdim, and third, it is a professional step by means of which a person is assigned to a trade union. (Ben-Meir, 1978, p. 146) The present discussion deals with the second aspect of this threefold phenomenon.

Hevrat ha'Ovdim (HHO) is the holding company of the Histadrut's economic ventures. Table 2.2 presents some indicators of the economic scope of this sector. The figures are conservative estimates of the Histadrut's economic activities. They cover only the larger companies, and those where share of ownership amounts to fifty percent or more. As a whole, between a fifth and a quarter of the Israeli economy is owned by the Histadrut and operated through the HHO. The operative directorate of the HHO is the twenty-nine member Managing Committee (Va'ada Menahelet), chaired by the secretary of the HHO. The Managing Committee is elected by the HHO secretariat (6 members). The secretary general of the Histadrut serves as the chairperson of the secretariat. Three more institutions serve as democratic organs of legislation and membership control. These are the Convention (1,501 members), the Council (501) and the Executive Committee (151). All three forums function in dual capacities. They convene periodically, sometimes as the legislative organs of the Histadrut, and at other times, as the legislative bodies of HHO. In many instances, these meetings are scheduled on successive days.

Table 2.2: Hevrat ha'Ovdim: Some economic indicators (1982) (Percentages). *

Percent of Total Israeli:	Year	
	1982	1983
Industrial Investment	28	27
Industrial Sales	27	28
Industrial Export	23	25
Industrial Employment	19	20
Construction	15	13
Beginning of New Housing	12	8
Agricultural Production	86	87
Wholesale Sales	12	– **
Life Insurance	27	24

* Source: Hevrat Ha'Ovdim, 1982. The Economic Department and Culture and Education Enterprises.
** No data.

The Histadrut-owned sector can be divided into two main parts, the administered and the self-managed. The first includes all economic enterprises which are under the direct ownership of the Histadrut. In these enterprises, all directors and general managers are appointed by the HHO. The second type includes cooperatives, moshavim and kibbutzim, but is of peripheral relevance to our present discussion which will therefore deal solely with the administered sub-sector of the HHO.

Can the executive bodies of HHO be regarded as an employers' association? Hardly so. All members of its executive bodies are either elected through party lists or nominated on the basis of their political affiliation. They are not people "whose considerations stem from their status as owners of capital invested in profitable targets." But that is not the main point. Work conditions in Histadrut-owned enterprises are fixed by the executive bodies of the Histadrut. The bylaws of the federation designate the Trade Union Division (TUD) as the ultimate authority for this purpose. Therefore, whenever disagreement arises between the TUD and the secretariat of the HHD, the former's views take precedence. Therefore, HHD is not a forum which is "free to enter negotiations and to take contractual obligations, without intervention, neither of government nor [and in particular] of a trade union." Ben-Meir, himself a former high-ranking functionary in the Histadrut establishment, presents nine reasons why the HHD can serve as a powerful tool for the promotion of the Histadrut's class struggles. With these considerations in mind, the HHD is a very peculiar type of employers' association:

1. Industrial relations in the Histadrut owned sector are not determined solely by the laws of supply and demand. Criteria of social justice and promotion of the interests of the workers are of primary importance.

2. In times of confrontation in negotiations with employers outside the HHD, the Histadrut can order its own sector to adopt its demands and implement them in its enterprises. In this way, the TUD may be able to demonstrate to its counterparts the feasibility of its demands.

3. During long strikes, when reserves in the strike fund become exhausted, the Histadrut plants can employ the strikers and supplement their subsistence.

4. In times of strikes, when solidarity of employers prohibits employment in substitute jobs, HHD can supply work even if it is uneconomical to do so.

5. The HHD can start a multiplier effect, boosting the economy in times of depression.

6. By avoiding layofs in times of recession, a deterioration of the economic situation can be avoided.

7. The Histadrut administers and owns many funds. These may be used for supplying loans to employers, private and public, to create or at least keep jobs.

8. The Histadrut can offer a wide range of opportunities for retraining in its vocational schools and thus can reduce unemployment.

9. The Histadrut can adopt long range planning and tie the HHD's employment to future levels. (Ben-Meir, 1978, pp. 193-195)

Considerations like these minimize the involvement of HHD in union-management negotiations. Traditionally, the terms of agreements undersigned by the CBEO and the TUD, have been automatically adopted by the Histadrut owned sector. Industry and plant level negotiations are customarily conducted behind closed doors, and their outcomes are usually to the benefit of labor representation. The Histadrut has managed to safeguard its sector from external determination, and even in hard economic times has not been forced to make wage or employment cuts. Such an approach can stand moderate economic fluctuations, but extreme depressions have had disastrous effects. Such was the case in 1927, when Solel Boneh, the major Histadrut owned contracting company closed its doors, and more recently, in the mid 1980's, when various construction and industrial companies fell into massive deficit.

Employer's Associations — Conclusion

As we see, national employers associations do exist in Israel, but their scope is less than that of the Histadrut, and they are less tightly organized. Inter-sectoral employer interaction in the sphere of industrial relations is almost nonexistent. The Coordinating Bureau of Economic Associations is a tenuous confederation of independent partners, and its importance is determined less by the representation needs of the employers than by its leaders' personalities. The specialized employers' associations are much more solid and stable institutions. The most influential among them is the Manufacturers Association (*Hit'achadut Ha'taasiyanim*), which in 1975 represented a total of 1,040 firms, employing almost 50 per cent of Israel's industrial workers. This organization, in spite of fulfilling strategic functions in the realm of industrial relations in general, and strike insurance in particular, is much less centralized than the Histadrut. The individual employer within the association is much more autonomous than his counterpart on the union side—the local workers committee.

A trend towards centralization is clearly evident among employers in the public and the Histadrut sectors. The Civil Service Commission can be singled out as the most important actor in the public sector arena. Its paramount status stems from its direct linkage with the government and its policies. It serves both as a direct wage and salary regulating agency for the Israeli civil service and as an indirect reference framework for other public and semi-public employers.

Labor Representation — The Trade Union Division of the Histadrut (TUD)

The hub of labor relations in Israel is the Trade Union Division of the Histadrut. The unit is simultaneously an administrative section of the Federation's bureaucracy, a political position and a comprehensive assemblage of union representatives.

The administrative body of the Histadrut is divided into ten divisions: (1) The Trade Union Division, (2) The Organization Division, (3) The Division of Social Security, (4) Hevrat ha'Ovdim, (5) The Center for Culture and Education, (6) Na'amat (Volunteering Female Workers), (7) The Industrial Democracy Division, (8) The Central Consuming Authority Division, (9) The Bursar Division, (10) The Division of Administration, Personnel and Planning. Of all ten divisions the TUD is regard as the most important. During the last thirty years, whenever an insider was elected to the post of the secretary general of the Histadrut, he had formerly been the head of the Trade Union Division (Becker, Meshel, Kessar). In most cases, the head of this division also serves as an acting secretary general whenever the elected office holder cannot fulfill his duties, for personal or political reasons.

The primary positions of the TUD are occupied by political personalities. The chairperson of the division has always been a member of the Labor Party (or its predecessors), and a political flavor adheres to the secretaries of most Trade Unions. They are elected to their positions through a system of party lists. (This characteristic is somewhat less typical for the representatives of the professional unions.)

An impressive variety of unions send their functionaries to the Plenum of the TUD (160 members) and to its Coordinating Committee (30 members). With the exception of very few occupations almost all salaried workers in Israel are represented by the TUD of the Histadrut. This noteable situation has the following reasons: (1) approximately sixty percent of the Israeli population are Histadrut members, (2) an additional five to seven percent of the population are members in two independent religions movements (ha'Poel ha'Mizrachi and Po'alei Agudat Israel), that joined the TUD (and some other Histadrut organs) without being required to merge completely with the General Federation, (3) almost all collective agreements undersigned in Israel, are with the TUD or its affiliated unions. According to the Law of Collective Agreements (1957), a collective agreement covers every and each employee in a given unit, whether he/she is a member of the representative union or not and, (4) a wide variety of extension orders have been issued by the Minister of Labor and Welfare extending the validity of collective agreements to non unionized parts of the Israeli economy.

THIRD PARTIES

Third party services are supplied by the government through the system of labor courts (Ben-Israel, 1978) and by the Department of Labor Relations in the Ministry of Labor and Welfare (Galin and Krislov, 1979).

Labor courts were established in Israel in 1969. Their involvement in collective bargaining is limited to rights disputes and to enforcing labor and management observance of labor legislation. The labor court has two levels, dealing with local and national claims. The number of collective disputes claims submitted to local courts increased from 6 in 1970, to 30 in 1974, 66 in 1978, and 130 in 1981. Most of the claims were initiated by management in the course of strikes. The labor court is usually regarded by all parties as a facilitative rather than as an executive institution.

The substance of collective labor relations is that the relationships, including the solution of disagreements and disputes, will take place between sides [i.e. management and union], and not through disregarding or concealing them. (Hausman and Goldberg, 1977, p. 856a).

The Department of Labor Relations is empowered by the Settlement of Labor Disputes Law (1958) to supply both compulsory mediation and voluntary arbitration. It has been the policy of the Department since its inception to avoid the use of compulsion.

THE HISTADRUT AND ITS ENVIRONMENTS

When founded in 1920, the Histadrut had 4,433 members. By 1979 its membership had risen to 1,495,000. This tremendous growth influenced its structure, but had very little impact on its governing principles. Throughout its history, the Histadrut has emphasized its generality, politicality, and centralization. All wage earners and 'non-exploitative'[1] self-employed workers are expected to join the Histadrut, and, as noted above, in 1977 sixty-five per cent of the total Israeli population was affiliated to it (Economic and Social Research Institute, 1981, p. 2). Its legislative governing bodies are based on a proportional party system determined by elections held every four years. All executive positions are assigned by coalition key. A Histadrut member is first of all a member of the General Federation of Labor and only through this affiliation does he become a member of a particular trade union. Central institutions, rather than specific unions or localities are, thus, its primary sources of authority.

As can be seen in Table 2.1, the national-level industrial relations system varies substantially from ownership sector to ownership sector. As a mixed economy, Israel has, like the West, a private sector of a capitalistic structure and a welfare-state public sector. It also has a unique Histadrut-owned sector. Management representation on the national level differs from sector to sector, but the Trade Union Division of the Histadrut represents wage earners irrespective of sector. This feature of the Israeli irs, as well as the uniquely high level of unionization, places the Histadrut in an extremely powerful position. Both the positive and negative implications of this unique position will be elaborated below.

The Histadrut's special status can also be discerned from the third party column in Table 2.1. Whereas the classic trade union sits on one side of the bargaining table as the representative of labor, the Histadrut serves as a third party both on the national industrial relations system level, in the Histadrut owned sector and on the local level, where it functions through its local Labor Councils (Mo'atsot Po'alim). Such a role on the local level exists outside Israel, but to a much lesser degree. The Collective Agreements Law (1957) stipulates that there are only two parties to a collective contract, the employer, or an employers association, and the union that signed the agreement. A local workers' committee is not regarded as a legal party for this purpose, but is looked upon as part of the national union and is expected to act in compliance with the code of the national union (Hausman and Goldberg, 1977, p. 52). Since local union/ national union disputes are thus rendered totally internal affairs, the Histadrut holds third-party status in many local disputes, a situation frequently welcomed by local employers.

The Histadrut, as a complex organization, has both external and internal environments. Externally, it communicates, among others, with the state. On the internal perimeter the Histadrut deals with its subordinate units. On the face of it, the continuum of external front—Histadrut—subordinate Histadrut units is a unidimensional phenomenon. The Histadrut should comply with state law, while subordinate Histadrut units should comply both with state law and Histadrut bylaws. In fact, the situation is not so simple. The Histadrut negotiates with the state. It is not subordinate to it. In some areas—wage fixing is a clear example—the government holds routine rounds of negotiation with the Histadrut (or with one of its subunits). In other areas such as the shaping of economic or welfare policy, the involvement of the Histadrut is less routine. Different governments, finance ministers and secretaries general have taken different approaches. The Labor Party has seen the Histadrut as a legitimate partner in a wider range of issues than has the Likud Party. Some Likud Party finance ministers, Simha Ehrlich for example, were more ready to negotiate with the Histadrut on non-union specific topics than others (such as Yoram Aridor), while some secretaries general of the Histadrut, like Ben-Aharon, conceived the mission of their organization to be wider than did others (such as Meshel).

The relationships between the Histadrut and its subsidiaries are also not clear cut. In the early 1960s, Hevrat ha'Ovdim, the holding company of all Histadrut sector enterprises, was no more than a small, low level staff unit in the Executive Committee of the Histadrut. Later it become a much stronger unit headed by Yaacov Lewinson, a strong figure, and staffed with economists. The relationships between the central body of the Histadrut and its local extensions are also not of the same kind. The three largest workers' councils, those in Jerusalem, Tel-Aviv and Haifa, are relatively independent from the financial point of view. The budgets of all other councils are kept under the supervision and administration of the Organization Division of the Histadrut.

Some unions are more independent than others. The Teachers' Union, for example joined the Histadrut in 1942. It was, and still is, a large union, controlling an independent bank and other financial assets. When it joined the Histadrut, this union insisted on keeping its autonomy. By the assigning of it to a special status in the Histadrut organizational chart, its claim was respected. The Teachers' Union is therefore directly subordinate to the secretary general and not to the head of the Trade Union division, as are all other unions. Similar arrangements have crystallized over the years for other white collar and professional unions. The engineers, physicians and the lawyers have kept their own independent professional associations. This alternative organizational arrangement allows them a wider choice than usually accorded to affiliated unions.

Thus, as we can see, discussing both the external and the internal environments of the Histadrut is a much more realistic approach than dealing with it as an independent and unified entity.

The Relationships between the Histadrut and the State Political Elite

The trend toward an increase in TUD autonomy was preceded by an expansion of the Histadrut's independence from Israel's political elite, or to be more specific from the leadership of the Labor Party. Becker who served as a secretary general during the 1960s believed that both Histadrut leadership and government ministers were the organ of the party.

> I have never believed and never will, that the delegates of the party in the two most central executive arms—the government and the Histadrut—should be allowed to fight one another, using means like demonstrations, strikes, protest declarations, etc. I believe that they must adhere to party discipline and demand its involvement. They should try and bring the party to adopt their views. If they fail, they ought to resign. (Becker, 1982, p. 243)

He also expressed this another way:

> The major factor which stood behind the generality of the Histadrut and safeguarded its uniqueness was the Labor Party . . . *the party* (emphasis in the original) formulated its policy in the Histadrut, and its agents were the carriers of this policy. This party served as the pivot joint that connected between its spokesmen in the state and in the Histadrut. Just as the party discussed and reached decisions on the central problems of the state, so did it discuss and reach decisions on the principal issues of Histadrut life.... The secretary general of the Histadrut, Pinhas Lavon (1949-50), and myself were assigned to shape the patterns of mutual relations between the government and the Histadrut and we did it, through the party and its institutions. (1982, p. 24)

Becker regarded the labor movement as the most crucial factor. It's *raison d'etre* was primarily ideological, both socialistic and Zionist. The leading apparatus for promoting ideology is the party, in this case the Labor Party or its predecessor, Mapai. The party was conceived as a superstructure entity with exclusive authority to determine in detail a binding policy. Becker does not deny the existence of disagreements inside the party.

> These struggles [between cabinet ministers and Histadrut leadership] were frequently very bitter, but they were usually run in the closed forums of the party and the public at large was unaware of their existence." (1982, p. 242)

It will be recalled that Ben-Aharon succeeded Becker in 1970. On the surface, they seemed like extreme opposites. Becker had a weak image. His public speeches were calm and moderate and he had as solid a faith in the party as any politician can have. He was a city dweller and served for many year in the ranks of the Histadrut. Ben-Aharon, on the other hand, was regarded as a man of principle, who had demonstrated his independence by resigning from his ministerial position in 1962. An energetic speaker and a talented writer, he was a member of Kibbutz Giv'at Hai'im and was sent to fulfil many duties during his long public life. Despite their differences, they shared a devoted belief in the socialistic and Zionist values of the Israeli labor movement. But Becker was a conformist, while Ben-Aharon was a prototype of the nonconformist. Ben-Aharon, says Gothelf (n.d., p. 29) believed that

> The General Federation of Labor, The Histadrut, is in need of the spiritual-ideational guidance of the political party. The Histadrut cannot produce ideas for Hevrat ha'Ovdim, for the nature of the Israeli society, for the distribution of national income and the product of labor, for peace and war. The Histadrut is dependent for life and death on the social-political creativity of the party.

Still, argues Gothelf, Ben-Aharon believed that the party must shape the general policy of the Histadrut, but not get into its ways of implementation, fixing of exact percents for wages, cost of living allowance (COLA), etc. As noted in the introduction, Ben-Aharon was a great believer in the people. He was interested in revitalizing the bureaucratized Histadrut by bringing rank-and-file members into its representative bodies. This populist approach brought him into continual conflict with the party establishment. While Becker regarded party leadership as composed of three equal-status components, the government members block, the Histadrut leadership bloc, and others, Ben-Aharon identified a hierarchy, with party leadership located in state government. Under this constraint, Histadrut leadership has a permanently inferior status. Only pressure from below can counterbalance the authority of party-government leadership. In an interview, Ben-Aharon argued that the government had failed many secretaries general of the Histadrut, including himself. This was because the interests of government and the Histadrut were not identical.

Therefore, Ben-Aharon supported the following six principles:

1. The state must refrain from involvement in the ir sphere.

Many examples can demonstrate this point. On September 15, 1971, in the midst of widespread labor unrest, the Knesset held a debate on the state of labor relations. Although he, himself, was a member (MK) of Knesset, Ben-Aharon stayed away. On May 15, 1972, he resigned his office, only taking it back when wide popular support materialized. This act was a response to a mediation effort which was initiated first by Mr. Almogi, the Minister of Labor, and later by Prime Minister Meir.

An extreme expression of this principle was reported by the press on January 7, 1971. Ben-Aharon criticized Finance Minister Sapir for discussing wage issues in his budget speech. "Wages are not connected with the budget speech," argued Ben-Aharon, "because they are based on free negotiation between the Histadrut and the employers, and are not under the jurisdiction of the government and the Knesset."

2. The relationships between the Histadrut and the government are an issue open to coordination and not dictate.

This thesis was announced by Mr. Asher Golan, who served as a representative of the Histadrut in the price committee on June 30, 1972.

> Up till now, the Histadrut was a branch of the party. This was very convenient to government since Histadrut steps were coordinated with government prior to their implementation. Today [1972], the secretary general of the Histadrut represents an authentic position which he is ready to coordinate with the state, but not to bind by command.

This policy led Minister Bar-Lev to accuse [unspecified people] of establishing a separatist state, which did not recognize the contiguous state, and was even fighting a war of attrition against it.

3. The state and the Histadrut must avoid being superimposed.

Political life is highlighted during election periods. Therefore, argued Ben-Aharon, an effort should be made to separate state and Histadrut election dates. This stance has been ratified by both his successors.

4. The party must allow significant leeway to its representatives in the Histadrut.

This principle has been applied time and again. For example, after a long series of meetings a clear wage policy was agreed upon by a widely based and respected nineteen-member party committee. Ben-Aharon requested (January 11, 1970) that no decision be made by the committee and that the policy draft be brought for discussion and decision to the executive committee of the Histadrut (185 members).

5. The Executive Committee is the legislative forum of the Histadrut.

Its members are elected indirectly on the basis of party affiliation. Both coalition and opposition parties are represented in it. Still, the labor party has managed to control this panel since the establishment of a unified labor party. Therefore, this setting is controlled by the Histadrut bloc of the Labor Party. Non-Histadrut bloc functionaries of the party are, nevertheless, excluded from it. A few months after the events noted above, on May 5th, a plan to establish a center for the Trade Union Department with 107 members, many of whom were regular members of their unions, was accidentally leaked to the media. The clearest sign of criticism relates to the fact that the plan was initiated by Ben-Aharon without ever having been discussed in any party setting. Then, on October 12th, the press reported that the central committee, the executive organ of the Histadrut, had discussed a demand for an increase in cost-of-living compensation. While Meshel, then the deputy secretary general proposed waiting for the party's decision, Ben-Aharon disagreed. He demanded an immediate Histadrut decision, followed by a struggle with the party.

6. An effort should be made to encourage 'authentic' popular leadership, and common membership involvement in the Histadrut.

An organization, any organization, prefers the established to the unculti-
vated. A union is no different. The spontaneous leader who gains members'
support, is a threat to the established functionaries of the union. A classic
example of this kind is the leader of the stevedores in Ashdod Port, Yehoshua
Peretz. This workers' committee chairman gained the support of his fellow
workers and expressed his contempt for Histadrut authority. Becker, who
tried to discipline disobedient shop stewards initiated an appeal against him
and his colleagues in the internal judiciary court of the Histadrut. This trial
proved very unconstructive and, eventually, the dispute was settled out of
court.

Ben-Aharon adopted a much more supportive approach towards Peretz,
and this exposed him to continuous criticism by the press, government and
the public. Nevertheless, Ben-Aharon regard Peretz as the prototype of the
authentic leader as continued to support him. Peretz reciprocated with respect
and even with an act of crossing a picket line, during a strike of foremen
which was repudiated by the secretary general.

In his conclusion to a discussion of the prospects for the Histadrut in the
1970s, Ben-Aharon stated:

> Whatever you present as signs of crisis etc., are, as far as I am con-
> cerned, one of the great miracles. What degree of loyalty, patience,
> acquiescence, idealism (call them by less flattering terms if you wish) of
> Histadrut members to the social, administrative and democratic
> regime which exists here for years and years, when nobody but those
> who work here justifies it. And there is no way to change it. (Gothelf,
> n.d., p. 36)

Ben-Aharon was the standard bearer for this acquiescent public. He hoped
to make popular support his trump card against the Histadrut establishment
and the leadership of the Labor party. When the moment of truth came, this
hope of support was not realized as effectively as he hoped. On November
18th, 1973, after winning only a moderate victory in the general elections of
the Histadrut, Ben-Aharon resigned and opened the door for his successor,
Yeruham Meshel.

The Histadrut that the new secretary general inherited was very different
from that bequeathed by Becker. It was a kind of *enfant terrible* of Israeli society. Many myths of harmony had been exploded, but a new and consolidated
Histadrut did not emerge. The degree of Histadrut autonomy increased, even
though this was bitterly criticized on a wide front. A political upheaval, in the
form of a Labor Party defeat in parliamentary election was needed to consoli-
date Ben-Aharon's beginning. This defeat would have been for Ben-Aharon
his least preferred development. Still, it managed to confer a state of semi
autonomy on Secretary General Meshel. This development will be described
in more detail below.

The Relationship between the Histadrut as a General Federation and the TUD

The Histadrut is not a trade union, although one of its functions is the running of trade union activities. Only if we agree to and understand the distinction between being a union and engaging in a union's function, can we explicate the relationships between the Histadrut and its Trade Union Division. The ten division structure of the Histadrut has been delineated above. Even a cursory glance can convince us that the Histadrut is not a federation of trade unions. The wide scope of Histadrut activities makes it a strange combination of political movement, economic enterprise, trade union, social security agency and cultural institute. No one of these functions describes the Histadrut in full. It is a unique body, much more than the sum of its divisions.

The first clause in the Histadrut's constitution explains this unique feature:

> The Histadrut unites all workers in the country, who live of their own work without exploiting others, for the arrangement of all the settlement, economic and even cultural concerns of all the workers in the country, for the purpose of establishing a society of Hebrew labor in Eretz Israel.

With this wide platform in mind, the Histadrut served as a major tool in the establishment of an economy, in the creation of a society, and in the revitalization of a culture. Before independence, the Histadrut acted as a quasi-state. Even at present the secretary general of the Histadrut can argue quite convincingly that Israel *is* the Histadrut. His claim has much more validity than the well-known statement, "The U.S.A. is G.M." In the early days of the Histadrut (1920-40), its political center was engaged primarily with the nationwide problems of economy, security and culture. The trade union function was decentralized, and implemented by local labor councils. It was not until 1940 that a trade union department (not division!) was established. The increasing involvement of the Histadrut, as a national-level body, with issues of industrial relations created endemic tensions between the roles of secretary general of the Histadrut and head of the TUD.

At first, the tensions were conceived of on a personal level. The personal relations between secretary general Becker (1960-69) and Meshel, his TUD head, were unbearable. (In his autobiography, *Of Time and Men*, Becker mentions Meshel only five times, and even then, only in impersonal terms). Ben-Aharon, who succeeded Becker, preferred to appoint a weak head of the TUD, so as to be able to dominate the trade union sphere. Meshel, who followed, preferred an obedient nominee with long-term ambitions. He chose Kessar, assuming that Kessar would avoid any disruptive action that would endanger his chances of serving as Meshel's successor. His logic proved to be sound. When he took over the role, Kessar nominated a candidate of marginal status, Mr. H. Haberfeld. This choice assured the loyalty of the new nominee.

This tactic thus followed the one adopted by all former secretaries general. If there is a change in strategy, it seems to be in another direction. Kessar allows Haberfeld much wider discretion than has traditionally been approved. Kessar spends most of his time and energy in promoting macro-social objectives like narrowing the income gap through the legislation of a minimum wage act, securing a welfare type of medicine by consolidating the Histadrut's ailing Sick Fund, by securing low levels of unemployment, by avoiding cancellation of production projects, by fighting stagflation, by supporting the normative and ideological substructure of the Histadrut, and by vetoing any use of decrees in industrial relations issues.

This strategy, if followed consistently, will create an autonomous TUD, allowed to act on the basis of exclusive IR criteria, without substantive sensitivity to economic or political considerations.

Note to Chapter 2

1. A 'non-exploitative' independent worker according to the bylaws of the Histadrut is a person who is either a salaried worker, a member of a cooperative or a kibbutz, a housewife, or an employer of no more than three workers.

3

The New Economic Policy and the Autonomy of the Israeli irs

June 1985. A national unity government, led by the two major political blocs, the Labor and the Likud parties, tries to fight a rampant two digit inflation. The arsenal of solutions seems exhausted. Promising tripartite package agreements, agreed upon by the government, the Histadrut and the private sector Coordinating Bureau of Economic Organizations, achieve meager results. Prime Minister Peres (Labor) and Finance Minister Moda'i (Likud), assisted by prominent economists from the academia prepare a drastic secret program to solve the almost unsolvable crisis. The comprehensive economic stabilization plan includes the following main points:

1. An annual $750 million cut in the state budget.
2. A devaluation of the Sheqel by 18.8 percent.
3. An *ad-hoc* income tax of 8.3 percent on companies and self-employed.
4. A tax on high standard houses and apartments.
5. A partial compensation for low income families.
6. A three percent cut in public sector employment.
7. Increased mobility in the public sector.
8. A price hike caused by cuts in subsidies of basic foods and transport, followed by a three months price and wage freeze.
9. Gradual exemption from the price freeze following a decrease in the rate of inflation.
10. Encouragement of savings, aimed at encouraging economic growth.
11. A promise to keep all present public savings unharmed.

The plan was approved by the government after a marathon meeting lasting nineteen hours. The plan called for extreme labor market related steps such as wage cuts and sacking of employees, with implementation envisaged through emergency decrees.

Most of the details of the program were leaked to the press during the week preceding the decision of the government. Although the leaders of both the Histadrut and the employers' associations were notified by the prime minister a few days preceding the government plenum, essentially they were faced with a *fait accompli.*

The following description of the Histadrut's struggle against this policy can serve as an additional introduction to this book. Through it, I hope to show the rationale behind the book's title, *A State within a State: Industrial Relations in Israel*.

The function of a political systems, says Niklas Luhmann, is the making of binding decisions. "A decision is binding whenever, and for whatever reasons, it succeeds in effectively restructuring the expectations of those affected and thus becomes the premise of their future behavior." (1982, p. 145) In the present instance, the Israeli political leadership acted as though it monopolized the political arena. The program was pushed through the executive and legislative bodies, both government and Knesset. Only then, when policy formulation presumably ended and implementation started, the real hard phase of negotiations and reformulation got under way. But let's keep a temporal order and present our case step by step.

The 1984 parliamentary elections in Israel ended in deadlock. Neither the Labor Party nor the Likud Party could form a coalition with other smaller parties. The only possibility remaining was a national unity coalition based on equal representation of each major political bloc. A rotation agreement was reached on the position of prime minister. Shimon Peres was to hold the position for the first two year term, while Yitzhak Shamir was to take over for the following two years. The country was immersed in two major problems, the first, a costly war in Lebanon and the second—galloping inflation. Prime Minister Peres ordered a partial withdrawal from Lebanon. Thereafter, the economic problem took priority.

As noted above, a promising tripartite package agreement proved to be much too mild a solution for the ailing economy. Still, the Labor Party could not afford a defeat in the prospective elections in its stronghold—the Histadrut. Yisrael Kessar, the new secretary general of the Histadrut, who had succeeded to the post after the long term served by Yerucham Meshel, stood for election for the first time. Kessar, a Yemenite in origin and a Tel-Aviv University master in Labor Studies, ran a personal, American-style, election campaign and won a solid majority. Immediately after the elections, Prime Minister Peres asked two prominent economists, Professors E. Berglas and M. Bruno, to prepare a comprehensive program for salvaging Israel's ailing economy. The plan was prepared in complete secrecy with the full cooperation of the Finance Minister, Mr. Y. Moda'i (Likud). While various wage-price-tax freeze phases were adopted, the situation called for a more drastic move. The last week of June, 1985 (23.6 – 27.6) started with many press leakages. *Davar*, the Histadrut-owned newspaper, reported on Thursday, June 27th that

> the discussions now taking place involve items like abolishing subsidies and certain payments of the National Insurance Institute (NII) including child and old age allowances, partial or complete cancellation of the Free Education Act and a rejection of the demands to

extend government coverage of health costs . . . These radical economic steps which are being discussed with the Prime Minister will require modification of present legislation and a wide political consensus.

Sha'ar, an economic newspaper reported that

. . . a substitute for the package deal is in preparation. A team, headed by the director general of the Finance Ministry has locked itself in a hotel room and is busy preparing a tough program: among other steps, a 25 percent devaluation of the Israeli Sheqel, stabilization of the currency and its replacement, preventing an influx of currency into the economy, and cancellation of subsidies, are under consideration. It is reported that the Histadrut leadership has been informed.

The market showed signs of nervousness. An immediate decision had to be made. The English language newspaper, *The Jerusalem Post,* reported that on June 25th Peres had held meetings with Moda'i (finance minister), Zamir (the attorney-general), Amorai (deputy finance minister (Labor)) and Professors Bruno and Berglas, on June 26th with Moda'i, Mandelbaum (chancellor of the central bank) and Sharon (minister of industry and commerce), and on the 27th with Hurvitz (president of the manufacturer's association). All these meetings indicated that major decisions were pending. On Friday, June twenty-eighth, *The Jerusalem Post* reported:

. . . .*Treasury Considering Governing By Decree* . . . Under the regulations being considered, workers in the public sector would have to give up part of their wages, thousands could be sacked within two weeks and the working conditions of those remaining would be worsened. The regulations could practically abolish collective wage agreements and present legislation, and leave workers in the public sector without trade union protection.

On the same day Yisrael Kessar, the secretary general of the Histadrut meets the Prime Minister and learns of the impending policy. The Histadrut's response comes from Mr. H. Haberfeld, head of Trade Union Division who warns that "the government will fall if emergency decrees for sacking workers are issued." A similar message is delivered by Kessar to the secretary-general of the Labor Party, Mr. U. Baram that "if the news reported by the media on the intention of the government to invoke emergency decrees in place of work agreements is true, an extreme confrontation between the government and the Histadrut as well as an unbearable situation for the party will be created." On Saturday night, Kessar is once again invited to Peres's apartment. There, Moda'i tells a shocked and bitter secretary general that "from now on nothing depends on an agreement with the Histadrut." (Haaretz, 5.7.85).

Sunday, June 30th, is a busy day. Both the government and the Histadrut Executive Committee meet. At 7:30am, there are parallel consultative meetings of the Labor and Likud ministers. Peres addresses Labor ministers, while Moda'i meets with Likud ministers. Afterwards, at 9:30am, the government convenes. On the agenda—a five year plan prepared by Mr. Gad Yaacobi, the Minister of Economics. Participants prefer to cut discussion short on this topic. They are anxious to get into the "real" stuff—the new economic program, scheduled for a second meeting at 2:30pm.

At 10am, Kessar addresses the legislative forum of the Histadrut, the Executive Committee. Preceding the public debate is a phone call by Kessar to Yaacov Shamai, the head of the opposition Likud Party minority in the Histadrut. Kessar tells Shamai of the new plan and offers to join him in opposing the program. Shamai agrees. A wall-to-wall consensus is established in the Histadrut.

Only partial disclosure of the new policy is permitted. Kessar reports that the government plans to adopt a resolution including: a) a wage and price freeze for three months, b) returning to the wage level standards of January, 1980, c) a layoff of three percent of the public sector employees, d) a one-time three percent cut in the wages and salaries of public sector employees, e) the imposition of a tax on training funds, and f) a further cut in subsidies. "All this," stressed Kessar,

> will be done by emergency decree. That's the first time since the establishment of the state that an effort is being made to run labor relations by emergency legislation. Even during our wars, wage and cost-of-living allowances have never been regulated by such decrees.

Later, in the afternoon Kessar will tell Peres, "wage cut decrees will serve as a casus beli."

Peres is aware of Kessar's outrage. He sends econvoys to Histadrut headquarter and even invites Kessar to meet him during the government session. At 6:30 am, Peres leaves the government meeting joined by three other Labor Party ministers (Shachal, Gur and Yaacobi). After two and a half hours Kessar leaves angry and unconvinced. The only concession he manages to obtain is that the prime minister will not apply his formal authority to issue emergency decrees until negotiations with Kessar end (*Haaretz*, 1.7.85).

At 9:00 am, after nineteen hours of deliberation, "white smoke" is seen. The government has approved the program, fifteen ministers voting for it, seven against and one abstaining.

The Histadrut response is prompt and clear. Kessar approves the calling of a general strike. A strike committee is established. Both coalition (Labor) and opposition (Likud) join. A twenty-four hour general strike is scheduled for the next day, Thursday, July 2nd.

Meanwhile, Kessar makes sure of essential support for his prospective moves from the strong workers' committees. The secretary of the Ashdod

Port workers and the chairman of the telephone engineering workers are called to meet Kessar. Both line up with him.

The Jerusalem Post describes Tuesday's happenings in the following words:

> With the country at a virtual standstill due to the one-day general strike, Prime Minister Shimon Peres yesterday decided to postpone implementation of several of the major elements of the new economic program. Meeting with Histadrut secretary general Yisrael Kessar and trade union department chairman Hayim Haberfeld immediately after the Knesset voted to approve the program, Peres agreed to postpone implementation of the emergency decrees regarding the freezing of wages, cutting the cost-of-living allowance and dismissing public service. (3.7.85)

Seventy of the one hundred and twenty Knesset members voted for the economic program, with nineteen against. The issue was regarded as a vote of confidence for the government. Therefore, the most Kessar—as a Knesset member of the ruling party—could do was to state that he had not taken part in the voting. Knesset member Shamai, the head of the Likud minority opposition in the Histadrut, left the hall while voting took place.

Negotiation between the government and the Histadrut continued. The government refrained from applying the decrees. However, unless explicitly abrogated by the government, they were still due to take effect at noon, July 7th. The Histadrut called a general strike of state employees. A government phone vote, hastily arranged after midnight, extended the suspension of the decree and made the calling-off of the strike possible (10.7.85). July 16th. brought another sign of defiance. The Histadrut and the CBEA (Coordinating Bureau of the Economic Associations), signed a renewed cost-of-living allowance agreement. Since the abolishing of all institutionalized links between wages and prices was a declared goal of the new economic policy., the renewed contract indicated the dissatisfaction of both union and employers with government interference in labor-management relations. The Minister of Finance reluctantly approved the agreement, even though he refused to act in the customary fashion by applying the agreement to public sector employees.

Negotiations between the government and the Histadrut continued for a few more weeks until a typical compromise had, in effect, been established. The emergency decrees were left to die quietly. The Histadrut succeeded in regaining its quasi-sovereignty on its traditional territory: terms of employment. Negotiation, not legislation, was reestablished as the name of the game.

The best indication of this effect came on July, 25th. The government had hoped to barter its authority to impose emergency decrees for an effective and quick process of lay-offs in the public sector. For this, a centralized sacking procedure was essential. The Histadrut leadership was none too keen to agree to such a mechanism. It preferred to maintain the roles of individual local and national unions—exactly what the government was eager to avoid. Nevertheless, "The negotiations were interrupted without a centralized agreement on employee sacking," reports *Haaretz*, and

> an effort was made to create an image of a new impasse and crisis. In fact, an understanding developed between the Histadrut and the government: the government does away with the emergency decrees, the government pays public sector employees a fourteen percent compensation for increased prices, and the government decides to lay off six percent of its employees. Sacking procedures will follow current collective agreement. (26.7.85)

This understanding included a concession by the Histadrut not to reimburse public sector employees in full for the increased cost of living. The complete figure was 18.8 and not 14 percent. It allowed the government to layoff six percent of its employees, and not three percent (+ a 3% wage cut) as had been specified in the original economic program. However, this increased discharge was still dependent on standard lay-off procedures, which made it a desired, but almost unattainable, target.

On June 5th, five days after the announcement of the new economic policy, Israel Kessar was asked in a press interview why he had chosen to focus his campaign on the procedural issue of emergency decrees and not on substantive issues like wage cuts or layoffs. His answer was:

> I raise my voice firstly on the decrees, because all other issues stem from them. If the decrees are sustained, I can continue protesting as much as I like. The cancellation of the decrees means that the government enters into dialogue with the Histadrut on all these issues. Then, we can negotiate what is forbidden and what is allowed. We will fight the decrees day and night. If, after discussion we reach agreement, I will be very happy. (*Ma'ariv* 1.7.85)

Two days before, an editorial in *Haaretz* expressed a different view:

> The Histadrut must respect the will of the Knesset. It is the duty of the government to rule, given the confidence of the Knesset. The Israeli regime does not accept a condominium between the government and the Histadrut. (3.7.85)

Kessar's strategy, however, proved successful, while the *Haaretz* editorial proved unrealistic.

This short case-history demonstrates the existence of an autonomous industrial relations system in Israel. "The autonomy of a system," argues Luhmann "refers to the degree of freedom with which the selective criteria of the system can regulate the relations between system and environment." (1982, p. 142) Collective agreements stipulate sacking procedures; cost-of-living-allowance (COLA) agreements link earnings to prices. Adopting contractual procedures for the first issue is a perfect indicator for the autonomy of the Israeli irs. Agreement on a modified compensation procedure, close enough, but not identical to, the COLA machinery, is a respectable surrogate, and not a real threat to this autonomy. Maintaining autonomy

> depends on the environment's giving the system time to insert its own ways of processing information. In order to save time and use it rationally, a system sets up its own timetables that cannot be fully coordinated with timetables in the environment. (Luhmann, 1982, p. 143)

Contract expiration dates are set autonomously by the irs. An effort to change them through legislation failed. An agreement between the private sector employers' associations and the Histadrut is another demonstration of the same feature.

A second precondition for sustaining a system's autonomy, following Luhmann is legitimacy. That is, it needs general acceptance and authorization to make decisions. Neither the prime minister nor the finance minister would have negotiated with the Histadrut unless such acceptance and authorization were imputed to it.

A symbolic confirmation of this Histadrut attribute was granted by the prime minister, who left a government meeting in session, accompanied by some of his colleague ministers, in order to meet a Histadrut delegation. His failure to convince them is an impressive indication of their autonomy.

4

Strike Management:
Norm and Practice

Introduction

We can envision two extreme models of strike regulation. On the one hand a state of laissez-faire, in which any organization of workers can start a strike with no external constraints imposed. The industrial relations arena is a stage for a power game between managements and unions. On the other hand, society may limit the degrees of freedom available to the union to such an extent that its mere existence, not to say operations, becomes problematic. Pure power is the name of the game in the first extreme, while indisputable managerial authority is the source of order in the second. No democratic society can resort to either of the two extremes.

Even a superficial visit to the U.S.A. can provide evidence for the assertion that it tends toward the first model. I can demonstrate my assertion with the following short example: On the door to a supermarket called "Ralph's" this announcement was posted sometime around the end of October 1988:

Because of the probability of a labor dispute in the near future
RALPH'S
Is now accepting applications for temporary employment as:
truck drivers/general warehouse personnel/office clerical
meat cutters/meat wrappers/seafood clerks
bakery plant workers
supermarket clerks & cashiers
automotive workers/maintenance engineers

Applications are available thru the store director

This announcement tells a very clear story. Ralph's was engaged in contract negotiations with a union, which represented its employees. Management came to the conclusion that the disparity of views between it and the workers' representatives was too wide to be solved without the use of power. In a war, act like you're in a war. By issuing this announcement the management gained both a viable option to continue and run its stores in the event of a strike and dispatched a straightforward message to the union. "We are ready! Can you beat us?"

The typical Israeli scenario is very different. An announcement on the radio informs *everybody*, both union members, the employer and the general public, that a strike has been declared for the next day. On the following day, *nobody* comes to work. If the strike is important enough to be covered by the Israeli TV, a typical story is presented. A reporter visits the place of work, and finds a locked building. When he tries to enter the site, the security guard, who is an employee of a security service agency, peeks out of the building and tells the reporter: "It's closed. There's a strike." No one even bothers to assemble a picket-line. The rules of the game are clear and simple. No one tries to bring the dispute into the open, let alone to start a physical clash. The real game takes place around the negotiation table, in official, semi-official or even unofficial talks.

The Israeli state has selected a unique middle-of-the-way structure. The actors of the industrial relations system are allowed an almost limitless freedom, *but* they are expected to exhibit self-restraint by conforming to the bylaws and norms of their representative organizations. The cornerstone of the Israeli irs normative structure is the collective agreement.

> A collective agreement has only two sides—the employer, or an employers' organization, and the labor union that undersigned that agreement. The workers' committee [the local union] is not a 'third party' to a collective agreement, it is a part of the union organization. (Hausmann and Goldberg, 1977, p. 52)[1]

This stipulation treats the national union as the major representative of the workers' community. It envisions a dominant general federation of labor, which negotiates, signs and takes care of the implementation of all the web of norms in Israel. Such a superpower has never actually existed in Israel. It can hardly exist in any democratic society. Decades ago, the pre-independence Israeli irs was managed locally. In those days, the local workers' councils (Moatsot Ha'Poalim)—the regional extensions of the Histadrut—were the most prominent union actors of the IR arena. Some councils gained a more militant image than others. The most famous for its power and influence was the workers' council of Haifa, which was nicknamed "Red Haifa." Political factors increased the importance of the Jewish national level organizations, and were the ones that negotiated with the British administration. They were the factor which prepared the Yishuv (the Zionist Jewish community) for the establishment of an independent state. The pull toward the center led to the establishment of the Trade Union Department in 1941 (Shirom, 1983, p.126).[2] In its first years "the main activities of the Department were concentrated in the shaping of a national and industrial wage policy, in the definition of the operative goals of the trade unions in issues of welfare and in the fixing of the organizational accords for new national unions" (Shirom, 1983, p. 126).

We can learn more from this citation by way of omission, if we ask ourselves what is *not* explicitly mentioned as a routine task of the department. It didn't engage in national-level wage negotiations, it didn't conduct plant-level negotiations, and it interfered as little as possible with the established unions. That is clearly *not* an image of a superpower. The predominance of the center developed later, mostly after the establishment of the state. These years brought the collective agreement, and the union organization which backs it up, to a paramount status. This standing was recognized and honored by the central bodies of the state. The high court stated that "the collective agreement is of superior status in industrial relations, and whoever cares for his money should avoid doing anything which implies a jeopardizing of, or a conspiracy against, it" (Cited by Hausmann & Goldberg, 1977, p. 65).

This jurisdiction put the collective agreement above and beyond the individual agreement. An employee is not allowed to give away a right that is bestowed on him by a collective agreement. Thus, no employee has the discretion to exchange his social benefits, pension privileges or even clothing that he receives from his employer, for any thing he may be more interested in getting. The court has warned employers who make such an individual agreement that they may find themselves in a position where they are required to make double payment, once to the worker when the agreement is made, and then, later, when this same worker, or his descendants ask for payment under the terms of the collective agreement. The mere fact that the worker was aware of the exchange, or even was interested in it, would not be a sufficient cause for refusing such a renewed demand.

The logic behind this point of view is clear. Whenever there is a need to choose between a collective and an individual good, and so long as we deal with industrial relations, the collective takes precedence. Even though in a specific situation both the individual worker and his employer may gain from a specific, narrowly tailored transaction, in the long run, when you apply a collectivistic perspective, the institution of collective negotiation may be hampered. In this framework, the balance is between cases where a strong employer tries to extract from his workers concessions which the union tries to avoid and a situation where individual workers negotiate with their employers exclusive compensatory schemes. In the Israeli case, the risk of the former outweighs the benefits of the latter. This rationale is logical only under very strict normative circumstances—when it is agreed that collective are more important that individual criteria.

When this presumption is accepted, many social control and mobilization challenges are redundant. For example, what is the most important problem a union faces when calling a strike? In many cases, the most difficult challenge a union faces is not the employer, who stands on the other side of the barricade, but the rank-and-file, whose support is a prerequisite for running an effective stoppage. Not all union members are required to show active support. The mere act of avoiding showing up at the plant is of significant importance. But, if a threat of strikebreaking exists, then at least part of the members for at least part of the time must show more active support. Their participation in a picket line is needed. Sometimes, their involvement in illegal actions is essential. Mass demonstrations, violence against scabs, or even plain sabotage, were, and still are, typical items on the protocols of many industrial disputes in many parts of the world.

Without a pronounced backing by a union's membership, strikes are an empty threat. This being so, unions have devised many techniques to mobilize support. They arrange rotating teams of participants in the picket line, they assemble their members and report to them about the developments in negotiations, they call for support announcements from various sympathetic organizations, and publicly post such letters of support. Unions must invest a significant amount of their scarce resources in assuring internal support. They are relieved from these requirements when they are safeguarded by institutionalized means. When the employer regards the hiring of strike-breakers as unthinkable, when he believes that directly communicating with his employees during a strike, thus bypassing their union, is immoral, then the union is relieved of the need to activate morale boosting devices. The union can then limit its activities to pure negotiation. Any observer of the Israeli stage can find many clues to the dominance of such institutional considerations.

A high level of institutionalization of the collective bargaining process leads unions and employers to rationalistic behavior, shaped by economic considerations. That was the view promoted by Snyder (Snyder, D. Institutional setting and industrial conflict: comparative analyses of France, Italy and the United States, *American Sociological Review*, Vol. 40, No. 3, 1975). Snyder suggests that irs's can be divided into two models, one shaped mostly by external political variables and the other conditioned by economic considerations. Italy and France were identified as having politically determined IR institutions, while the U.S.A. after World War II was found to approximate the economy-dependent type. Judged on the basis of its level of institutionalization, Israel could be expected to act like an extremely rational system.

A rational union functioning in the framework of a favorable institutional setting, so believes Snyder, will adopt an economic union model of action. Such a union, suggests Friedman (1972) prefers collective negotiations on the plant level to a legislative effort on a national-political level. It adopts an industrial or a craft structure, rather than a multi-industrial or whole-economy pattern. It regards the strike as an appropriate union means, and avoids using it in a nationally coordinated action that has political overtones. An economic union of that type is a constant threat to a dominant national union. The material presented below deals with the correspondence between IR norms and their practice. It challenges the common assumptions that institutionalization and conformity are highly related phenomena.

The Workers' Committees Charter

In a setting as described above, the Histadrut, the major national union movement in Israel, has formulated its bylaws in an effort to control workers' committees.

THE HISTADRUT CHARTER FOR WORKERS' COMMITTEES

The designated Histadrut charter for workers' committees (*Takanon Vaadei ha'Ovdim*), includes a complete chapter dealing with procedures for calling industrial disputes, both strikes and sanctions.[3] The following clauses define the procedures for workers' committees:[4]

Chapter 3: Procedures for calling industrial disputes – Strikes and Sanctions.

1. A decision on assembling a workers' meeting, which entails a partial or complete cessation of work, requires the approval of the workers' council.

2. A decision on the calling of an industrial dispute in a single place of work, a plant or an office, will be brought by the workers' committee to the approval of the local workers' council.

3. A decision on calling a general or a partial (sanctions) strike must be accepted in a secret ballot by the body of the workers employed in a place of work.

4. A decision to call a strike is valid only if supported in a secret ballot by a majority of at least 50% of the total employees employed in this place of work.

5a. The secret ballot on calling a strike must be held at least five days after the convening of a workers' meeting. The meeting has to be convened by the workers' council under whose jurisdiction the place of work is included.

5b. Reporting to the workers in the place of work prior to the strike on the substance of the dispute and on the views of the management, will be done by the representatives of the workers' committee in the local workers' council or by the relevant Histadrut body, prior to the casting of the votes on strike declaration.

6. The voting on calling a strike will be cast in a ballot box with stationery supplied by the workers' council and under its supervision.

7. Calling a strike (after the ballot) [enclosed words part of original document], requires the approval of the workers' council under whose jurisdiction the place of work is included.

[Clause 8 not relevant here]

9a. If the strike is approved by the workers' council, an authoritative announcement will be made to the employer as stipulated by the law.

9b. The announcement on calling a strike, following the procedure as stipulated in the bylaws, will be delivered by an authoritative Histadrut unit, for a local strike—the workers' council, and for a national strike—the national union, whichever applies.

10. In case the strike or a step requested is not approved by the workers' council, a workers' committee can appeal to the Trade Union Department, or the Committee for Academic Affairs,[5] whichever applies. (General Federation of Labor, 1978, p. 12-13)

The bylaws, as cited above, exhibit a clear effort on the part of the Histadrut to supervise as closely as possible and to control the ways and methods adopted by the workers' committees in dispute management. The battery of control devices includes pre-notification and pre-approval of an intention to initiate an industrial conflict, a supervised general meeting and a secret ballot. Moreover, the assignment of the ultimate authority to call a strike or initiate sanctions stays in the discretion of the superordinate Histadrut unit. All these are a clear indication of the Histadrut's distrust of the institution of workers' committees.

The workers' committee, which is introduced in the preamble to a booklet widely distributed by the Trade Union Division (General Federation of Labor, 1978, p. 5) as "the elementary cell of the Histadrut in general and the trade union in particular," is the antithesis of the Histadrut in its rationale and composition. While the Histadrut is a centralized body, operated by a detached cadre of officials elected to their positions along party lines, the workers' committees are decentralized, run by immediate representatives of their constituencies, and elected mostly on a personal basis.

In a further discussion below, Snyder's hypothesis on the rationality of unions will be tested in greater detail. At present I am more interested in checking to what degree the actors in the Israeli irs follow the supposed norms of the system.

SOURCES OF DATA

Three sources will be used in this context. First, strike statistics will be presented and analyzed; second, findings from the industrial disputes study

(IDS) will be presented; and third, the main findings from the dissertation by H. Fisher (1978) will be cited. These three sources are not of equal weight.

Strike statistics are the most comprehensive of all three. These data are collected concurrently by two agencies, one run by the government and the other by the Histadrut. While governmental agencies have been replaced a few times during the last three decades,[6] the evolving axis for the field work has been the Institute for Economic and Social Research of the Histadrut. This unit has been involved in this area since the establishment of the state. Computerized strike statistics are available for the State of Israel for the period starting with the year 1965. These data will be heavily relied on in this work.

While strike data is comprehensive in scope, it is shallow in depth. The length of the research form is restricted by practical considerations. The forms are sent by mail with minimal follow-up. The informants are always biased representatives of a given side of a conflict. Very little effort can be, or is, invested in verification, or in complementary sources of information. Therefore, this valuable source requires supplementary sources.

Academic research is one such. The two studies reported below gained their data from similar sources, the immediate actors in each of the sampled conflict events surveyed. The IDS research design involved the collection of information from two levels of union officials and two levels of management, at plant level and the one above it.[7] The Fischer (1978) study interviewed the members of the workers' committees who were involved in the dispute, the union representative who handled the case and the general and/or personnel manager of the organization who was in office at the time of the conflict (Fischer and Jacobsen, 1982, p. 343). The IDS was run using a crisis research design and covered the disputes in real time, while the Fischer research adopted a post-hoc design. The method adopted by the IDS ended up with a sample of sixty-three strikes, strike threats and lockouts. This sample size was not planned in advance. Neither was the final date of data collection shaped by statistical considerations. An impending election threatened to interfere with the routine functioning of the Israeli irs. Therefore, a decision was made by the investigators to discontinue interviewing actors in new cases of conflict.

The design of the second study made it possible to use a proportional, stratified sample of seventy disputes, representing the strike population of the years 1972-74. The IDS can serve as a follow up for the Fischer study. It was carried out in 1977. As to their foci of interest, the main characteristic of the IDS is its time sequential nature. The actors were followed up, in some cases four times, over a period of four months. This allowed the detailed collection of data on the steps adopted during the development of a given dispute. The Fischer study, on the other hand, allowed an in depth investigation into the attitudes and values of the respondents.

These three sources allow us to investigate ten strike related norms. Some of these norms are state laws, others, Histadrut bylaws, and one, a typical clause in almost any collective agreement.

Table 4.1 allows us to follow these steps and see how far strike related procedures are adhered to. The three sources do not always tell a similar, let alone an identical, story. Nevertheless, we can try to extract from them some degree of understanding.

Table 4.1:   Strike-related procedures: Their sources and institutional status.

NORM	Official Statistics	Chermesh	Fischer	Institutional Status
1. Strike prohibited while a valid contract has not expired	x	x	x*	Contract
2. Workers' Committee should decide on calling a strike		x		Bylaws
3. A request for convening a workers' meeting should be referred to the Histadrut		x		Bylaws
4. A convening of a meeting should be approved by the Histadrut		x		Bylaws
5. A workers' meeting should be convened if a strike is planned by the Workers' Committee		x		Bylaws
6. A secret ballot should be administered for approval of a strike	x	x	x*	Law
7. The strike must be approved by a representative union (in most cases, by the Histadrut)	x	x	x*	Law
8. The Labor Relations Officer must be notified 15 days in advance	x	x	x*	Law
10. Notification should be made by a representative union			x	Law

*   Data were aggregated in a way which does not allow disaggregation.

DISPUTE MANAGEMENT NORMS AND THEIR DEGREE OF CONFORMITY

1. Strike prohibited while a valid contract has not expired.

Most Israeli strikes are called prior to the expiration of a collective agreement. The official statistics flatly reveal a solid seventy percent of the strikes as being in the illegal category. The figures do not differ significantly between the terms of two of the secretaries general of the Histadrut, Ben Aharon and Meshel, for whose administrations data are available. The figures of the IDS are even more extreme. Of the forty-one cases for which information is available, in forty (97.6 percent) the contract was valid during the dispute. Almost all contracts allow for strikes during the time of a agreement, but the legitimate reasons for strikes are always limited. Thus, it is clear that norm breaking is very common for this specific procedure. It should be remembered that the more acceptable category, when a contract is not in effect, is also quite an ambivalent case.

Israeli law stipulates that an agreement seldom expires. If no pre-specified acts have been adopted by one of the parties, or both of them, an agreement remains a binding contract even though its term has expired, until a new agreement is signed. Therefore, the only case where there are clear-cut conditions for a legitimate strike (all other norms being ignored for the moment) is the category of *no contract*. This is the case in a negligible 1.8 percent of the reported strikes. The comparison between the propensity to evade this procedure during the Ben Aharon and Meshel periods and also between Meshel's Labor and Likud sub-periods are revealing.

Ben Aharon was no doubt the most radical secretary general of the Histadrut, while Meshel was one of its most conservative leaders. Meshel experienced both an Alignment led government[8] and a Likud led government. All these differences had no impact at all on the propensity to circumvent the sanctity of the collective contract. It may thus be sounder to state that this assumed sanctity, that could be expected to confer a high degree of conformity on the procedure under current discussion, is no more than a myth. The norm was *not* to regard the contract as a binding agreement to avoid strikes, lockouts or sanctions. The directive not to strike prior the expiration of a contract was a dead paper procedure, and not a norm.

2. A worker's committee should decide on calling a strike.

A first possible step for a strike declaration is a decision made by a workers' committee. Not all strikes must originate at this level, but for plant level strikes it is most probable. The IDS shows an almost perfect adherence to this norm. Ninety-one percent of all covered disputes were discussed and agreed upon by the committees. As is probably clear to all, a valid test of conformity to a norm occurs when a party is tempted to deviate from it. In fact, the norm here delineated is seldom brought to such a test. A decision by a committee is

simultaneously an act made by a powerful active actor and a legitimate step
for calling a strike. Therefore, conforming to it does not attest solely to conformist behavior. It also demonstrates the power of a participating actor—the
workers' committee.

3. An application to the Histadrut to approve calling a workers' meeting
   must be made.

Whenever a workers' committee opts for a strike it is required by the
Histadrut's constitution to bring it to a workers' meeting. A meeting with a
strike agenda must be pre-approved by the authoritative unit, be it the local
labor council or the national union.

Table 4.2: Steps implemented by strike initiators.

Enacted	Did labor rep. approve a strike	Was a request for meeting requested from workers' council	Workers' meeting for calling a strike	Secret ballot for calling a strike	Workers meeting declared a strike	Was Histadrut approval requested	Strike reported to Labor Relations Officer	Strike reported to employer
Yes	91.1	30.6	85.2	26.4	67.3	72.0	72.7	92.6
n	(51)	(11)	(46)	(14)	(33)	(36)	(40)	(50)
No	8.9	69.4	14.8	73.6	32.7	28.0	27.3	7.4
n	(5)	(25)	(8)	(39)	(16)	(14)	(15)	(4)
Total	100.0%	100.0%	100.0%	100.0%	100.0%	100.0%	100.0%	100.0%
n	(56)	(36)	(54)	(53)	(49)	(50)	(55)	(54)

As we can see in Table 4.2, most committees (69.4 percent) don't bother to
follow this requirement. The workers' committee thus gains an important
asset, complete control of its relationship with its constituency. As long as a
representative body can keep this communication route under its complete
control, it gains a significant level of autonomy. This desired autonomy is
precisely the asset that the Histadrut bylaws were aimed at preventing.

4. A request for convening a workers' meeting should be referred to the
   Histadrut.

The first step a workers' committee is expected to take after contemplating
a strike call is to obtain the approval of the local workers' council to assemble
a workers' meeting for discussing the strike proposal. The Histadrut prefers to
keep its finger on the strike process from its earliest stage. Not all organized

places of work are regulated through the workers' council channel. For example, nationwide employers are supervised directly from the center. Therefore, the appropriate method to gauge conformity to this procedure is by distinguishing between local and higher level enterprises.

Table 4.3:　Histadrut approval of a meeting sought by level of irs.

Approval Requested	LEVEL		TOTAL
	Local	Higher	
YES	44.0	0.0	30.6
n	(11)	(0)	(11)
NO	56.0	100.0	69.4
n	(14)	(11)	(25)
TOTAL	69.4	30.6	100.0
n	(25)	(11)	(36)

$P\,(\chi^2 = 5.05023) \leq 0.0246$

Table 4.3 makes exactly this distinction. It shows that in only less than half the strikes (44.0 percent) where this procedure was appropriate was it conformed to. Fifty-six percent of the IDS disputes started without notification, let alone approval, of the representative union. Therefore, all subsequent steps will have been either unconstitutional, or at least, hard to supervise.

5.　Convening a meeting should be approved by the Histadrut.

The only step that a workers' committee is entitled by the bylaws to take independently, is to decide that it is interested in opting for strike action. Afterwards, each of the following steps must either be taken solely by the representative union or in coordination with it. As we have seen above, in most disputes surveyed by the IDS, the workers' committee abstained from applying for workers' council approval for calling of a meeting. However, the question remains as to whether this is because the official Histadrut organ is simply disregarded, or because of a suspicion that it will not grant the desired approval? We have no way of knowing what the response of the workers' committee would be if such an application were made. On the other hand, we do know the response of this Histadrut organ to those cases where such an application was actually made. Table 4.4 shows that in most cases (76.9 percent), the response was supportive.[9] If at all possible, then, the Histadrut does not block discussion of strike initiatives. The workers' committee, it appears, prefers to manage its affairs without reference to its superordinate Histadrut organ.

Table 4.4: Meeting convened with consent of the workers' council. *

	FREQUENCY	PERCENT
YES	10	76.9
NO	3	23.1
TOTAL	13	100.0

* Since most meetings were convened without seeking Histadrut approval, the sample size of the present table is very small.

6. A workers' meeting should be convened if a strike is planned by the workers' committee

A general meeting is a democratic method of formulating policy. The public is seemingly given the opportunity both to express its views and to shape decision making. It is, on the other hand, a medium constrained by its own structure. In an orderly meeting only one person at a time has the right to deliver his or her views. Under the constraints of time, this means that only a limited number of people can express themselves. This makes the freedom of speech a scarce resource. In the framework of a group discussion, it is the privilege of the chairperson to allocate this scarce resource. In a union meeting, the chairperson is not a neutral figure, but the head of a union body, or his representative. His or her aim is not so much to reach a considered democratic majority as to keep order. The easiest way to maintain order in a meeting is by adhering to the agenda and by approving the officially raised motions. This way, the meeting may be turned into a controlled form of what might otherwise become a risky ballot.

Meetings can thus be made efficient means for controlling the public instead of being used as an effective means of democratic decision making. When disorder erupts, meetings are quite a threat to a union's leadership. This may happen in various situations such as when a strike is mishandled. Such a case, however, is not relevant to a decision to call a strike. If at all, it is relevant to the calling off of one. Even then, such a level of popular criticism may be expected only when a strike drags on for a long period. Most Israeli strikes during the years under study were much too short for the build-up of a significant amount of opposition. In some cases, though, when rank-and-file mood is high and union leadership is perceived to be hesitant, a spontaneous replacement of leadership is a possible outcome of a meeting.

This can also occur when an high level of apathy and disinterest prevails among union members, and only a small, non-representative minority shows up to a general meeting. Such a low attendance may establish a setting where any decision may be possible. Surprisingly enough, this is a situation typical of meetings of unions of professionals, where the common member is much more interested and involved in his work than in union activity. At the universities, for example, strikes, faculty meetings and demonstrations may be regarded by many scientists as a gift of time to be used to catch up on research, etc. No wonder these meetings quite frequently lead to unpredictable outcomes and are avoided or postponed as often as possible by union leaders.

Meetings can serve many functions, tactical as well as substantive. The committee can use them as a symbolic gesture to tell their counterparts that they are serious in their strike threat. Calling a general meeting can mean adopting a non-reversible strike option. The saving of face and prestige may make it very difficult for a union to cancel a strike after gaining rank-and-file support for it without demonstrating significant achievements. Thus, an announcement of a scheduled meeting can serve as a negotiation device. A meeting can be used as a channel for communicating plans, presenting policy and assigning tasks. As such, a meeting serves as a one-way rapport method from the source of authority—the committee—to the public. Such manipulation can be exploited by strong and authoritative leaders, but any encounter between rank-and-file and elected officials can get out of control and end up with expressions of disenchantment or even impeachment.

Calling a meeting may also mean no more than adhering to a normative protocol. If the Histadrut bylaws require an approval of a strike by a general meeting, then such a meeting must be held. A test of good faith is needed under such circumstances. A meaningful test has to indicate to what degree the plant level union leadership has exposed itself by opening the stage to criticism. The running of a secret ballot may be a valid test for such a claim. A more radical purpose for running a general meeting is to open the door for membership participation in union decision making. Here, once again, the follow-up of a secret ballot can indicate whether this was the purpose of assembling a meeting or not.

Communication with the rank-and-file is an important means of spreading information, consolidating support and incorporating members' views in the decision making process. Its exact function cannot be inferred from the mere calling of a meeting. It is the complete set of steps which is adopted by an authority that allows U.S.A. to try and judge its meaning and purpose. I will postpone an evaluation of this aspect until we gain greater acquaintance with the various scenarios adopted by the plant level union representatives. Our data show that workers' committees tend (85.2 percent) to assemble general meetings prior to the calling of a strike. This is an indication of at least one point—members are *not disregarded* by their elected officials. I choose this double negative expression to allow a more elaborate discussion later on.

7.   A secret ballot should be administered for approving a strike.

While in most reported disputes covered by IDS, the plant-level union representatives called for a meeting prior to declaring a strike, only in about one in four (26.4 percent) was such a meeting followed by a secret ballot. The unequivocal purpose of a ballot requirement is derived from the basic democratic assumption that any significant policy decision should preferably be made by the concerned public. This assumption is frequently blended with a more pretentious belief: the public is more responsible than its leadership. The IDS findings indicate that neither of these assumptions is brought to a meaningful test in the Israeli case.

A common surrogate for a secret ballot is the general meeting. This method, as we saw above, has its pros and cons for the plant level union body leadership.

As can be seen in Table 4.2, running a ballot is the exception, and not the rule in Israeli disputes. Under such circumstances, the workers' community has only a very limited control over the typical industrial dispute. It is a closed game, played by the union, be it the plant level workers' committee or the legal representative body, and management. This exclusion of the rank-and-file from the process requires the existence of an institutional setting in which conformity to union policy and union security are taken for granted, that is, are indisputable.

8.   A strike must be approved by a representative union (in most cases, by the Histadrut).

The Histadrut bylaws require that a strike, even if approved by the members of a local union by a secret ballot, must also be condoned by an authoritative Histadrut organ. This procedure assigns the final power of determination to a body characterized by a wider scope of judgment than the local union officials. This way there is a greater chance that the policy of the Histadrut will be implemented and that the national union will not find itself committed to decisions it dislikes.[10] This approach is doubly important when we remember that the strike fund is run on the national level and that an "irresponsible" strike can easily exhaust resources accumulated with endless effort. As can be seen in Table 4.4, in almost three out of every four disputes the approval of the Histadrut has been requested. These figures seem very high. If they are valid and taken at face value, then the Histadrut can claim a very high level of control in this domain. I would not rush to make so sweeping a statement. Such local application to the Histadrut may often be a formal approach, which tries to maintain the forms of legality, while including the implied threat of "take it or leave it. We are going ahead whether you approve or not."

This interpretation continues a trend suggested by Friedman's (1963) study on workers' committees. In this study, Friedman found that most of his interviewees, who were a representative sample of committee members in industrial plants, chose not to commit themselves to an unconditional conformity to the Histadrut. Instead, they stated that their compliance "depended on the specific circumstances of the case." This conditional conformity cannot be interpreted as a meaningful acceptance of Histadrut authority. My reservation for the topic under current consideration may seem unsubstantiated, but compliance data, as presented by Fischer and by the official statistics make it more convincing. Fischer drew her sample from a list of 251 disputes. Only 103 (41.0 percent) of these conflicts gained the approval of the Histadrut. Nevertheless, all but twenty-three of these cases[11] ended in strike action. Thus, only in very few cases did a denial of approval by the Histadrut prevent a strike from taking place. In other words, it is nice having the Histadrut's support, but it is not essential. Strikes can, and do get called without the consent of the official representative union. This is so despite the fact that Fischer reports, "when members of workers' committees are asked what has to be done before calling a strike, their first reaction, in almost all the cases was: "apply to the Histadrut" (Fischer, 1978, p. 72). The official figures for this topic are quite detailed and longitudinal.

The percentage of strikes approved by the Histadrut, as presented in Table 4.5 and the analysis of variance shown in Table 4.6 can be used for a detailed examination of the Histadrut's propensity to approve strikes. Four variables are included in this analysis: the identity of the secretary general of the Histadrut (Secretary), the ruling party in the Israeli parliament (Party), the number of strikes in a given month (N) and a measure of time trend (BSMONTH). An all time total approval mean of 39.7 percent characterizes the 1965-86 era. It starts with the high Becker[12] figure (42.9), continues with a long drop lasting 171 months during Ben Aharon's and Meshel's secretariats and ends with Kessar's increase of approval rates (49.2). The party line break shows an almost identical figure for both Labor and Likud dominated governments (38.2 and 38.7 respectively).

Table 4.5: Percentage of strikes approved by the Histadrut (by secretary general and ruling party).

Sec'y general	Party			Total
	Labor	Likud	Nat. Unity	
Becker	42.9			42.9
Ben Aharon	37.3			37.3
Meshel	31.7	40.1		36.6
Kessar		48.5	51.3	49.2
TOTAL	38.2	38.7	49.5	39.7

Table 4.6: Percentage of strikes approved by the Histadrut (by secretary general and ruling party) – Analysis of variance.

Source of variation	Sum of squares	DF	Mean square	F	Sig of F
Covariates	1265.741	2	632.870	1.594	.205
N	36..344	1	361.344	.910	.341
BSMONTH	904.397	1	904.397	2.277	.133
Main Effects	5812.359	5	1162.472	2.927	.014
Secretary	5779.846	3	1926.615	4.851	.003
Party	32.513	2	16.257	.041	.960
Explained	7078.099	7	1011.157	2.546	.015
Residual	101272.202	255	397.146		
TOTAL	108350.301	262	413.551		

Only the first phase of the National Unity government is covered by the present source. However, it discloses a much higher level of approval (49.5 percent). The cross-tabulation of secretary general by Party does not add too much to our comprehension of the approval tendencies. Half the cells of this table are empty. Becker and Ben Aharon served in a purely Labor-governed period, while Meshel was the only one to experience long periods of both Labor dominated and Likud dominated governments. Kessar's encounter with a Likud government was almost too short to draw any conclusions from it, lasting only two months. Most of his term was during the reign of the National Unity government.

This government had a unique feature. The position of the prime minister was held in rotation, first by the Labor Party leader (Shimon Peres) and then by the Likud Party leader (Yitshak Shamir). Our current data source covers only the first period. The analysis of variance treats two variables as covariates. This way we can control, at least statistically, two possible influences, the first, that the Histadrut leadership behaves differently in periods of high and low strike activity, and the second, of a linear time trend developing during the twenty-two years (1965-86). The analysis of variance shows clear results. A non-significant impact of the covariates (.205), a significant coefficient for the main effects (.014) stemming completely from the differences among the four secretaries general (.003), leaving the differences in composition of the governments extremely non-significant (0.960). Strike approval by the Histadrut is thus shaped by the policy of the union movement. It is not determined by political considerations.

9. Notification must be made to the Commissioner of Industrial Relations 15 days in advance.

A freeze period is a common means for facilitating reconciliation and preventing conflict. This idea led the legislators to include the following clause in the Settlement of Labor Disputes Law (1957):

"5a. Required notification of a strike and a lockout.
...a party to a dispute is required to notify the other party and the Principal Labor Relations Officer on each strike or lockout...fifteen days at least prior to its beginning."

With a process as complicated as an industrial dispute and with institutions having procedures as long-drawn-out and tedious as the judiciary or the bureaucracy, fifteen days were considered the minimal duration needed for successful intervention. A precondition for any action by the Labor Relations Officer is the institutionalization of an effective method of notification. As can be seen in Table 4.7, the reception this clause initially encountered was quite favorable. More than forty percent of the strikes were prenotified to the Commissioner at least fifteen days in advance during the Ben Aharon[13] period. However, this proportion fell steadily and severely. During the Meshel/ Labor Party era only 27.6 percent of the strikes complied with the letter of the law, with similar observance percents for the Meshel/ Likud (28.9), the Kessar/Likud (25.0), and the Kessar/Unity Government (22.3) periods. With figures as low as these, the impact of the Indus-trial Relations Department, the Labor Ministry unit assigned to deal with industrial conflict, cannot be regarded as significant.

Still, is this whole picture? Is the Labor Relations Officer deprived of information on impending and prevailing industrial disputes? The data from the IDS seem to refute this conclusion.

Table 4.7 shows that the Commissioner is kept out of less than a third of the running disputes and is informed about the other two thirds. If so, how can we explain the discrepancy between the two sources? One possible reason is linked to the wording of the law. Clause 3 of the Law of Industrial Disputes Resolution (1957) defines the parties to a dispute:

In a labor dispute between an employer and his employees, or part of them, the parties to the dispute are the employer and the employees' organization representing the majority of the employees concerned in the dispute, or where there is no such employees' organization as aforesaid, the representation elected by the majority of those employees either for any matter or for that labor dispute workers whether it is for any subject or for the given labor dispute. (State of Israel, Ministry of Labor and Social Affairs—Labor Laws, Jerusalem, 1989)

The exclusive outcome of the wording of clause 3 is that in a dispute between an employer and his employees, or part of them, and not only in a dispute between an employer and an employees' organization, the employer and the employees' organization that represents the majority of the employees related to the dispute, are the parties to the dispute. Only where there is no employees' organization representing as required, comes the elected representation—the workers' committee, or any similar representation. (Hausmann and Goldberg)

This legal specification of the parties to a dispute is relevant for the specification of a notification body. The Labor Relations Officer is required to limit his information reception to the legal parties to a dispute. As can be seen in Table 4.7 the legal party on the union side, the representative union, has notified the Commissioner in less than four out of every ten disputes (35.6+1.7=37.3 percent). Still, the Commissioner was uninformed in only one out of four disputes (27.1 percent). For all other cases, more than a third (35.6 percent), it was the legally denied, but the functionally active, workers' committee, that reported the impending strike to the official. If this explanation is accepted, then the Labor Relations Officer was regarded as a fully relevant participant in the conciliation process in most of the disputes even as late as 1977, the year data for the IDS were collected. It was up to the Commissioner to decide whether or not to intervene in a dispute, information on which reached him in a legally dubious way. We have no data on how the Commissioner responded to the notifications he received that were not in accordance with the letter of the law.[14]

Table 4.7: Labor relations officer notified of planned strike (by secretary general and ruling party)

LABOR OFFICER	PERIOD					TOTAL
	Ben-Aharon	Meshel Labor	Meshel Likud	Kessar Likud	Kessar Nat.Unity	
Notified	41.0 (160)	27.6 (95)	28.9 (177)	25.0 (9)	22.3 (71)	30.1 (512)
Not notified	59.0 (230)	72.4 (249)	71.1 (436)	75.0 (27)	77.7 (248)	69.9 (1,190)
TOTAL	22.9 (390)	20.2 (344)	36.0 (613)	2.1 (36)	18.7 (319)	100.0 (1,702)

$P (\chi^2 = 33.355) \leq .000$

A strike is a game which requires at least two players, an employer, or his representative association and a group of employees, or their union. Therefore, it is little wonder that most employers are notified of an impending strike. In an under-institutionalized setting, and the Israeli industrial relations system is clearly not of this type, the representatives of the workers may prefer that their identity not be disclosed to the employer. Under such circumstances, a surprise action, speaking for itself, may be selected. In Israel, unions seldom try to hide their responsibility for organizational action. Thus, notification to the employer of an imminent strike is almost self-evident. Table 4.8 shows that in only 6.9 percent of the disputes was the employer not notified of a planned strike.

10. Notification must be made to the other party at least 15 days in advance.

The disclosure is not made by same agents in all disputes. In local disputes, it is the local workers' committee that tends to be the communicator (54.3 percent), while in higher level disputes, it is mostly the representative union (56.5 percent). Still, this official notification is more or less a ritualistic act. Most employers know of an approaching strike even prior to its official reporting. This is the case however an official notification is made. The IDS data show that employers know in advance that a strike is at their gate in more than four out of five dispute cases (78.6 percent). Approximately the same figure holds for disputes where a notification is to be made by officials of the representative union (88.0 percent), by the local workers' committee (77.8 percent) or by neither (75.0 percent). This aspect of strike management will be discussed in the next paragraph.

Table 4.8: Reporting of the strike to employer by level of irs.

Source of Report	LEVEL		TOTAL
	Local	Higher	
Official Representative	34.3 (12)	56.5 (13)	43.1 (25)
Local Representative	54.3 (19)	34.8 (8)	46.6 (27)
Both	2.9 (1)	4.3 (1)	3.4 (2)
Neither	8.6 (3)	4.3 (1)	6.9 (4)
TOTAL	60.3 (35)	39.7 (23)	100.0 (58)

$P (\chi^2 = 3.1746) \leq .365$

11. A notification should be made by a representative union.

Let us return to Table 4.8 and look at Table 4.9. We are not only interested in the mere fact of pre-notification. We paid no attention to the year the data were collected. Now we will turn both to the identity of the notifier and to the period this information reflects. Let us deal with these two points one by one. First, the issue of the source of strike notification. As we are already aware of, only a representative union, in most Israeli cases, the Trade Union Division of the Histadrut or a member National Union is authorized to submit the official notification forms on a scheduled strike. Any other procedure does not comply with the requirements of the law. Still, as we can see in Table 4.9, in only slightly more than a third of the cases (35.6 percent) does the notification take the necessary form. In a similar percentage of cases, notification is accomplished by the workers' committee. You may think, so what? What does it matter who transmits a piece of information? As long as it reaches the right address, it serves the same function. However, the Labor Relations Officer is constrained by law to deal only with legally received information. Therefore, he may either ignore the dry letter of the law and initiate his intervention, or conform to his official task and let valuable information go begging. No detailed data on this point are available.

Table 4.9: Reporting of the strike to labor relations officer by level of
            irs.

Source of Report	LEVEL		TOTAL
	Local	Higher	
Official	33.3	39.1	35.6
Representative	(12)	(9)	(21)
Local	38.9	30.4	35.6
Representative	(14)	(7)	(21)
Both	2.8		1.7
	(1)	(–)	(1)
Neither	25.0	30.4	27.1
	(9)	(7)	(16)
TOTAL	61.0	39.0	100.0
	(36)	(23)	(59)

P $(\chi^2 = 1.2061) \le .752$

What is the propensity of different employees' organizations to notify the Labor Relations Officer? Official figures on this topic are available for the year 1981-86. As we may remember, the IDS was carried out in 1977. So, even though not of the same quality and contents, the data from these two sources may help us identify a time trend, with the IDS as the first point in time and the official strike file, as the second. Table 4.10 shows a very clear distinction. While workers' committees tend to ignore the requirements for pre-notification, the established unions tend to comply with them. Workers' committees[15] delivered their strike intentions to the official address only once in six cases, while representative unions tended to conform to the requirements of the law in about half of the cases! So, when we compare the IDS figures with those presented in Table 4.10, we see a meaningful change. Semi-official notification almost ceased. Only those who were officially required to notify did so. However, this change has even greater significance. Not only was there a cessation of informal, but constructive practices, but the proportion of notified intentions to strike drastically decreased. Of the total number of strikes for which information is available, 666, almost three quarters (74.2 percent) were called by workers' committees. Only one out of four strikes was called by a representative union, and of this quarter, only in half of the cases was the Commissioner informed, clear evidence of the disregard of the authority of this official position.

Table 4.10: Notification of labor relations officer by strike initiator.

Source of Report	LEVEL		TOTAL
	Local	Higher	
Official Representative	33.3 (12)	39.1 (9)	35.6 (21)
Local Representative	38.9 (14)	30.4 (7)	35.6 (21)
Both	2.8 (1)	( )	1.7 (1)
Neither	25.0 (9)	30.4 (7)	27.1 (16)
TOTAL	61.0 (36)	39.0 (23)	100.0 (59)

$P (\chi^2 = 1.2061) \leq .752$

SUMMARY AND CONCLUSIONS

The general view we get from the data presented in this chapter can be summarized thus:

1. The Israeli irs is a two-tier structure on national and organizational levels. These two levels have very different features.

The national level irs is both formal and conformist. It includes a solid union movement, the Trade Union Division of the Histadrut, and a formal third party system, the Labor Relations Officer. A Labor court does exist, but the statistical evidence for its evaluation is too meager to be instructive. Employers' associations do exist, but their influence on strike activity is negligible. The national level union movement tries to control the IR arena by methods of codification and resource management. The workers' committees charter is the set of Histadrut bylaws as established by the national movement. It is paternal and stresses centralization. The monopoly held by the Histadrut on union resources, especially of the Strike Fund, serves as a complementary means for restricting organizational level union from independent activity.

The national union tends to adopt two seemingly contradictory strategies. On the one hand, it sticks to the letter of the law whenever it applies to it. This approach is evident as far as notifying the Labor Relations Officer of an impending strike. On the other hand, it serves as a buffer for its lower level units, the workers' committees. In the majority of the cases, whenever a workers' committee applies for the assembling of a workers' meeting with a strike plan on the agenda, this request tends to be approved. When a strike is declared by a union subdivision, this initiative is usually approved. This latter phenomenon has become more evident with time. The Histadrut of Becker's period was more restrictive than that of Ben Aharon and Meshel. Kessar brought this permissive policy to a new high.

2. The workers' committees function in a very different mode. They tend to take the Histadrut's support for granted. Therefore, their IR actors' set includes two and only two figures, their member community and their employer. The employer is both notified and updated on forthcoming events. An impending strike is regarded as a two-player game, the employer being the second. The committees' attitudes toward their rank-and-file are manipulative rather than representative. They tend to convene meetings to distribute information. They avoid as much as possible the transfer of the ultimate right of decision to their membership. Plant-level union leaders know that their environment regards them as indisputably legitimate representatives of their laity. Their employers may fight them, but the employers' arsenal is normatively fixed. It never includes means like strike breaking or authority usurpation. They feel safe under the Histadrut's wing, regarding it as an unconditional defensive umbrella, not a resource, whose availability is dependent on loyalty and conformity.

One way of gaining a more comprehensive view of conformity to strike related norms is by superimposing some of these norms on a process variable. Such an approach is demonstrated in Table 4.11.

Three strike related norms are incorporated in Table 4.11. The required stipulation that a request be sent to the representative organ of the union to approve assembling a general meeting to discuss the calling of a strike, the requirement to call a general meeting prior to the decision to go on strike and the provision to run a secret ballot before any strike action is enacted. As we can see, in only one of six strikes (17.8 percent) were all three prescriptions of this scenario adhered to. This figure increases drastically when we remove the ballot provision. Almost half of the disputes (44.4 percent) conform to the two other institutional requirements. An interesting figure is the one relating to the complete disregard of any institutional provision. In only one case (2.2 percent) did the plant level union representative body call a strike without any prior consultation or approval of anyone else.

The six profiles shown in Table 4.11 exhibit six different conformity patterns. A subordinate union body which adheres to all three requirements can be labelled as *conformist*. Such a unit is orthodox in both directions, downward, towards its rank-and-file, and upward, accepting unconditionally the bylaws of the mother organization, the Histadrut. This approach may, but need not be, a balanced approach. The courtesy downward may, under the present institutional setting, merely be conformity to formal union rules.

Table 4.11:   Conformity profile by Histadrut approval.

Conformity profile	Profile Specification	Approval		TOTAL
		Yes	No	
Conformist	Follow all	23.3 (7)	6.7 (1)	16.7 (8)
Constituency taken for granted	No ballot	50.0 (15)	33.3 (5)	41.7 (20)
Formal upward conformity	Request to Histadrut	20.0 (6)	0.0 (0)	12.5 (6)
Authentic representation of membership	Meeting + ballot	0.0 (0)	26.7 (4)	10.4 (4)
Exclusive dominance	Only meeting	3.3 (1)	33.3 (5)	16.7 (6)
Complete disregard	None of above	3.3 (1)	0.0 (0)	2.1 (1)
	TOTAL	66.7 (30)	33.3 (15)	100.0 (45)

$P(\chi^2 = 20.43750) \le 0.0010$

The second profile is the no ballot type. Here the workers' committee gains the approval of the representative union to call a meeting, and afterwards sets up such a meeting. If we take the avoidance of running a secret ballot as a meaningful political act, then, this forfeit of unsupervised democracy may indicate a take them for granted approach toward union members.

Following this approach, the minimal conformity needed for running a successful negotiation process with an employer can be achieved without taking the risk of a ballot. If a strike is called, neither will members show up nor will the employer try to hire strike breakers. If so, why bother with too much democracy? It is important to note that this profile is the most popular in the IDS sample. We may label this profile as the *takes constituency for granted* type. More than four out of ten (44.4 percent) of the surveyed disputes adopt this style. One out of eight disputes (13.3 percent) goes further in *adopting formal upward conformity*. The Histadrut is requested to approve a meeting, while such an assemblage never takes place. Is this an illogical profile? Why petition for assembling a meeting and then not do so?

Two different reasons might explain such a seemingly strange combination. First, the petition for convening a meeting may have been dismissed by the union, and second, the application may have achieved its aim by bringing the employer to concede to the workers' committee's demands. The design of the study dismisses the possibility of both explanations. The study sample included disputes which went beyond the secrecy of plant negotiation or committee/union politics. The researchers sought access to the surveyed enterprises only after they became public events. If so, another explanation must be offered. The application to the union to approve convening a meeting may have been a step in dispute management, the notification serving manipulative purposes. Even if not approved by the Histadrut, it serves as a clue to the employer that the committee contemplates the use of more extreme steps than quiet negotiations. Although such a threat is not always sufficient for achieving desired goals, it may play a supporting role. Another conformity profile is the one which exhibits no reference to the Histadrut for convening a meeting, but adheres perfectly to the internal circle, the relationship with the rank-and-file. Those officials who adopt this profile can be regarded as the *authentic representatives* of the members of their union. One out of ten disputes of the IDS discloses this profile.

Another quite popular conformity profile is the *exclusive dominance* type. Here, the plant level union officials assume a dominant role. They don't apply for anyone's approval of their actions. They call for a meeting, using it as a means for transmitting conflict-related gestures *vis-à-vis* the employer, allocation of supervised information and assuring compliance. An unsupervised meeting without a ballot option serves this aim quite satisfactorily. The last available profile is quite infrequent. It may be labelled the *complete disregard* type. This genre exhibits a union leadership devoid of any public overseeing. Here the plant-level union representatives make all strike related decision by themselves with reference neither to their rank-and-file nor to the Histadrut officials. The IDS includes only one such case. This was a defiant body, running a lone wolf campaign. Its endurance depends very much on its instrumentality for union members. A dissatisfied workers' community may easily lead to replacement of officials.

Table 4.11 tells another interesting story: conformity profiles are related to strike approval styles. A request for strike approval is confirmed if and when upward conformity is adopted. *Conformists, unions taking constituency for granted* and *formal upward conformists,* gain Histadrut approval for their strikes more than do those who tend to attune to their rank-and-file. *Authentic representatives of their membership,* and *exclusive dominants,* on the other hand, are over-represented in the unapproved strikes category.

Only *conformists* enjoy the best of both worlds. They maintain smooth communications to both upper and lower union echelons. All others make a choice. The Histadrut seems to be aware of this choice and sanctions it. It is worthwhile noting that in five of each six disputes local representatives do prefer to make such a choice and not to follow the *conformist* route.

Notes to Chapter 4

1. This is a quotation from: Appellate case No. 32/3-4, Port of Ashdod Foremen's Committee of Shinua vs. Israel Ports Authority, *Israel Labor Cases*, Vol. 3, [1972], p. 225.

2. This department developed in time to the status of a Division of Trade Unions.

3. In the Israeli terminology, union sanctions are all actions initiated by workers or their union, which come close to complete cessation of work, but do not reach it. Slowdowns, work-to-rule actions, overtime bans, selective transfer of phone calls, are typical examples of such sanctions.

4. Comparable clauses specify the requirements set for other local unions, which are not under the authority of the local Workers' Councils. Their logic is identical. A local union must be supervised by a higher level union. No professional action is permitted unless approved by a higher echelon Histadrut forum.

5. The Trade Union Department was structured during the 1970s into two subdivisions, one under the direct control of the Head of the Trade Union Department, Mr. Y. Meshel, dealt with all blue collar and semi-professional unions, the other called the Committee for Academic Affairs, headed by the vice-head of the department, dealt with the issues relevant for unions of academic professions.

6. The following agencies took part in this venture: the Central Bureau of Statistics and the Labor Registration Division in the Ministry of Labor and Welfare.

7. The upper level officials were interviewed only if their part in dispute administration was deemed primary by their lower level counterparts.

8. The Labor Party has undergone many divisions and unifications. Since the mid 1960s Mapai (The Workers Party of Eretz Israel), which was the leading socialist party, formed a quasi federationist structure with two smaller parties, and a confederation with the left wing socialist party, Mapam. This framework was called the Alignment (Ma'arach).

9. This figure is based on a sample of thirteen cases. Therefore, it must be taken cautiously. Still, it should not be taken as the total number of valid responses to this topic. If we add those responses in which there was no application to the workers' council, we reach a sample size of twenty-five. This is a figure of 41.7 percent of the total study sample.

10. Secretary General Becker, in a private interview, phrased this approach in somewhat different terms: "The wider the approving forum, the more responsible will the final decision be."

11. Fischer reports on difficulties in gaining information in cases where the degree of normative compliance was complete. She regards a case of perfect compliance as an event where there was no binding contract, a notification was delivered to the Labor Relations Officer, the His-

tadrut disapproved the strike, and the strike was canceled. Therefore, her minimal figure of complete compliance may underestimate this phenomenon in the population, while the IDS figure of complete conformity may be more accurate.

12. Data available for the years 1965-69.

13. No data are available on this topic for the Becker period.

14. The following finding of the IDS may indicate that this semi-legal notification to the Commissioner was not always followed by meaningful actions. In response to a question concerning whether any demand evaluation was relegated to a third party, the typical response was: none (85.7 percent). For those disputes where a notification was made by a workers' committee, the tendency was much stronger (55.0 for none), *but*, the typical third party route was a bi-partite committee (30.0 percent) and not an arbitrator (5.0 percent) or a mediator (5.0 percent). The arbitrator or mediator referred to may or may not have been the Labor Relations Officer.

15. Local and national workers' committees were collapsed into a single cate-gory for the reproduction of Table 4.10. Their propensities to notify the Labor Relations Officer were almost identical.

5

Strikes in an Action Framework: Israeli Strikes and Their Context

Introduction

Strikes have one feature in common, they all begin and end. They differ, however, in many other aspects. While some strikes are spontaneous responses to threatening stimuli, most are planned. As such, they are typical examples of a social action. Action, following Parsons (1949), "is a relation between an actor and a situation." This relation has two temporal characteristics, first, it is a continuous process and second, it is future oriented. As acts, we can approach strikes from two major angles, their characteristics and the situation which surrounds them. An actor, usually a union, conducts a strike. Another actor, usually management, serve as its object. Strikes have a cause, or a rationale. They are conducted following a discernible method, leading to an outcome, though neither the method nor the outcome is fixed. A strike can be approved or disapproved by the legal authority. The initiating union can explicitly specify goals for a given stoppage, or it can convey its message more indirectly. Although unions can achieve their objectives through strikes, they may end in complete disaster. Strikes are, therefore, complicated acts. Their modes of enactment may change from time to time and from case to case.

In this chapter I shall discuss the changes in strike enactment during the years 1965-1987. Strikes, however do not happen in the vacuum. Like any other act, they take place within a context, a set of given constraints. Usually, strikers take as given the political and the economic features of their country. Therefore, the macro social characteristics of Israel are part of the context of Israeli strikes. These givens do not end on the macro-social level. Unions face a set of givens on the level of their action as well. Most unions under most circumstances do not repudiate the legitimacy of the institution of ownership. An owner may be a private party, but may, however, be public or even the union's own labor movement (in Israel, the Histadrut). Moreover, enterprises engage in economic activities. They manufacture cars or supply medical services. Seldom, if ever, do unions demand, or push toward, a rerouting of economic activity. They accept the activity of their workplaces. Therefore, for the sake of strike analysis, both the sector of ownership of an enterprise and its economic branch are part of the context. We should incorporate information on these aspects in our description. We should, however, treat them as constraints on the irs, not as part of it.

I shall distinguish between two types of contextual constraints on strike activity, the immediate constraints and the macro level constraints. The major political developments both on the state and on the Histadrut levels accompany almost each step of the analysis. We will compare the union composition of strikes during the Labor Party period to that of the Likud Party. We will see the differences in the rate of strike approval during the tenures of the early secretary generals of the Histadrut and their successors. The governing party and the identity of the Secretary General of the Histadrut will serve as independent variables for subsequent analysis. The more mundane features of the context, those of ownership sector and economic branch will be described in a separate section.

First, I will deal with the actors involved in Israeli strikes. Since strikes are a collective endeavor, I will concentrate on the collective representatives of workers, the unions. Next, I will present the *immediate* context of strikes. Then, we can discuss strikes in terms of their action features. Since any action is to some degree voluntaristic, we will look for the what's, how's and why's of strike activity. What did the striking unions do or abstain from doing while embarking on the strike route? Why did they opt for a strike? What did they try to achieve? How did they take action? Did they follow the due course of the law and Histadrut bylaws? Did they gain Histadrut approval? Did they notify the Labor Relations Officer? And, finally, how successful were they in achieving their goals.

All these aspects may differ from strike to strike. However, I do not plan to deal with these differences in the coming chapter. Rather, I wish to show the changes over time. What were the most significant changes in the style of striking in Israel between 1965 and 1987? In so doing, I hope to identify important developments in the industrial relations arena.

Any study of strikes in a given target area, be it a country, an industry, or a community, starts with a statistical introduction. Is this essential? Can it be done routinely or should it be tailored to fit the particular circumstances? Statistical data is presumably a prerequisite for an "objective" investigation. Nevertheless, I am still disturbed by a comment I heard many years ago in my macro-economics class. If one day our "housewives," some of whom may nowadays be male, decided to exchange their sites of activity, each going to clean, cook and wash in their neighbor's house, the official economic statistics would drastically change. Our gross national product would actually multiply by two. Not one single cup of tea would be added, but in the world of statistics a revolutionary change would take place. This paradox has led me to ask myself what we can learn from statistical data.

We may be interested in strikes for many reasons. An economist may ask, "how do I measure the economic costs of strikes?" For him a day of stoppage during a recession may have a totally different value than a day of idleness during a period of prosperity. A political scientist or a sociologist, on the other hand, may be interested in strikes as an indication of the prevailing dissatisfaction with societal establishments. For him, the value of lost product may be of peripheral importance. He will be interested in body counts. How *many* people were involved in strikes and not *whose* production has been lost.

The technology of the collection of strike statistics shapes their form more than their substantial application. The collecting agency, be it the Institute of Economic and Social Research[1] or the Central Bureau of Statistics in Israel, or the Bureau of Labor Statistics in the U.S., typically send forms to its sources of information. The published figures include the total number of returned forms—the number of strikes, the sum of reported people involved in strikes—the number of strikers, and the number of man days idle because of strikes—the sum of the multiplication of the number of reported participants in strikes and the duration of their abstention from work caused by reported strikes. I can envisage a change in the structure of worker representation, very similar to the above mentioned rebellion of housewives, where instead of strikes being led by local unions, a national union is established. This organizational change would cause a *decrease* in the number of strikes in official statistics. Anyone looking for the number of persons involved in strikes in a given period would be misled by these figures. The published numbers indicate the number of *times* workers participated in strikes and not the number of *people* who were involved. And, as a last illustration, the volume of mandays lost may give a deceptive notion of the cost of strikes. A change in the occupational, or in the industrial composition, of the strikers may be concealed by a stable figure of lost man days.

Strike Patterns—A General View

When people say that Britain under the first post World War II Labor Party government had a severe strike problem, what do they mean? When they suggest that the labor market warms up with the level of economic activity, what are they indicating? Do they imply that the number of strikes increases? That more workers are engaging in strike activity? That, on the average, workers stay out of work for longer periods because of strikes? That more working days are lost because of strikes? Or do they have in mind a claim that a larger part of the national product has been lost because of strikes? That the welfare of the population at large has been significantly affected by strike activity? All these possible meanings, and many others, can lie behind either of the opening statements. Even though we seldom acknowledge these distinctions, they are still very significant. The impact of a single long general strike is not the same as that of many smaller strikes. I will refer to the distinctions between many versus few, large versus small and long versus short strikes as differences in strike patterns.

The strike pattern concept is a major contribution to the methodology of strike research. The idea was developed almost simultaneously by two pairs of researchers, Britt and Galle, and Shorter and Tilly and has since been applied in various research studies. The strike pattern concept approaches strikes as a phenomenon with three dimensions, frequency, breadth and duration. The number of man days idle is regarded as a volume, the sum total of the multiplication of those three factors.[2] *The number of man-days idle is a multiplication of the number of strikes, the average size of a strike, and the average duration of striking per striker.* The concept of frequency x average breadth x average duration is important not only for the fact that it manages to decompose a make-believe solid entity, the measure of man-days idle. More importantly, it inspires a rethink and integration of past research findings. Stern suggests the following ideas about the components of strike patterns:

> *Frequency* represents the decision to take or call a strike... The *breadth* of participation measures the mobilization of workers for strike activity [and] *duration* represents the time it takes parties to settle after the 'rational' calculation to take or call a strike has been made. (Stern, 1978, p. 39)

These ideas should not be taken as the only possible rationalizations of the three dimensions of strike patterns. Still, they do call for separate theoretical explanations for each of the three. Adopting the strike pattern construct we can run comparisons across time and space. The more complicated distinctions of strike impact, those referring to their different economic or social costs must await future research. Their conceptualization is still in its preliminary stages. Nevertheless, I shall deal with part of them in chapter 8.

Table 5.1   Strike patterns by the dominant party and the identity of the secretary general of the Histadrut 1965-87.

P E R I O D			Strike Measures			
Dominant Party	General Secretary	D a t e s	Strikes per 100 Days	Average Strike Size	Average Duration	Period in days
Labor	Becker	1. 1.65* - 15.12.69	51	315	2.14	1,810
	Ben-Aharon	16.12.69 - 18.11.73	42	687	2.70	1,433
	Meshel	19.11.73 - 17. 5.77	31	1,081	2.10	1,277
Likud	Meshel	18. 5.77 - 15. 5.84	27	3,162	2.71	2,525
	Kessar	16. 5.84 - 23. 7.84	39	5,325	2.25	98
Unity	Kessar	24. 7.84 - 31.12.87**	41	3,179	1.32	1,257

*   Data available since this date. Administration started in 1962.
** Data available until this date. Administration continues beyond.

Since the volume of strikes is a three-dimensional issue, reviewing it requires the adoption of a strategy. Luhmann's (1982, pp. 229-254) system approach helps us make the choice. Luhmann sees social evolution as a process of differentiation, following three phases: segmentation, stratification, and then functional differentiation. *Segmentation* divides society into *equal* subsystems. *Stratification* divides society into *unequal* subsystems, and *functional differentiation* organizes society around special social functions. Israel shows an increasing resemblance to a functionally differentiated society. First comes the differentiation of roles. Ethnic and filial affinities lose much of their importance as the determinants of role assignments. This is the trend for the Jewish majority. The continuing Arab-Israeli conflict hampers a similar trend for the large Arab minority.

This long lasting conflict has made the army a major institution in Israeli society. The Israeli Defense Forces (IDF) form a functionally differentiated system. The daily need to defend the state has created constant pressures for achievement and specialization. Efforts to engage the army in fulfilling functions beyond that of defence have either been failures or have been rejected. The latest example of failure is an educational project for underprivileged draftees, which was initiated by the then Chief of Staff, General Raphael Eytan. This was a well-meant project, but its operation was closely tied to the beliefs of a single person, General Eytan. The project dwindled in time to minor importance.

The use of military titles as a means of promoting political views is another example of the mingling of military and political domains. This tendency has been under wide criticism for many years. On the other hand, the army has made an important positive contribution towards the differentiation of the wider society. The daily need to cope with uncertainties has forced the army to stress achievement. During peace time, armies serve ritualistic functions. Such functions may hinder functional differentiation. The Israeli case shows that armies can promote such processes. Since the army is a hierarchical organization, has a very wide recruiting policy and a relatively small number of positions in high command, it is a very competitive setting. Such settings have a peculiar characteristic. Their high rate of attrition exports high-quality personnel to their environment, which is the case with the Israeli Defense Forces.

This produces three types of job seekers for the civil labor market: a large number of junior officers, who leave service after a short enlisted career, a smaller number of officers who leave the army after reaching their personal peak on the promotional ladder, and an even smaller number of higher ranking officers who reach retirement relatively early, after twenty years of service. The younger ex-officers pursue their careers through the channels of higher education. They combine the high achievement values of the army with the abstract thinking modes of academic learning. The second and the third groups look for a second career. The most essential asset of these ex-army officers is their operative abilities. These three post-service groups differ in age, ability and experience. They all contribute to the disengagement of Israeli society from primordial criteria and to the stimulation of functional criteria.

The economic sphere more and more stresses achievement criteria as the only legitimate yardsticks for job selection and promotion. The political upheaval of 1977 brought a capitalistic (using Israeli terminology, liberal) ideology to the fore. While the economic accomplishments of the Likud administrations were less than impressive, their ideological implications did promote further specialization and self-reliance.

A highly differentiated society is not only a society structured along functional lines. It is a society in which each *domain* follows a functionally differentiated script. Therefore, we should analyze strike data both on the societal and the irs levels. Since any process of differentiation is time related, temporal milestones can help identify its impact. The developments in the wider society make it useful to relate strike pattern figures to the major contemporary political developments. Therefore, strike data will be broken down into three sub-periods, for the Labor Party (1965-77), Likud Party (1977-84), and the National Unity coalition (1984-87) days.

As has been made abundantly evident throughout this book, the Histadrut is is a major actor in the Israeli irs. Developments in the Histadrut, therefore, are likely to shed light or reflect developments in this system. Since the Histadrut is a democratic political organization, changes in its leadership correspond to stages in system changes. The periods of administration of the four secretary generals we are dealing with are basic phases of system evolvement. Presenting strike pattern figures broken down by Histadrut administration, then, is a second criterion for data analysis.

The twenty-three years under study will be divided into six sub-periods, corresponding to both political and irs bench marks: Labor as dominant party and Becker as the Histadrut secretary general (Labor-Becker), Labor and Ben-Aharon, Labor and Meshel, Likud as the dominant party and Meshel as the secretary general, Likud and Kessar, and National Unity government and Kessar.

What are the benefits of this six sub-periods breakdown of strike data? It allows us two types of generalization, one relating to the operation of units on sub-national levels (industry, sector, regional, etc.) and the other, on the functioning of the national labor market itself.

Some variables divide the national labor market into smaller segments, sector of ownership, economic branch and regional distinctions for example. Since both private and public sectors have their own irs, a comparison between sectors by their strike pattern features shows us the IR implications of the type of ownership. If we relate sector-level economic, political, technological and IR variables, we can identify the relationships between their corresponding systems in a specific domain. We may find that the irs of a public sector is more (or less!) sensitive to political influences than the private sector.[3] (Reshef & Bemmels, 1989)

Other variables depict the way the national-level labor market functions without showing finer distinctions. When we observe the changes in the involvement of the labor court, the Histadrut, or any other agent in strikes, in relation to the changes in rate of strike approval, we get a notion of the way the total Israeli labor market acts. We could actually run a two-level analysis, the changes of strike approval rates by sectors, for example, differentiating between national and sectoral developments. Such a level of detail, however, would be well beyond the degree needed for the present work.

Before we can get into the corpus of the data, we must make one more decision: whether to use crude strike data or standardized measures. It is tempting to use simple measures. On the face of it, in an analysis of a single case, one can draw conclusions from changes in the number of strikes, or the number of man-days lost in strikes. The comparison of strike frequency across time and space is more difficult. The six sub-periods here presented are very unequal in length. They range between ninety-eight days (Likud as dominant party and Kessar as the secretary general of the Histadrut) and 2,525 days (Likud/Meshel). Therefore, we present our data in a standardized form, as the number of strikes per 1,000 days.

Still, why not adopt a one year yardstick as a common denominator? If we did so, we could run a comparison with any annual strike statistics from anywhere in the world. *Technically* this may be done, but substantially this comparison would be meaningless without further controlling for size. Stern (1978, pp. 35-36) showed that standardization can and has been carried out using various criteria, the population size, adult population size, number of employees and number of union members. Most studies selected their standardization criteria on the basis of mere convenience. My present concern is, however, substantive and convenience must be a secondary consideration. From a pure methodological standpoint, the population at risk of a given threat, be it strikes, car accidents or pregnancy, should serve as the denominator for standardization. What, then, is the population at risk in the case of strikes? The intuitive answer is that organized workers are the carriers of industrial conflict. If assumed valid, the number of organized workers should serve as standardizing factor. But, as we all know, strikes are not individual level actions. There is no way to compare the odds that a thousand union members will take part in a strike to the odds that a single employee will participate in a stoppage. The valid standardizing criteria are contingent on the structure of the labor force.

A simple example can clarify my point. Assume we compare two hypothetical societies of the same size. In the first country the only existing enterprises employ ten employees, all of whom are members of the same union, and all the unions are plant unions. In a second country, all employees are employed by the same employer and unionized in the same union. Would we expect both societies to have the same level of strike activity? Clearly, the second society would experience many fewer strikes than the first. (The strike size in the second case would be, however, much larger.) And what if either of these societies moves from a biannual contract system to a three year system? We can easily agree that the population at risk for strikes is not the number of organized workers. It is either the number of negotiating parties or the number of negotiating opportunities. If so, is it at all possible to compare different societies using a valid standardizing stick? It must be very difficult, if, indeed it is possible at all. My task, however, is rather simpler since I am restricting the present analysis to a single—Israeli—context.

Strikes in Israel since it gained independence (1948-1987)

Any description of Israeli strike patterns and their change since the establishment of the state encounters two major problems. First, in spite of the short period under consideration, less than forty years, the size of its working population has drastically increased. The number of salaried employees multiplied by a factor of 5.87 from 1949 to 1986. From 184,800 employees at the beginning of the period it increased to 1,084,900. Thus, any raw figures of strike activity are meaningless. This aspect of relativity is relevant not only to manpower statistics. If there is a place where it is true to say that numbers are in themselves meaningless, unless you compare them to a specified frame of reference, it is Israel. It is a country, for example, where an inflation of four hundred percent per year (1985) made any nominal monetary comparisons worthless. It vastly increased its geographical size in six days, during the Six Days War of June, 1967. This same territorial expansion was cut drastically as the result of the peace treaty with Egypt in 1977. Therefore, Israel's size is not a commonly agreed upon absolute. Standardizing figures is therefore inescapable. Executing this procedure is required only for one strike pattern dimension, that of frequency. The two other measures are standardized in their accepted form.

The second problem is methodological. Until 1960, only stoppages of a day or more were included in the official strike statistics. A suspected increase in the occurrence of very short strikes, mostly labelled as workers' meetings during work hours, led to a widening of the definition. Since 1960, strikes of two hours or more are reported and registered. This policy change may modify all three strike pattern measures. It leads to the identification of a larger number of strikes from 1960, which may (or may not) exhibit the striking strategies of different categories of workers. It has direct impact on the average strike duration, decreasing this aspect. The only feasible way to avoid invalid conclusions is to present parallel statistical data, both for the minimal and the maximal definitions.

Table 5.2 presents Israeli strikes according to the minimal definition. Only disputes which lasted at least one day are included in it. Table 5.3 portrays the same phenomena based on the more inclusive definition. Figures are neither available for the years 1960-64 for Table 5.2, nor for the period 1949-59 in Table 5.3.

Table 5.2:   Israeli strike statistics: Duration of one day or more.

YEAR	No. of Salaried Workers	Average Duration	Average Breadth	Strikes per 100,000 Salaried Workers
1949	184,800	11.07	98	29
1950	253,300	6.05	126	28
1951	314,000	11.76	128	24
1952	332,000	4.14	149	28
1953	326,200	4.02	105	26
1954	369,400	5.93	148	22
1955	368,900	5.47	113	24
1956	367,100	9.76	155	20
1957	419,900	44.84	63	14
1958	432,300	14.50	126	11
1959	455,700	5.33	115	11
1960	472,600	na	na	na
1961	532,400	na	na	na
1962	574,700	na	na	na
1963	615,500	na	na	na
1964	638,100	na	na	na
1965	634,400	2.80	346	33
1966	638,900	2.89	234	33
1967	585,600	4.08	136	18
1968	649,500	2.17	428	11
1969	689,100	2.30	513	13
1970	709,200	5.38	398	18
1971	744,400	4.32	293	17
1972	787,200	3.41	536	16
1973	821,700	3.35	1463	9
1974	833,600	3.38	234	7
1975	850,400	2.36	731	11
1976	854,800	3.01	1,019	12
1977	884,500	2.91	1,220	12
1978	931,400	4.91	2,934	8
1979	960,200	2.56	2,013	10
1980	972,000	2.62	1,113	8
1981	999,400	2.52	3,416	9
1982	1,020,100	2.46	7,979	9
1983	1,052,300	7.92	1,536	8
1984	1,074,000	2.89	2,654	11
1985	1,081,700	2.00	2,401	9
1986	1,084,900	3.26	1,126	9

na = Not available.

Table 5.3: Israeli strike statistics: Duration of two hours or more.

YEAR	No. of Salaried Workers	Average Duration	Average Breadth	Strikes per 100,000 Salaried Workers
1949	184,800	na	na	na
1950	253,300	na	na	na
1951	314,000	na	na	na
1952	332,000	na	na	na
1953	326,200	na	na	na
1954	369,400	na	na	na
1955	368,900	na	na	na
1956	367,100	na	na	na
1957	419,900	na	na	na
1958	432,300	na	na	na
1959	455,700	na	na	na
1960	472,600	3.42	107	29
1961	532,400	4.69	209	23
1962	574,700	6.43	261	25
1963	615,500	1.48	686	20
1964	638,100	2.14	347	21
1965	634,400	2.37	314	45
1966	638,900	1.90	301	45
1967	585,600	2.64	178	24
1968	649,500	1.76	418	16
1969	689,100	2.21	437	16
1970	709,200	2.80	684	23
1971	744,400	2.02	525	23
1972	787,200	2.69	520	21
1973	821,700	3.07	1,274	12
1974	833,600	1.93	380	9
1975	850,400	1.54	966	14
1976	854,800	2.85	936	14
1977	884,500	2.08	1,553	14
1978	931,400	4.86	2,651	9
1979	960,200	2.04	2,131	12
1980	972,000	2.37	1,089	9
1981	999,400	2.52	3,416	9
1982	1,020,100	2.16	7,488	11
1983	1,052,300	5.19	2,025	9
1984	1,074,000	1.88	3,548	14
1985	1,081,700	1.14	3,618	12
1986	1,084,900	1.89	1,516	13

na = Not available.

Each of the first eight years of independence shows between twenty and twenty-nine full day and above strikes per 100,000 salaried workers. From 1957 on many fewer strikes erupted. The only deviant years, excluding those years for which no figures are available, are the years 1965-66. The extreme numbers for these years point to the turmoil in the industrial relations arena aroused by a reform in standards and classifications implemented in the public sector. The missing lines of Table 5.2 can be compensated for by the information available in Table 5.3. Here we can see higher relative strike frequency at the beginning of the reported series, the years 1960-67, than at its end (1968-86). A median year in the first phase shows 24.5 strikes per 100,000 employees, while a similar year in the second stage shows only thirteen strikes. So, both tables portray a trend of decrease in the tendency to call strikes.

An altogether opposite picture is found when we turn to the second strike pattern dimension, the average number of strikers per strike. The strikes of the twelve first years of independence (1949-60) for which statistics are available were very small. On the average no more than a hundred and fifty employees participated in an average strike. Starting in 1961 the breadth of strikes increased to several hundred. This trend continued, with the exception of the year 1973, in which the Yom-Kippur War took place, and which shows a exceptionally large average strike figure (but a small number of strikes), until 1977. Then, simultaneously with the political upheaval which threw the Labor Party into opposition after forty-seven years of stable majority (albeit with coalition partners), the average breadth of strikes changed its scale. Their size increased to the thousands. This scale was maintained to the end of the reported period even when a national front government, with a Labor Party representative as its prime minister, replaced the former Likud government.

The major characteristic of Israeli strikes is their short duration. Ever since strikes of two hours length and above were reported, only once (1962) did this measure surpass six days. Still, back in the first years of independence (1949,1951,1957,1958) the pattern was one of much longer strikes. This downward trend of strike duration is less prominent, but on the whole it holds.

Table 5.4: Strike measures and time correlation coefficients for two strike data sources.

	SF	AB	D	MDI
Coefficients for Strikes of 2 hours +	-.6898 (27) P=.001	.6929 (27) P=.001	-.2367 (27) P=.117	.5788 (27) P=.001
Coefficients for Strikes of a day +	-.7378 (33) P=.001	.6073 (33) P=.001	-.3253 (38) P=.023	.5102 (33) P=.001

SF = Frequency of strikes per 100,000 salaried workers.
AB = Average strike breadth. D = Average strike duration.
MDI = Number of man-days idle

Table 5.4 summarizes the trends of strike patterns in Israel. A regression coefficient of -0.69 is found for the trend of standardized strike frequency of two hours and above, (-0.74 for the one day and above series), a coefficient of

0.69 for strike breadth, (0.61 for the less exclusive series), and a coefficient of -0.24 for strike duration (-0.39 for the second set).

A separate discussion of the three strike pattern dimensions is inconclusive regarding the general trend of strike intensity in Israel. Has it increased, as may be concluded from its breadth, or has it moderated, as evidenced by its frequency and duration? If we turn back to the strike pattern formula, we find that the volume of strikes, i.e., the number of man days idle as a result of strikes, is a multiplication of frequency, breadth and duration. The last column of Table 5.4 gives us a clear answer: the volume of strikes in Israel shows an upward trend. The regression coefficient of time on the number of man days idle is 0.58 (0.51 for strikes of one day and above). The increase in average strike breadth more than compensated for the decrease in both the frequency of strikes and their duration

STRIKES IN ISRAEL SINCE 1965—A MORE DETAILED DESCRIPTION

Prior to any description of the changes in the attributes of strikes, the more basic picture, the *crude* dimensions of the Israeli strike pattern, frequency, average breadth and average duration, must be drawn. Table 5.1 presents these basics.

Israeli strikes are very short. Few Americans would regard a two or three days stoppage as a "real" strike, but it is the average duration in Israel.

Table 5.1 shows us the statistics for Israel, broken down by their corresponding dominant party and secretary general. The first dimension of the strike pattern, the frequency of strikes, has a curvilinear **U** shape. The second—the average size, has a trend of increase, and the last—duration, does not show a systematic trend. The volume of striking, the number of mandays idle due to strikes, has a curvilinear trend. For the frequency dimension, the lowest point is the Meshel/Likud period. For the volume of striking, the highest point is the Kessar/Likud period. Because of the unreliability of this short period as a frame of reference, the Meshel/Likud period should be selected as the maximum point for strike volume.

As we can see, the frequency of strikes in Israel has a clear **U** shape. Table 5.1 shows a decline during the Meshel's era (1973-84) and two climaxes at the beginning and the end of the years under study. The identity of the Secretary General of the Histadrut and *not* the dominant party, determined this trend. Both pairs of two periods, of Meshel and of Kessar, exhibit a similar level of strike frequency, despite changes on the political level.

One clear trend developed during these twenty-three years. Strikes became much larger. While an average strike during the Becker era mobilized 315 workers, a sixfold number took part in a typical stoppage during Meshel's and Kessar's second terms.[4] The determining factor of this trend is neither a single secretary general nor a specific dominant party. The figure increased both when the Histadrut leadership changed and when a political upheaval occurred during the administration of a specific Histadrut functionary.

The only significant change in strike duration occurred in the Kessar/ National Unity government period. If shown to be lasting, this is a significant development in Israeli strike patterns. An average strike duration of 1.32 days is a phenomenon of major importance. If this short duration persists, then it can serve as a clear indication that Israeli strikes have become purely symbolic acts. A duration as short as this can only be a gesture, the meaning of which is widely acknowledged and used as a communicative means for negotiation. Only in very extreme and unique strikes, such as shutdowns of electricity or water, can a strike as short as this cause significant damage. It can only be either a demonstration of power or a symbolic gesture of dissatisfaction.

Who Are the Strikers?

UNION IDENTITY

Any listing of Israeli unions will include many which strike very seldom. Our discussion will, therefore, proceed in two stages. First, a discussion of those unions that do take part in industrial disputes to a considerable degree. Then, unions will be grouped on the basis of their members' occupation. This classification will allow a more comprehensive analysis

Top Striking Unions, A Union Specific Discussion

A few unions account for a significant percentage of the total strike count. Exactly the same unions remain at the top of the list for the entire period under investigation. Their ranking, however, is not completely stable. For the period as a whole,[5] *Histadrut ha-Pkidim* (The National Union of Clerical, Administrative and Public Service Employees—UCAPSE) has a high first place (22.9 percent of all strikes for which union affiliation was reported). Second comes *Histadrut Ovdei ha-Medina* (The National Union of Government Employees in Israel—NUGE) (11.3 percent), and then, *Histadrut Poalei ha-Matechet* (National Union of Metal, Electric and Electronic Workers) (9.7 percent), *Histadrut ha-Morim* (Israel Teachers Union) (4.0 percent), and the *Irgun ha-Morim ha-Al-Yesodi'im* (Union of High-School Teachers, independent union, unaffiliated with the Histadrut). These five unions account for more than half of the strikes (55.2 percent).

Three major switches in ranking occurred during the years under consideration:

a. The Union of Government Employees lost its standing to the Union of Clerical Workers. The formation of the first union was an expression of the belief that state employees share a dominant common denominator and deserve a common union. This extreme industrial conception—a single union for all the employees of one huge employer, the state—proved very ineffective. The variety of occupations in the civil service was too complex and unwieldy to be represented by the same union. The first to quit were the professional groups, engineers, economists, physicians and their colleagues. Other skilled occupations, like technicians, followed suit. All these groups saw the unified union as a threat to their identity and specialized privileges. As a result, various groups split from the union, or at least shifted their identification from this union to their craft frame of reference. One way or another, while the Union of Government Employees ranked first (63 strikes) during the Ben-Aharon era, with the Union of Clerical Employees second (33), this order was later reversed. During all following periods, the Union of Clerical Employees initiated more than double the number of strikes called by the Union of Government Employees . Detailed figures are presented in Table 5.5.

Table. 5.5: Summary strike pattern features for strikers' union and period.

Period	Strikers' Union	F^1	$Size^2$	D^3	MDI^4
Meshel-Labor	Printing, binding	6	73	2.8	1,292
Meshel-Likud	"	3	146	5.4	2,492
Kessar-Likud	"	20	700	1.0	14,286
Kessar-Unity	"	4	239	1.1	998
Ben-Aharon	Assoc. of nurses	1	60	10.1	842
Meshel-Labor	"	8	3,317	4.5	116,897
Meshel-Likud	"	1	2,750	3.7	8,119
Kessar-Unity	"	18	4,697	2.4	196,613
Ben-Aharon	Social Workers	3	1,005	1.9	5,255
Meshel-Labor	"	1	2,600	1.0	2,036
Meshel-Likud	"	1	3,500	0.5	2,228
Kessar-Unity	"	6	1,363	0.9	6,579
Ben-Aharon	Gov't Employees	62	917	2.5	141,535
Meshel-Labor	"	34	1,461	1.3	62,961
Meshel-Likud	"	27	4,027	1.2	125,153
Kessar-Likud	"	41	293	2.2	25,816
Kessar-Unity	"	31	4,755	0.5	73,006
Ben-Aharon	Building Workers	1	242	1.9	652
Meshel-Likud	"	6	339	2.7	5,031
Kessar-Unity	"	6	563	1.0	2,995
Meshel-Labor	"	10	204	2.9	6,056

Table 5.5 cont'd

Period	Strikers' Union	F	Size	D	MDI
Kessar-Unity	"	10	276	4.0	11,335
Becker	Clerical Employees	3	196	0.9	472
Ben-Aharon	"	48	667	1.7	53,897
Meshel-Labor	"	63	989	1.6	98,884
Meshel-Likud	"	65	2,023	2.5	328,248
Kessar-Likud	"	92	10,826	1.1	1,057,480
Kessar-Unity	"	130	1,874	2.6	626,985
Ben-Aharon	Graduate Engineers	2	692	0.3	401
Meshel-Labor	"	2	15,667	2.4	86,922
Meshel-Likud	"	2	6,166	1.0	12573
Kessar-Likud	"	31	10,333	8.9	2,801,020
Kessar-Unity	"	4	504	3.1	6,139
Ben-Aharon	Diamond Workers	3	59	6.3	1,026
Meshel-Labor	"	2	285	12.2	5,427
Meshel-Likud	"	2	1,302	9.4	29,040
Kessar-Unity	"	2	427	5.9	3,990
Meshel-Labor	Aircraft Industry	2	120	7.7	1,439
Meshel-Likud	"	0	19,500	1.0	7,723
Ben-Aharon	Histadrut Industries	9	249	2.6	59,58
Meshel-Labor	"	12	217	4.7	11,902
Meshel-Likud	"	4	661	7.5	19526
Kessar-Unity	"	1	65	6.0	310
Ben-Aharon	Metal, Electric, Electronic	33	398	3.1	40,655
Meshel-Labor	"	28	307	5.6	48,547
Meshel-Likud	"	26	397	4.9	50,358
Kessar-Unity	"	44	265	3.5	41,033
Ben-Aharon	Wood & Paper Ind.	3	356	4.8	4,759
Meshel-Likud	"	4	241	4.1	3,533
Kessar-Unity	"	2	119	9.1	2,582
Ben-Aharon	X-ray Tech.	1	20	1.0	14

Table 5.5 cont'd

Period	Strikers' Union	F	Size	D	MDI
Kessar-Unity	"	5	27	5.9	749
Ben-Aharon	Textile, Garment & Leather	15	470	4.6	31,830
Meshel-Labor	"	13	293	6.6	24,307
Meshel-Likud	"	7	312	7.1	15,839
Kessar-Unity	"	13	176	11.3	25,346
Ben-Aharon	Road Transport	1	22	4.0	61
Meshel-Labor	"	6	509	1.1	3,381
Meshel-Likud	"	1	82	1.4	135
Kessar-Unity	"	1	350	14.0	3,898
Becker	Longshore-men & Sea Port	15	251	2.8	10,508
Ben-Aharon	"	17	244	1.7	6942
Meshel-Labor	"	13	957	1.9	22,645
Meshel-Likud	"	8	238	1.4	2,585
Kessar-Likud	"	31	69	2.7	5,806
Kessar-Unity	"	2	260	0.4	151
Ben-Aharon	Rubber & Tire Ind.	3	334	1.4	1,333
Meshel-Labor	"	5	203	9.6	9,123
Meshel-Likud	"	2	190	7.8	3,499
Kessar-Unity	"	4	306	8.1	9,924
Meshel-Labor	"	2	54	2.6	219
Ben-Aharon	Lifeguards	1	25	24.0	419
Meshel-Labor	"	1	9	3.0	21
Ben-Aharon	Media & Creative Arts	2	117	0.9	216
Ben-Aharon	Agricul. Workers	8	64	6.3	3,121
Meshel-Labor	"	2	63	3.0	439
Meshel-Likud	"	2	1,029	1.9	3,929
Kessar-Unity	"	2	1,727	0.3	1,128

Table 5.5 cont'd

Period	Strikers' Union	F	Size	D	MDI
Kessar-Unity	"	1	18	1.0	14
Ben-Aharon	Technical Engineers	3	4,182	1.0	14,351
Meshel-Labor	"	4	5,130	0.3	5,316
Meshel-Likud	"	5	893	0.6	2,403
Kessar-Unity	"	6	604	0.9	3,603
Meshel-Labor	Pharma-cists	1	1,350	0.5	529
Meshel-Likud	"	1	877	1.5	1,588
Kessar-Likud	"	10	150	1.0	1,531
Kessar-Unity	"	1	1,000	4.0	3,182
Becker	Teachers, Aguda	6	428	1.9	4,498
Ben-Aharon	"	2	967	1.2	2,373
Becker	High Sch. Teachers	23	473	1.2	13,255
Ben-Aharon	"	18	308	13.1	73,192
Meshel-Labor	"	3	57	1.9	345
Meshel-Likud	"	6	6,346	2.3	88,270
Kessar-Likud	"	10	7,000	0.3	17,857
Kessar-Unity	"	23	3,443	0.9	73,368
Ben-Aharon	Medical Assoc.	2	3,440	12.3	88,724
Meshel-Labor	"	1	2,500	1.0	1,958
Kessar-Unity	"	4	1,102	1.0	4,383
Becker	Teachers' Union	13	701	1.3	12,188
Ben-Aharon	"	10	54	3.6	1,858
Meshel-Likud	"	16	13,455	2.1	437,091
Kessar-Likud	"	31	17,200	1.0	520,408
Kessar-Unity	"	24	20,372	0.7	325,221
Ben-Aharon	Journalists	1	230	6.1	1,970
Meshel-Labor	"	1	100	1.0	78
Meshel-Likud	"	3	255	6.8	4,783
Kessar-Likud	"	20	450	1.0	9,316
Kessar-Unity	"	6	389	14.7	36,487
Ben-Aharon	Ceramics & Glass	1	147	5.0	513

Table 5.5 cont'd

Period	Strikers' Union	F	Size	D	MDI
Kessar-Unity	"	1	70	4.0	223
Ben-Aharon	Misc. Non-Histadrut	6	622	1.0	3,759
Meshel-Labor	"	6	1,561	0.9	8,965
Meshel-Likud	"	2	27	12.6	535
Kessar-Unity	"	1	20	4.0	64
Ben-Aharon	"	17	1,827	1.1	33,545
Meshel-Labor	"	31	1,518	2.2	101,860
Meshel-Likud	"	24	10,732	2.2	551,181
Kessar-Likud	"	10	800	0.3	2,041
Kessar-Unity	"	27	6,851	1.2	214,956
Ben-Aharon	Wood & Paper	1	555	11.0	8,502
Meshel-Likud	"	2	496	19.8	15,562
Ben-Aharon	Coopera-tion Cen.	1	3,110	0.8	1,628
Becker	Human. & Soc. Sci.	1	30	1.0	17
Meshel-Labor	"	3	588	2.0	3,739
Meshel-Likud	Electric Company	1	1,300	2.0	2,059
Meshel-Likud	El-Al	3	1,896	27.5	144,512
Meshel-Likud	Airport Authority	2	570	1.7	1,970
Kessar-Unity	"	3	388	0.4	537
Meshel-Labor	"	9	38	14.9	4,817
Meshel-Likud	"	3	368	76.8	78,308
Kessar-Unity	"	3	101	1.6	520
Meshel-Likud	Restaur't. & Hotel	0	325	0.2	32
Kessar-Likud	"	20	4,150	1.5	123,214
Kessar-Unity	"	9	240	3.1	6,489
Kessar-Unity	Physio-therapists	1	125	90.0	8,950
Meshel-Likud	Watchmen, Security	0	100	1.0	40
Kessar-Unity	"	1	100	8.0	636

Table 5.5 cont'd

Period	Strikers' Union	F	Size	D	MDI
Kessar-Unity	"	4	570	0.6	1,313
Meshel-Likud	Working Youth Org.	0	220	1.0	87
Kessar-Likud	"	10	1,000	2.0	20,408
Meshel-Likud	Biochem., Microbiol.	1	1,677	2.0	3,984
Kessar-Unity	"	6	648	2.1	7,559
Ben-Aharon	Sr. Acad. Staff	1	700	12.0	5862
Kessar-Unity	"	1	7,000	0.3	1392
Ben-Aharon	Jr. Acad. Staff	3	594	14.9	24,721
Meshel-Labor	"	1	350	1.0	274
Meshel-Likud	"	0	500	1.0	198
Ben-Aharon	Academic Staff	1	1,100	1.0	1,535
Meshel-Likud	"	2	4,845	1.0	7,674
Meshel-Labor	"	15	344	1.6	8,282
Meshel-Likud	"	5	22	4.5	499
Kessar-Unity	"	1	100	2.0	159
Meshel-Likud	Unorganized	1	20	7.4	117
Becker	Unknown	3	82	3.6	976
Meshel-Labor"	"	9	758	4.6	30,211
Meshel-Likud	"	4	121	2.7	1,164

1. No. of strikes per 1,000 days.
2. Average no. of strikers per strike.
3. Average duration per striker.
4. Sum man-days idle by strikes /1,000 days.

b. The most active striking union of the blue collar workers is the National Union of Metal Workers. It is the only "trade" union on the list of the five most active unions. For the BenAharon and Meshel periods, it ranks third in number of strikes. An increase from some 30 to 44 in the number of strikes per 1,000 days during the Kessar term moved it up to the second rank.

c. A similar rotation of ranking developed for the two teachers' unions. Two unions represent teachers in Israel: one affiliated with the Histadrut, the *Union of Teachers,* and the other independent, the *Union of High School Teachers.* The latter union was the more militant of the two in the Ben-Aharon period. Since Meshel's time, the ranking shifted, the Histadrut affiliated union calling more strikes than the smaller, independent, union. Still, during the most recent Kessar period both unions initiated a similar number of strikes (24 by the Teachers' Union and 23 by the High School Teachers' Union).

Most major unions exhibit a similar U-shaped trend for the standardized strike frequency dimension. They show higher strike frequency in the early and late periods than in the middle ones. Although similar, they are not identical, because the timing of the lower figures differs. For the Union of Government Employees and the Union of Metal Workers, the Meshel/Likud period is the lowest, for the Teachers' Union it was the Ben-Aharon period, and for the High School Teachers' Union—the Meshel/Labor term. The Union of Clerical Employees is the only exception. The more recent the period, the higher the number of strikes called by that union. Why does this union, the largest in size, deviate from the trend? Two possible explanations come to mind. The first relates to the extension of jurisdiction. Since, however, no meaningful change in demarcation was carried out in this period, this explanation is unsatisfactory. The second looks more appropriate. It focuses on the deterioration in the quality of industrial relations in specific segments of the economy represented by this union. Two major sections of this union organize local government employees and workers in the banking industry. A financial deterioration in these sub-branches may be the reason for the steady rise in strikes initiated by the Union of Clerical Employees.

Most major unions show an increase in average strike size. Strikes called by the Union of Government Employees, the Union of Clerical Employees, and the two teachers' unions reach their highest figures in the Kessar era. Still, the industrial relations system of the educational domain in the Ben-Aharon term (elementary teachers) and the Meshel/Labor period (high-school teachers), is more locally contained than in Becker's time.

Two opposite trends in duration developed for the unions of Clerical Employees and of Government Employees. While the duration of strikes called by the former increased, those declared by the latter decreased. Thus, during the Ben-Aharon era, an average civil service striker abstained from work for 2.43, and a Clerical Employees' Union member for 1.68 days, respectively, but in the Kessar/Unity period these figures became 0.49, and 2.56 days each. Strikes by non-professional state employees, therefore, took the form of symbolic, very short gestures, while strikes of clerical workers outside the civil service evolved into longer, more concrete cessations of work. This trend may reflect the impact of two unrelated processes, the crystalization of a symbolic code between state bureaucracy and its representative unions and the financial collapse of local government in the 1980s.

On the whole, different unions changed their strike patterns in different ways. This variety serves as a clue to the relative autonomy of individual unions. Four of the five most active unions are members of the same General Federation of Labor. Their industrial actions vary both in their pattern and in the way that pattern changes. The two teachers' unions, on the other hand, do not share the same organizational affiliation. Their strike patterns, however, changed in very similar ways. The peculiar function of the Histadrut in Israeli industrial relations can explain these two sets of developments. The Federation supplies institutional backing for its affiliated unions. By implication, it does so for unaffiliated unions as well. The individual unions, however, use this generalized resource in various ways. The strategy of a union is therefore determined by two factors. The national-level union organization supplies a constant factor, and the economic, political, or technological constraints of their industry/craft/employer irs add their set of specialized factors.

A short reference to the ports is appropriate. The ports provided a volatile setting for strikes and lockouts in the 1960s and the early 1970s. This situation changed during the Meshel/Likud term. Ben-Aharon's policy encouraged the Union of the Ports Operation Workers, and other unions connected to the Ports Authority, to act in a militant way. In that period these unions called 5.5 percent of Israeli strikes. Meshel abandoned this policy, opening the way for economic factors to make an impact. A deteriorating demand for the services of Ashdod Port, stemming from strike-induced frustration on the part of importers and exporters, led to the replacement of the local union leadership, which then adopted a non-militant approach. Consequently, strike figure decreased to 4.2 percent in the Meshel/Labor period, to 2.9 percent in the later Likud period, and to nil in the Kessar/National Unity period.[6]

Union—Major Occupational Categories

On a high level of generalization we can classify unions on the basis of their members' occupational affiliation. Traditionally, unions represent blue collar workers. Unions of white collar employees have followed their path. Professional unions, meaning unions that represent physicians, lawyers, engineers and the like, are a more recent phenomenon. Unions of technicians and para-professionals, occupy the middle ground between the blue collar workers and the professionals. They are another significant type. As a residual category, some unions fit no clear-cut occupational classification and are classified as unions of mixed type.

Table 5.6 shows the distribution of the standardized frequency of strikes by the type of union representing the workers involved in strikes. It shows that we can divide striking unions into three by their striking tendencies. A third of the strikes is called by blue collar unions, a third by white collar unions and the rest, by all other unions. This presentation, however, overlooks the changes which developed on this level over time. The only category which kept its relative representation intact is that of the white collar unions. As we have seen above, there were shifts among unions, but the general figure stayed around a third. The percentage of strikes by blue collar unions, on the other hand, shows a downward trend. In the first two periods, blue collar unions accounted for close to 40% of the strikes. In the middle period this percentage changed to 33% and at the most recent period, to 26%. Strikes by para-professional unions underwent a dramatic increase. Both their percentage and absolute number went up, doubling in percentage terms from 6.2 in the Ben-Aharon term, to 12.9 in the Kessar/National Unity period.

Table 5.6: Summary strike pattern features for union type and period.

Strikers' Union Type	Period	F[1]	Size [2]	D[3]	MDI[4]
Blue collar	Becker	19	216	2.6	10,865
White collar	Becker	3	196	.9	472
Para-professional	Becker	19	621	1.4	16,687
Professional	Becker	23	462	1.2	13,272
Blue collar	Ben-Aharon	117	347	3.7	150,947
White collar	Ben-Aharon	110	808	2.2	195,433
Para-professional	Ben-Aharon	19	956	1.6	27,939
Professional	Ben-Aharon	31	670	9.6	201,660
Mixed	Ben-Aharon	27	1427	1.1	40,374
Blue collar	Meshel-Labor	120	337	3.6	145,554
White collar	Meshel-Labor	97	1,153	1.4	161,845
Para-professional	Meshel-Labor	24	2,938	2.1	147,116
Professional	Meshel-Labor	13	3,530	2.2	95,882
Mixed	Meshel-Labor	45	1,243	2.0	115,641
Blue collar	Meshel-Likud	86	428	4.2	156,464
White collar	Meshel-Likud	91	2,607	1.9	453,401
Para-professional	Meshel-Likud	28	7,943	2.1	468,661
Professional	Meshel-Likud	22	3,767	5.2	430,299
Mixed	Meshel-Likud	34	7,827	3.0	778,566
Blue collar	Kessar-Likud	133	870	1.6	186,061
White collar	Kessar-Likud	133	7,585	1.1	1,083,296
Para-professional	Kessar-Likud	31	17,200	1.0	520,408
Professional	Kessar-Likud	82	5,006	7.0	2,850,133
Mixed	Kessar-Likud	10	800	0.3	2,041
Blue collar	Kessar-Unity	107	304	3.5	112,532
White collar	Kessar-Unity	161	2,427	1.8	699,991
Para-professional	Kessar-Unity	53	10,901	0.9	526,185
Professional	Kessar-Unity	51	2,081	1.4	148,040
Mixed	Kessar-Unity	34	5,463	1.2	216,078

1. No. of strikes per 1,000 days. 3. Average duration per striker.
2. Average no. of strikers per strike. 4. Sum man-days idle by strikes/1,000 days.

Their standardized number climbed from 31 to 51 respectively. Unions of professional employees hardly struck at all in the Meshel era, but their number shows an all time high in the most recent periods.

If we turn to the three dimensions of strike pattern, we see once again the traditional **U**-curve form of strike frequency. The main core of all types of union adheres to this curve. The only pronounced exceptions are the para-professional unions, which more than doubled their frequency of strikes during the twenty-three year period. From a low of nineteen strikes per 1,000 days (Becker), the number increased steadily to a figure of fifty one in the Kessar/National Unity period. Not only did the para-professionals increase their strike propensity, they expressed their increased militancy by organizing much larger strikes. This a very pronounced aspect of the union type break-down. Blue collar unions, basing their jurisdiction on small to average sites, kept a similar average strike size figure for the whole period. A typical blue collar union strike involves less than 500 workers. All other union types kept increasing their strikes size. None of these groups had reached an average strike size of a thousand in the Ben-Aharon term.[7] All mobilized more than two thousand for an average strike by the end of the period. Still, no one single union type made as radical a size increase as did the para-professional unions. From an average size of 956 workers in the Ben-Aharon period, they increased to 2,938 in the Meshel/Labor, to 7,943 in the Meshel/Likud, and to 10,901 in the Kessar/National Unity periods—an increase of 1,140 percent!!

We can use another method for approaching strike patterns, a three dimensional graphic presentation of the three components of the strike phenomenon. We can draw a separate three dimensional cube for each type of union in each period. This way we can clearly identify the strike pattern differences among union types. If we fix a common scale for each period, we can run a comparison among the various union types for a given period. If, on the other hand, we choose a common scale for a given union type, we can perform a comparison among the various periods for a given union type.[8]

Figure 5.1 reveals the strike pattern characteristics of union types along four of the periods covered by the present work. Let us skip the Becker period (period I) since very little data were available on this topic for this period. The five union types exhibit distinguishable patterns. In the Ben-Aharon period (II) unions of blue collar workers have a many-small/medium sized duration pattern, white collar workers act in a many-medium sized/medium duration pattern, paraprofessionals—in a few-medium/long pattern, para-professionals—in medium frequency/medium sized-long strikes and mixed unions—in medium frequency-large/short duration actions. The frequency dimension is the most stable of all. Unions of both blue and white collar workers tend to strike frequently. Unions of professional employees start (in Ben-Aharon's days) with few strikes, but end up with a medium frequency.

The trend for mixed unions is the reverse. In the earlier years they called a medium number of strikes, but latterly the numbers had diminished.

Fig. 5.1: Strike pattern characteristics of union types by period.

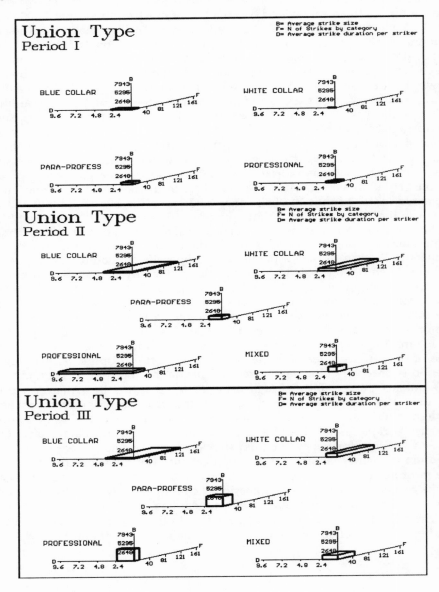

108

Table 5.7: Summary strike pattern features for occupation[1] and period.

Strikers' Occupation	Period	F[2]	Size [3]	D[4]	MDI[5]
Scientific-Academic	Meshel-Likud	24	3,004	0.9	67,171
Technical, Professional	Meshel-Likud	55	6,539	2.4	860,729
Managers	Meshel-Likud	2	183	1.9	577
Clerical	Meshel-Likud	71	10,490	2.7	2,004,630
Service	Meshel-Likud	16	722	1.1	12,366
Agricultural	Meshel-Likud	3	1,065	1.2	3,994
Skilled Workers	Meshel-Likud	88	565	3.7	181,354
Unskilled Workers	Meshel-Likud	19	347	5.0	33,507
Scientific-Academic	Kessar-Likud	71	4,714	8.5	2,847,959
Technical, Professional	Kessar-Likud	71	8,501	0.9	547,735
Clerical	Kessar-Likud	122	8,150	1.1	1,059,357
Service	Kessar-Likud	20	4,150	1.5	123,214
Workers	Kessar-Likud	71	463	1.3	42,092
Unskilled Workers	Kessar-Likud	31	170	4.1	21,582
Scientific-Academic	Kessar-Unity	43	1,995	1.0	83,520
Technical, Professional	Kessar-Unity	87	7,099	1.0	613,648
Managers	Kessar-Unity	1	591	0.5	235
Clerical	Kessar-Unity	126	2,663	1.8	599,979
Sales	Kessar-Unity	6	1,727	0.6	5,489
Service	Kessar-Unity	32	1,390	2.6	113,451
Agricultural	Kessar-Unity	2	77	1.6	292
Skilled Workers	Kessar-Unity	99	342	3.6	121,532
Unskilled Workers	Kessar-Unity	9	623	1.0	5451

1. Reliable data available for the year 1981-87.   4. Average duration per striker.
2. No. of strikes per 1,000 days.   5. Sum man-days idle by strikes /1,000 days.
3. Average no. of strikers per strike.

109

Strike breadth distinguishes between white and blue collar unions. The former act mostly on a plant level, leading to narrow scope strikes. The later, on the other hand, being employed mostly by public sector employers in public services, tend to mobilise a larger number of participants. Strikes of the other union types, para-professionals, professionals, and mixed, act in a more volatile fashion. Both para-professional and professional unions tend to switch from medium to wide sized strikes. Their peaks and sloughs do not, however, coincide. Paraprofessional unions called wide strikes during the Meshel-Labor, Meshel-Likud, and Kessar-Unity periods, indicating a trend towards wider strike mobilization. Professional unions, on the other hand, show peaks of wide activity during the Ben-Aharon and Kessar-Likud periods. These seem to coincide with strikes of physicians.

No systematic differences can be identified for the duration aspect of the strike pattern. This component oscillates in a non-systematic way, prone to being shaped by the peculiarities of a very few large strikes.

As I have tried to show, the three dimensional graphic presentation can facilitate identification of trends and distinctions. However, a parallel inclusion of both tables and figures may distract the reader's attention. I will therefore single out the tables as a more concise source and only they will be presented in this chapter. All figures will be given as an appendix at the end of the book.

STRIKES BY OCCUPATION[9]

As we have seen above, strikes are collective events. Collectivities of employees take part in them, collective agreements being their ultimate goal. An occupation, on the other hand, is an individual level characteristic. When we try to relate individual-level attributes to actions of higher level units, we run into methodological and substantive problems. Let us take a hypothetical strike in an industrial plant. What is the occupation of its participants? Depending on the technological level of the plant, the majority of the workers can either be skilled or unskilled, although some are most probably clerks, while others are professional or other technical workers. How can we classify the strike? By its largest sub-category? By the identity of the leading sub-category? As an unclassifiable case? If we insist on following prudent coding procedures, most strikes do not fit any single occupational classification. As a matter of fact, *only* craft strikes are classifiable along occupational lines. (Such strikes, on the other hand, are very difficult to grasp using economic branch schemes). So, here, once again, we must choose the lesser of two evils: either we abandon occupational classifications, or we follow imperfect methods.

This dilemma has afflicted the collectors of strike data in Israel. As a result, we are now in the worst of all possible situations. Occupational coding is available for the years 1965 to 1972. But, the adoption of a new classification for occupation served as an opportunity to drop occupational information from the reporting forms. Later, it became clear that an important aspect of industrial strife had been lost by this omission. Therefore, in 1981 this item was added, this time on a much more desired secondary category level. When I came to analyze the data I found so much inconsistency in the older data[10] that I decided to abandon it. Therefore, Table 5.7 covers a period starting in 1981, three and a half years after the Likud came to power. As a corollary, the weighting of the data for the Meshel/Likud period was adjusted. The figures in Table 5.7 only take into account the period for which occupational data are available.

Three major categories account for the majority of Israeli strikes both in the Meshel and Kessar periods. They are the skilled workers, the clerical workers, and the technical-professional employees. These categories of occupation account for the majority of Israeli labor power. While skilled workers were the most frequent striking category in the Meshel period (31.7 percent of the strikes), clerical workers ranked higher in the Kessar/National Unity period (31.0 percent). The change in strike frequency clearly shows this switch of ranking. The number of strikes called by skilled workers increased from 88 in Meshel's time to 99 in that of Kessar, while the corresponding figures for the clerical workers were 71 and 126! Technical-professional workers kept a stable third rank position for the whole period. They declared 55 strikes per 1,000 days in the Meshel term and 87 in the Kessar/National Unity period. The occupational data clearly show that strikes are means used by the more central and established groups of workers. The small number of strikes called by unskilled, sales, service, or agricultural workers are not a sign of their solid and satisfactory work conditions. They are most probably an expression of their vulnerability and powerlessness.

The average size of a strike changes for the various categories. Skilled workers are mostly concentrated in small to medium workplaces. Therefore, their strikes mobilize up to a few hundred personnel. Clerical employees and technical workers are employed in larger settings and their strikes encompass thousands. Still, while strikes of the former category declined on the average, those of the latter did not.

STRIKES BY THEIR INITIATORS

The most active actors on the workers' side are the members of workers' committees and national committees. Strikes called by the former account for four out of ten declared strikes, while two to three out of ten are called by the latter. The more established Histadrut organs, the local workers' councils and the national unions, account for much less—10 percent by the first and 16 percent by the second.[11] Table 5.8 shows these developments.

Table 5.8: Summary strike pattern features for union declaring strike and period.

Period	Declaring Union	F[1]	Size[2]	D[3]	MDI[4]
Meshel-Likud	Workers' Com.'	54	370	4.23	84,973
Kessar-Likud	"	143	360	1.66	85,531
Kessar-Unity	"	158	501	3.58	283,397
Meshel-Likud	Action Com.'t	2	92	4.21	923
Kessar-Unity	"	27	2,178	3.00	176,765
Meshel-Likud	National Com.'t	31	2,474	1.26	96,131
Kessar-Likud	"	112	1,102	1.24	153,806
Kessar-Unity	"	104	6,490	0.79	534,386
Meshel-Likud	Workers' Council	17	207	5.53	19,470
Kessar-Likud	"	31	325	1.13	11,224
Kessar-Unity	"	45	224	6.58	66,854
Meshel-Likud	Nat'l Union	21	24,159	2.35	1,193,195
Kessar-Likud	"	82	23,000	2.32	4,359,694
Kessar-Unity	"	49	9,138	1.26	556,795
Meshel-Likud	Lockout	9	347	46.62	147,410
Kessar-Likud	"	20	112	13.80	31,684
Kessar-Unity	"	14	1,422	4.07	82,860

1. No. of strikes per 1,000 days.
2. Average no. of strikers per strike.
3. Average duration per striker.
4. Sum man-days idle by strikes /1,000 days.

The size of a workers' committee constituency limits the scope of strike mobilization. National committees and national unions, on the other hand, have a much wider jurisdiction. Still, the size of strikes called by national committees more than doubled between the Meshel/Likud and Kessar/ National Unity periods, while the average size of strikes declared by the more established national unions was reduced by 60 percent (from 24,159 to 9,138). The duration of industrial disputes tells us a story too complicated to be entangled by global statistics. It is interesting to note, though, that strikes initiated by workers' councils are longer than any other worker-launched stoppages. The longer duration may show that these Histadrut organs act on the frontiers of the institutionalized industrial relations systems. Therefore, any gain in such a domain cannot rest on past achievements. It is a venture requiring effort and patience. In a similar vein, employer-commenced disputes or lockouts are usually much longer than the average strike. During the

Meshel/Likud period an average lockout lasted for almost forty-seven days, almost unprecedented in an Israeli setting.

The Context—Sector of Ownership and Economic Branch

As discussed above, the *context* of strikes has a variety of aspects. First, a strike takes place in the context of an industrial branch—manufacture, public services, transportation, etc. Different industries have different propensities to strike. Many sources discuss this point (Kerr and Siegel, 1954, pp. 189-212). In the present case I am not going to deal in depth with strike propensity. This is impossible to carry out without including a detailed discussion of the appropriate frame of reference (number of plants, number of negotiations, size of work force, etc.). The present analysis will deal only with strike figures and their changes over time.

STRIKES BY ECONOMIC BRANCH

Three major economic branches account for almost four out of five strikes of the 1965-87 strikes: public services (39.4 percent), manufacture (25.1 percent), and transportation-storage (14.5 percent). Both the public services and industry follow the same strike frequency trend. Their maximum values are at the beginning (Becker) and at the end (Kessar/National Unity). However, their maximum values differ. Manufacture has its lowest point earlier (Meshel/Labor) than the public services (Meshel/Likud). Considering the strong impact these branches have on the total number of strikes, it is no wonder that the trend of total strike frequency adheres to this shape. Strikes of transportation employees have an inverse **U**-shape. Their *minimums* are at the beginning and at the end of the period under investigation, while their peak is in the Meshel/Labor term. The **U**-shape trend is found also in agriculture, water-electricity, construction, commerce and individual services. The pervasiveness of the **U**-shape shows quite convincingly that strike frequency is *not* determined by factors related to the specific economic branch.

The few exceptions to this trend (mining, finance and transportation) should be analyzed separately. For example, one of these exceptions, transportation-storage, is understood only in the context of the establishing of the Israel Ports Authority, the closing of Tel-Aviv Port and the development of the Ashdod Port. Individual level characteristics, like the personality of Yehoshua Peretz, the leader of the Ashdod Port workers, are indispensable factors as well.

Strike size expanded almost everywhere. The structure of the labor market constrained this trend in manufacture, individual services, and mining, while the paucity of strikes in the electricity and the water branches prevented the crystallization of a size trend in this branch.

No durational trend has evolved in the major branches. For those secondary branches where a trend is identified (agriculture, mining, construction and commerce), it takes the shape of an inverse **U**. At this moment I can suggest no ready explanation for this trend.

As a whole, the economic branch variable has very limited explanatory power for the time trend changes in strike pattern dimensions. It may explain the limits imposed on strike size in industry or in individual services, but cannot explain the outburst of strikes in a certain period in the ports. It may or may not explain the propensity to strike, but we are not dealing with this issue here.

A much less important development, but still worth mentioning, is in agriculture. This economic branch has seldom been a significant setting for industrial conflict. Since, world-wide, rural workers are mostly seasonal workers, are dispersed over a wide area and have many employers, unionization campaigns have seldom proved successful, despite the wide publicity achieved by leaders such as Cesar Chavez in isolated cases. Without organization, no collective action is possible. In the absence of strong unions, pressures to improve the working conditions of agricultural workers tend to be channeled into political alternatives.

The Israeli setting differs from the conventional pattern. Agricultural workers are mostly seasonal workers. However, those workers who work with the same employer for a few consecutive years gain a semi-tenured status. Their terms of employment are negotiated between their representative union and the Farmers' Association. Agricultural workers are employed in small numbers by many employers, but the larger firms sign collective agreements with the union of agricultural workers. These contracts serve as models for the whole industry. While rural workers are employed in a peripheral segment of the economy, work in agriculture has been a valued activity, the ultimate realization of the Zionist dream. Thus, even though the take-home pay of agricultural workers has always been relatively low, working in orchards and farms has had its own non-monetary worth.

The Six Day War (June, 1967) serves as a landmark for many developments in the Israeli society. The status of rural employment is one of them. A large influx of Arab workers from the occupied areas began to supply the larger part of the demand for hired manpower. This change in the ethnic composition of the workers changed the climate of industrial relations. The Israeli rural labor market lost its unique character and took on the style of a typical country. As a corollary, stoppages almost disappeared. The 6.4 percent figure of the Becker term decreased to the negligible 1.2 percent of the Kessar/ National Unity period.

In recent years, the finance-insurance branch has become a significant source of industrial conflict. As we can see in Table 5.9, both the absolute number and the percentage of strikes in this section of the economy is on the increase. The banking industry was prosperous in the 1960s, strikes erupting there occasionally. For some short periods their number was even quite substantial (1977—13, 1979—14). Still, it never achieved the salience of 1987 (19 strikes). This increase parallels a rise of distrust by the employees and unions in the banking industry and its management. This attitude stems from official reports of mismanagement and well-publicized scandals. These may be transitory events, leading to the return of the banking branch to its traditional middle-of-the-road strike patterns.

Table 5.9: Strike frequency by economic branch and period.

Economic Branch	Becker	Ben-Aharon	Meshel-Labor	Meshel-Likud	Kessar-Likud	Kessar-Unity	TOTAL
Agriculture	6.4	2.9	1.0	1.0	2.7	1.2	3.0
	(59)	(17)	(4)	(7)	(1)	(6)	(94)
Mining	1.6	1.0	2.1	1.9	2.7	1.0	1.5
	(15)	(6)	(8)	(13)	(1)	(5)	(48)
Industry	27.9	27.3	24.7	24.1	24.3	22.8	25.7
	(256)	(162)	(96)	(161)	(9)	(116)	(800)
Elecricity, Water	1.1	1.2	1.0	1.8	0.0	1.2	1.3
	(10)	(7)	(4)	(12)	(0)	(6)	(39)
Construction	4.9	1.7	1.3	2.5	0.0	2.4	2.9
	(45)	(10)	(5)	(17)	(0)	(12)	(89)
Commerce, Hotel	4.0	3.0	3.6	2.4	5.4	3.5	3.4
	(37)	(18)	(14)	(16)	(2)	(18)	(105)
Transport, Storage	11.2	18.4	26.8	21.0	10.8	5.7	15.7
	(103)	(109)	(104)	(140)	(4)	(29)	(489)
Finance, Insurance	1.2	1.3	6.4	4.8	8.1	6.9	3.7
	(11)	(8)	(25)	(32)	(3)	(35)	(114)
Public Services	38.4	38.1	29.6	38.1	40.5	51.3	39.3
	(353)	(226)	(115)	(254)	(15)	(261)	(1224)
Individual Services	3.3	5.1	3.4	2.2	5.4	4.1	3.6
	(30)	(30)	(13)	(15)	(2)	(21)	(111)
TOTAL	29.5	19.0	12.5	21.4	1.2	16.4	100.0
	(919)	(593)	(388)	(667)	(37)	(509)	(3113)

The ownership sector is a cardinal feature of industrial relations in Israel. The large public sector, including that part of the economy owned by the government, the Jewish Agency, and local government, was in the foreground of industrial conflict for the entire period covered by this study.

Table 5.10: Summary strike pattern features for sector and period.[1]

Period	Sector	F[2]	Size[3]	D[4]	MDI[5]
Becker	Private	184	155	3.61	103,348
Ben-Aharon	Private	144	327	4.46	210,659
Meshel-Labor	Private	87	390	3.70	125,568
Meshel-Likud	Private	67	539	4.44	160,256
Kessar-Likud	Private	82	2,105	1.37	234,694
Kessar-Unity	Private	97	860	1.64	136,998
Becker	Histadrut	72	325	2.39	56,155
Ben-Aharon	Histadrut	40	1,125	1.32	59,987
Meshel-Labor	Histadrut	38	424	3.21	52,153
Meshel-Likud	Histadrut	23	1,870	2.06	86,768
Kessar-Likud	Histadrut	41	340	4.53	62,908
Kessar-Unity	Histadrut	49	1,407	2.07	141,130
Becker	Public	139	243	1.92	64,801
Ben-Aharon	Public	85	363	2.01	62,052
Meshel-Labor	Public	62	866	1.56	82,265
Meshel-Likud	Public	64	1,683	2.71	292,841
Kessar-Likud	Public	41	519	1.75	36,990
Kessar-Unity	Public	131	4,072	1.61	860,895
Becker	Multi-Sector	12	3,289	1.37	52,214
Ben-Aharon	Multi-Sector	11	6,575	3.24	238,080
Meshel-Labor	Multi-Sector	10	10,353	2.55	268,336
Meshel-Likud	Multi-Sector	19	23,617	2.65	1,189,355
Kessar-Likud	Multi-Sector	41	31,200	2.88	3,668,878
Kessar-Unity	Multi-Sector	30	5,084	1.60	245,182
Becker	Government	106	357	1.83	69,135
Ben-Aharon	Government	133	668	2.23	198,581
Meshel-Labor	Government	109	1,133	1.37	167,730
Meshel-Likud	Government	91	2,291	2.66	557,261
Kessar-Likud	Government	184	3,182	1.09	638,469
Kessar-Unity	Government	97	4,631	0.70	315,995

1. Reliable data available for years 1981-87.
2. No. of strikes per 1,000 days.
3. Average no. of strikers per strike.
4. Average duration per striker.
5. Sum man-days idle by strikes /1,000 days.

STRIKES BY SECTOR OF OWNERSHIP

No reliable figures on employment by sector are available, but crude estimates show that strikes in this sector account for substantially more than its share in the population. The private sector, on the other hand, has established a solid and a stable industrial relations structure, reducing strike involvement. The Histadrut sector has its own unique industrial relations system, that has succeeded, at least in the past, in keeping disagreements between management and unions from developing into fully fledged strikes. Table 5.10 provides the basis for a detailed analysis of this dimension.

The private, Histadrut and public sectors adhere to the total trend of strike frequency. For all three, the Meshel/Likud period[12] exhibits the lowest frequency figures. The other sectors show a surprisingly different trend. Excluding the Ben-Aharon term, the standardized number of strikes in the government sector showed an almost stable trend. The number of strikes per 1,000 days fluctuated narrowly in the range of 91 to 109 strikes, proportionally, a much narrower range than any other sector. Surprisingly, the number of strikes in the government sector is therefore *not* affected by political considerations! One might expect this sector to be the *most* politically sensitive sector of all. However, it appears that its internal problems are the most important determinants of its high dispute volatility. These problems called for the setting up of various public or professional committees,[13] and for legislative initiatives.[14] Israeli governments have always proclaimed the need to reduce the number of their employees and have shown a lamentable lack of power (or commitment) to do so. Neither economic constraints nor political changes made any real impact on this segment of the labor market.

A second sector which defies the general trend is the multi-sector segment. Multi-sector strikes are industrial actions initiated by collectivities of employees from more than one sector. Strikes of groups united by their common vocation, physicians, engineers, technicians, are typical examples. The functional criterion has become a prominent dimension of union affiliation. With its consolidation, more and more strikes cut through sector lines. The number of multi-sector strikes increased from the beginning of the period under study (1965) until the Kessar/National Unity period. There is no way of knowing if this phenomenon has reached its peak. All along it has been a threat to the very existence of a unified General Federation of Labor. The Histadrut has found a way to adjust to the craft dimension of unionization. It has never managed to find a complete solution to the industrial-versus-craft lines of unionization. The increase in multi-sector strikes is evidence for this. While the number of such strikes is not high, their size is exceptionally large, which makes them a very significant phenomenon.

The first dimension of strike pattern is *frequency*. All non-state sectors, private, Histadrut and public, had a minimal strike frequency when a political balance between the Labor (in the Histadrut) and the Likud (in the government) parties existed. Stern (1978) argues that each of the three strike-pattern components has its own meaning. The frequency of strikes represents a rational process of decision making. If so, the decrease in the number of strikes is evidence of a policy of self-restraint *on both sides*, unions and employees. Since this trend is found in most sectors, but *not* in the government sector, the source of this attitude of self-restraint stems from the political context of privately, Histadrut and publicly owned enterprises. It is not an attribute of the government as employer. Under this balance of power situation, unions are more hesitant in initiating strikes and employers are more reluctant in accepting the challenge (and calling lockouts). A situation of a monolithic labor power structure, on the other hand, inspires high levels of industrial conflict all through the economy.

Let us turn now to the second dimension of strike patterns, *average size*. Stern (1978) believes that this is a measure of the success in mobilizing support for a strike. The argument of mobilization, though, does not fit the Israeli context. Workers conform almost totally to their unions' announcements of strikes. An announcement in the mass media is usually enough to assure compliance. This being the case, this dimension is more a projection of the structure of the labor market than anything else. The trend for the overall economy shows a clear increase until the Meshel/Likud period, and a leveling out thereafter.

A trend of this form does not exist in any specific sector! In the private, public, and government sectors, the trend of increase does not stop. The size of striking unit reaches its maximum in the most recent, Kessar/National Unity period. The multi-sector segment reaches its peak during the Kessar/ Likud term. The Kessar/National Unity period shows a decrease in strike size. No discernible trend is identified in the Histadrut sector. Each period exhibits a different, unsystematic size. Thus, the growth of striking units is quite widespread. The Histadrut sector, however, is one area to which this process has not spread. Strikes in this sector are mostly limited to a specific plant. These plants may be as large as Kupat Cholim (Sick Fund), or as small as a local industrial plant (such as Chasin Esh). No coalitions have crystallized.

The most unsystematic dimension of all three strike pattern components is that of *average duration*. Fluctuations and lack of ability to explain its variance have been the lot of all research efforts dedicated to it. Stern (1978) believes that mostly local factors determine the pace of negotiation and its successful completion. Therefore, local factors explain the variance of duration. The only systematic changes in strike duration developed in multi-sector disputes. Their number is quite limited and they share several characteristics. They are economy-wide by definition, and therefore require a similar setting for their evolution. Multi-sector strikes have one more important feature in common, their proclaimed cause. Almost two out of three (63.0 percent) multi-sector strikes are triggered by wage and salary demands. That is much more than public (38.4 percent), private (42.9), Histadrut owned (46.6) or even government owned enterprises (51.0), and may explain their relative orderliness along the duration axis. Multi-sector strikes gain their maximum length (3.24 days) during the Ben-Aharon era. They maintain a quite stable length (more than 2.5 days) during the Meshel term. Their shortest spell was in the early days of Becker (1.37) and in the later days of Kessar (1.60).

The only systematic trend in Table 5.10 is the change that took place in the private sector. The Israeli economy did not evince a significant change in its sectoral composition. The distribution of strikes by sector of ownership, on the other hand, did change. The private sector managed to decrease its proportional representation from around a third to around a quarter. Better still, the number of strikes per 1,000 days changed from a three digit to a two digit figure. In the pre-Meshel period, the private sector was the setting for 184 (Becker) to 144 (Ben-Aharon) strikes per 1,000 days. In the subsequent period, the figure never exceeded a hundred. However, it gained its all time low figure during the Meshel/Likud period and has since tended to increase. The private sector model of industrial relations did not serve as a model for the various public sector segments.

The three major non-private sectors acted in three different ways. While the Histadrut sector strike frequency fluctuates without a conspicuous trend, the other two sectors tell us two separate stories. The frequency of strikes in the public sector shows a trend of decrease in the first five periods. In the Becker period, a record number of 139 strikes per 1,000 erupted. This number decreased sharply to 85 in the Ben-Aharon term and continued with 62, 64 and 41 strikes per 1,000 days for the following periods. The Kessar/National Unity period exhibits an abrupt increase to 131.

The frequency of strikes in the governmental sector stays relatively stable. The range of stoppages is between 91 (Meshel/Likud) and 133 (Ben-Aharon). The difference between the developments in the government sector and the other public sectors calls for an explanation. Why do these two non-private sectors not conform to a similar pattern? The answer may lie in the causes of strikes. Different causes triggered strikes in these two sectors. At the beginning of the period, wage demands were the stated cause of half or more of the strikes in both sectors. For both, the percent of strikes acknowledged to be caused by this issue shows a downward trend. For the public sector the percentage figures are 50.0, 53.3, 48.1, 29.6 and 3.7. For the government sector it is 60.7, 56.1, 48.9, 48.7 and 15.5. In the last period, wage demands ceased to be a major cause for strikes in these non-private sectors, but a compensating source of unrest—delays in payments—developed in the public sector. The budgetary situation in this economic segment, especially that of local government, triggered high industrial strife. The inability of municipalities and other local authorities to pay their salaries on time brought about many strikes. The government, on the other hand, managed to handle its accounting more effectively.

The Process—What, Why, How, and What For?

STRIKES VS. LOCKOUTS? WARNING STRIKES VS. WORKERS' MEETINGS

Being a social action, a strike is not an automatic or predetermined event. It is a premeditated act of selection. It takes one actor to initiate a strike, but two actors to actualize it. When an actor, be it a union or an employer, adopts a decision to stop operations, its counterpart may agree or disagree with this initiative. The agreement may not be on the *solution* to the impasse. It may be on the means adopted for pursuing this deadlock. A generous last minute offer by an employer, of course, can, often annul a decision to strike. However, many other options exist. An employer can test legal options: frequently, the courts can supply temporary aid. Alternatively, an employer may appeal to a higher authority, in the union hierarchy or in the political system. The choice to take up the challenge of a strike is not less conscious than the one to call it. What is more, it is possible to so manage the situation that the adversary is forced into a trap, and has no option but to initiate the strike. This undeterministic nature of industrial disputes leads us to the analysis of the distinction between strikes and lockouts, between warning strikes and workers' meetings. These distinctions are not absolutely categorical. They are a variety of outcomes following a process of social interaction and choice.

Strikes vs. Lockouts

Statistical data refer to strikes in more than one way. The term strike implies both a synonym for work stoppage and a narrower term referring to stoppages initiated by unions. The first use lumps together work actions initiated by unions and cases where employers initiate the halting of operations. At first glance one may wonder why official agencies dropped the distinction based on identity of the precipitating actor, but on reflection, we may be convinced that such a policy is not as arbitrary as it seems. A stoppage is not an isolated event, easily distinguished from those preceding and following it. Quite frequently, an actor is forced to choose either to halt operations, or to sustain disastrous damage to his vital interests. This may happen to unions or management. A probable outcome is either a strike or a lockout. In cases like this it is not meaningful to ask who initiated the stoppage. The event is worth consideration notwithstanding which party initiates the forthcoming standstill.

The Institute of Economic and Social Research has added a new item to its strike report form. This question asks whether the reported strike was a continuation dispute, meaning a strike or a lockout preceded by work sanctions, a strike preceded by a lockout, any other combination, or a conventional stoppage. In 3.3 percent of the reported cases, a lockout was preceded by drastic action on the side of the union (a strike or an initiation of work sanctions). If the *dispute* is what we are interested in, and not the specific form it takes, then these disputes can hardly be regarded as "pure" lockouts. Eighty-one of the disputes under review are either strikes preceded by sanctions or vice-versa. Are these "pure" strikes (or work sanctions)? Treating them as such turns the Bureau of Statistics into a producer of reality instead of serving as its dependable reflector. Therefore, there is a case for collapsing employer and union initiated cessation of operation in a single term, be it "strike" or any other term. Nevertheless, of the 892 responses to this recently added item, only 30 (3.3 percent) are in the gray area. One must therefore ask if it is worth losing information on a major aspect of industrial conflict just because *some* cases are difficult to classify?

With these considerations in mind, it can be stated that about one out of twenty stoppages is called by management. Contrary to common belief, the *number* of lockouts has not changed significantly in the last two decades. Seventeen to twenty-five cases per 1,000 days took place in each of the various periods under study. The Ben-Aharon period has the lowest prevalence of lockouts (17), while the Becker term time has the record high (25). These figures disclose no trend for the frequency of lockouts. Two consecutive periods have the highest and the lowest figures, while all following periods share an almost identical figure, 24 for Meshel/Labor, 20 for Meshel/Likud and Kessar/Likud and 23 for Kessar/National Unity. Even though the frequency of lockouts has changed in a non systematic way for the economy as a whole, a clear steady decrease evolved only for one single—the private—sector. Private employees adopt this drastic method less and less. At the beginning of the period, in Becker's day, fourteen cases of lockouts took place for each 1,000 days. The figures average between ten and eleven cases for each 1,000 days for most of the period under study. A drastic shrinkage in this figure emerges during the Kessar/National Unity period. Only *five* cases occurred in each of his two sub-periods. This decline in employer-declared stoppages parallels the decrease in the total frequency of strikes reported above.

Warning strikes vs. workers' meetings

Stoppages are classified not only by their initiators. Official statistics tabulate them also by their purpose and form. Detailed information on this aspect is available from the Meshel/Labor term on. For this fourteen year period, almost half of the stoppages are labelled as "standard" strikes, 28.2 percent are warning strikes, 14.8 percent are workers' meetings during working hours, 2.1—solidarity strikes, and six percent—lockouts. Calling a stoppage a "warning" clarifies its purpose. It is a message to the employer: "negotiate in good faith, raise concessions, or else..." Neither form of strike is time consuming. They can be as short as an hour, or as long as a few days. In most cases their duration is fixed in advance.

Do warning strikes differ from workers' meeting in their communicative value? Most probably, yes. The symbolic interaction between actors in an industrial relations system is a continuous process of sending and receiving messages. Strikes, lockouts, slowdowns, meetings, are all examples of symbolic gestures exchanged between actors. The choice of symbols is not and cannot be arbitrary. The selection of one symbol over another gives us important information on the changing context. A move from a mild to a more extreme gesture may mean that the former has been ignored, or has been responded to in a disappointing manner. The conflict of interest between the sides may have become more pronounced, the ideology of one actor (or both) may have become more radicalized, or the channel of communication may have become noisier. All these explanations may fit union-management relations.

The contextual constraints of an industrial relations system may be more or less favorable for compromises. Northrup and Young (1968) showed that changing economic conditions transformed peaceful places of work into conflictual sites. A recession may limit the resources available for distribution. Under such conditions, a marginal profit may turn into a loss, or a balanced budget may force a public utility into the red. Radicalization of action may be expected when a union is insensitive to the realistic alternatives, or when the situation is so drastic as to make stable employment and regular payment of wages problematic. The situation can also shift as a result of changes in the identity of power holders. A change of ownership, replacement of management or union leadership may be accompanied by a change of ideology. The greater the incompatibility of ideologies, the higher the probability of more extreme forms of action.

A change may also take place in the channels of communication. Lines of communication may become longer, external concerns may distract the parties from their negotiation and lead to a need for pronounced symbolic transmissions. Instead of a meeting, an explicit warning strike can be chosen. Instead of a restricted strike, an open-ended stoppage can be declared. The difference in form that strikes take in various sectors or at different periods can reflect these considerations. If warning strikes are harsher actions than meetings during working hours, a relative increase in the use of the former reflects an effort to overcome difficulties in union-management interaction.

Detailed information on types of strikes is available since the Meshel/ Labor period. Table 5.11 shows the number of meetings and the number of warning strikes per 1,000 days by ownership sector. Let us check the various sectors in sequence.

The government sector has a curvilinear trend. In the Meshel/Labor period, the number of warning strikes and meetings is almost the same (21 and 23 respectively). The Meshel/Likud period is completely different, with 33 warning strikes compared to 11 meetings. This clear escalation of industrial strife reflects an increasing tension in industrial relations.

Table 5.11: Number of working-time meetings and warning strikes per 1,000 days by period and ownership sector.

Period	Working Time Meetings				Warning Strikes			
	Private	Hista-drut	Public	Govern-ment	Private	Hista-drut	Public	Govern-ment
Meshel -Labor	11	0	6	23	5	10	13	21
Meshel -Likud	5	3	9	11	15	4	20	33
Kessar-Likud	(0)[1]	(10)	(0)	(41)	(31)	(10)	(20)	(92)
Kessar-Unity	20	10	12	28	18	14	29	29

1. Unreliable figures based on a very short period.

The tension could be seen as a derivative of the political disparity between the Likud and the Labor parties, but other indications disprove this notion. The percentage of approved strikes sank to its lowest level during this period. If it had been a case of a political conflict, a relaxation of strike-approval policy could have been expected. In fact, the policy was tightened. Therefore, explanations related to internal industrial relations seem more appropriate.

Did either of the parties become more militant as a result of an ideological shift? Did the external situation become less conducive to industrial peace, or did the noise in the negotiation channel increase as a result of new negotiators, a change in the negotiation structure, etc.? The data available for the present study can hardly test the validity of the various hypotheses. At the most it can test a few ideas and limit the number of possible answers.

While there was little change in the Histadrut during these years, some changes occurred on the management side of the government sector. New people were nominated to the position of the Civil Service Commissioner. The first was Abraham Friedman, a well known academic figure in the field of industrial relations. Mr. Friedman gained his first experience in labor relations as the head of the social research unit of the Histadrut. This was hardly a background alien to the union. His experience later included private business. Still, he was not a typical civil servant and thus might have upset the system.

A major impediment to orderly negotiations in the Likud administration period stemmed from political intervention in the negotiation process. This involvement was sometimes motivated, I suspect, by hostility towards the Histadrut. This seems to be the case with Finance Minister Yoram Aridor's involvement in a lengthy physicians' strike, perhaps motivated by personal, rather then ideological considerations. The involvement of Deputy Prime

Minister David Levy in an El-Al workers' dispute may have been similarly motivated. No one can penetrate the rationale behind the acts of politicians. The examples cited above were widely covered by the mass media, but that is only a tenuous proof of their validity. Both cases may be attributed to the inexperience of a new political elite, faced with the urgent need to monitor a turbulent system. Be it inexperience, political or personal considerations, the 1977 change of regime imposed difficulties on the government sector industrial relations system. The intensification in the forms of industrial conflict is a minor expression of these difficulties.

The Histadrut sector shows an altogether different pattern. The pre-Likud period exhibits a multiplicity of warning strikes (10) and no meetings. Such a pattern is a model for a radicalized industrial relations system. If true, this phenomenon is an outcome of the ideological incompatibility between the idea of an enterprise owned by the workers and the de-facto status of an employee. The Histadrut ideology regarded a conflict of interests between the employees of a Histadrut owned enterprise and those of the working class in general as improbable. Strikes were inconceivable. Formal and informal mechanisms were developed to cope with this inconceivable situation. Many grievances and disagreements were referred to bipartite committees and pressure was imposed on managers (in particular) and on leaders of workers' committees to avoid explicit conflicts.

All these means were effective. The number of strikes in the Histadrut sector always tended to be smaller than its share in the economy. Still, when conflicts erupted, they were more extreme and their results less successful for the workers. Michael and Barel (1977, p. 249-250) found similar results in their study of the 1960s. They report, "the lowest level of success in the Histadrut sector...medium in the public sector[15]...and high in the private sector". They continue, "it is worthwhile to notice that the highest proportion of strikes which ended with continued negotiation and arbitration was in the Histadrut sector" (p. 250). The Histadrut sector during the Likud period experienced a reduction in its level of conflict. The number of strikes decreased at a faster rate than that of all other sectors. The total number of warning strikes and meetings decreased by 30 percent, and almost half of these disputes took the form of meetings. The national political upheaval was a shocking experience for the Histadrut and the decrease in industrial conflict may be an expression for this feeling on the union-management relations arena. An increase in the level of industrial strife in the Histadrut sector accompanied the Kessar/ National Unity period. This trend was not more drastic in this sector than in other parts of the economy. At least there was no retreat to the pre-Likud level of intensity. The sensitivity developed during the Likud period seems to have persisted.

The public sector is characterized by a predominant tendency to hold meetings, which outnumber warning strikes throughout the period. However, this tendency is weakening.

Table 5.12: Summary strike pattern features for type of strike[1] and period.

Period	Strike Type	F[2]	Size[3]	D[4]	MDI[5]
	Workers'				
Ben-Aharon	Meeting	33	726	0.32	1,800
Meshel-Labor	"	43	1,717	0.45	33,010
Meshel-Likud	"	32	2,417	0.40	31,051
Kessar-Likud	"	51	300	0.28	4,296
Kessar-Unity	"	76	1,637	0.31	39,152
	Warning				
Ben-Aharon	Strike	52	3,831	1.05	47,692
Meshel-Labor	"	54	2,279	0.96	11,8437
Meshel-Likud	"	82	6,492	1.46	772,292
Kessar-Likud	"	163	1,408	1.15	263,663
Kessar-Unity	"	87	7,620	0.85	560,812
	Solidarity				
Ben-Aharon	Strike	11	272	0.82	621
Meshel-Labor	"	12	387	0.86	3,909
Meshel-Likud	"	6	3,315	0.97	17,901
Kessar-Unity	"	10	4,447	0.52	23,998
	Conven-				
Ben-Aharon	tional Strike	383	601	3.05	702,825
Meshel-Labor	"	175	698	4.05	490,580
Meshel-Likud	"	128	1,618	5.85	1,213,355
Kessar-Likud	"	153	11,874	2.39	4,342,296
Kessar-Unity	"	213	2,047	2.24	978,645
Ben-Aharon	Lockout	11	365	4.13	16,835
Meshel-Labor	"	24	338	6.33	50,312
Meshel-Likud	"	19	578	22.70	254,398
Kessar-Likud	"	20	112	13.80	31,684
Kessar-Unity	"	19	1,127	4.66	100,219

1. No detailed figures are available for Becker's period. Data for Ben-Aharon are limited to 322 days in 1973. Weighting was set correspondingly.
2. No. of strikes per 1,000 days   3. Average no. of strikers per strike
4. Average duration per striker   5. Sum man-days idle by strikes

The more recent the period, the higher the tendency for public sector actions to take the form of warning strikes and not meetings. A deterioration in the solvency of local government in Israel can explain this phenomenon. Economic difficulties made it increasingly difficult for local authorities to keep up with the demands of the unions. A deterioration in the atmosphere of negotiations followed. Of all sectors, the trends in the private sector are the most unsystematic of all. Meetings are the dominant pattern of the pre-Likud era, with warning strikes supplanting them during the Likud period, to be replaced by a near equality between the two forms in the Kessar/National Unity period. There is, however, no straightforward explanation for the various patterns. The proportions for the Meshel/Likʻud and the Kessar/ National Unity periods match the decrease in intensity of industrial conflict in this sector, but the low militancy pattern of the Labor period stays unexplained. The pattern dimensions of the various types of strike is presented in Table 5.12.

Since most strikes are of the conventional type, the pattern of conventional strikes approximates the pattern of total Israeli strikes (Table 5.1). The trends for other types are more interesting. A steady increase in workers' meetings and warning strikes replaces the typical **U**-shape of strike frequency. Since these are the most limited types of stoppages, they imply an increase in the use of conflictual gestures for industrial negotiations. The curvilinear form of the total number of strikes thus leads to an increase in the *percentage* of symbolic conflict gestures during the Likud period and to a relative decrease in such acts during that of Kessar. The industrial relations arena was therefore saturated with declarations and warnings during the Likud period and overwhelmed by conventional strikes during Kessar's time. As to duration, the shortest, as can be expected, are the workers' meetings. Their length is less than half a full working day. Warning strikes last for a bit longer, somewhere between a day and a day and a half. The duration of solidarity strikes is in between, more than a meeting and less than a warning strike.

THE 'WHY' ASPECT OF STRIKES

Wage demands are the most proclaimed cause for strikes almost anywhere and anytime. We can apply this near universal premise both as the conclusion of a discussion and its beginning. On the one hand, wage claims are the most logical issue to bring about a strike. People go to work to earn their living and in a modern society, no matter how much people earn, they believe that they deserve *more*. This issue is the underlying rationale of trade unions all over the world. Nevertheless, although wages keep rising, strikes do not disappear. Therefore, the relationships between earnings and strikes is not just a simple case of cause and effect. The relative and not only the absolute level of wages becomes a cardinal source for labor unrest. Wage increases cease to be a simple solution to workers' dissatisfaction. Sometimes, an increase won by one group raises demands for parity by others. Wage increase is therefore, in some circumstances, a cause of, rather than a remedy for, strikes.

Wage claims are the bread and butter of a union's activities. This endows such claims with the status of legitimacy. Therefore, when a union prefers to hide its true motive for protest, it covers it with a wage demand. This way, no one can expose the union to accusations of infringement of managerial rights.

Table 5.13: Frequency of strikes by reported cause and period.

Cause	P E R I O D						
	Becker	Ben-Aharon	Meshel-Maarakh	Meshel-Likud	Kessar-Likud	Kessar-Unity	Total
Wage & salary	47.7 (442)	50.8 (302)	43.8 (172)	45.3 (305)	36.8 (14)	32.6 (160)	44.8 (1,395)
Promotion	0.0 (0)	0.0 (0)	0.0 (0)	0.7 (5)	5.3 (2)	0.8 (4)	0.4 (11)
Union recognition	6.3 (58)	14.1 (84)	9.7 (38)	6.7 (45)	18.4 (7)	3.7 (18)	8.0 (250)
Delays in payments	13.1 (121)	5.1 (30)	4.8 (19)	13.5 (91)	5.3 (2)	27.3 (134)	12.7 (397)
Layoffs	14.2 (132)	10.8 (64)	10.9 (43)	13.2 (89)	23.7 (9)	16.7 (82)	13.4 (419)
Physical conditions	0.0 (0)	0.2 (1)	1.8 (7)	3.0 (20)	0.0 (0)	1.6 (8)	1.2 (36)
Organizational changes	0.0 (0)	0.0 (0)	0.0 (0)	2.2 (15)	5.3 (2)	5.3 (26)	1.4 (43)
Discipline	0.0 (0)	0.0 (0)	0.0 (0)	2.4 (16)	0.0 (0)	2.4 (12)	0.9 (28)
Work contact	0.0 (0)	0.0 (0)	0.0 (0)	0.0 (0)	0.0 (0)	3.5 (17)	.5 (17)
Lockout	4.9 (45)	4.2 (25)	7.9 (31)	7.3 (49)	5.3 (2)	4.9 (24)	5.6 (176)
Other	13.9 (129)	14.8 (88)	21.1 (83)	5.6 (38)	0.0 (0)	1.2 (6)	11.0 (344)
TOTAL	29.7 (927)	19.1 (594)	12.6 (393)	21.6 (673)	1.2 (38)	15.8 (491)	100.0 (3116)

If we accept the assumption that monetary compensation is the overiding consideration for working, then the finding that wage claims are the major source for strikes may serve as the end of an inquiry. If we prefer to assume that wage claims *may* be a source for strikes, but that many other causes are sometimes hidden in wage demands, then here our inquiry starts, not ends. Table 5.13 sums up the recorded causes for Israeli strikes.

Wage strikes are the cause most frequently reported for almost all periods. The only one when it is not the first, is during the Kessar/National Unity term, when wage demands were superceded by another wage related issue— late payment. Strikes caused by wage claims do not share the common **U**-shape, but show a steady decline. Wage related strikes, meaning strikes triggered both by wage claims and by late payment, do have this **U**-shape. Therefore, on the whole, the major factors explaining fluctuations in wage related strikes are those explaining the move between demands for wage increases and efforts to secure wage payments on time. This move is highly related to the level of economic activity. An increase in defensive strikes[16] accompanied the recession of the mid 1960s during the Becker term. The same happened during the recessionary period of Kessar. Wage strikes show a steady increase in size. Wage delay strikes, on the other hand, do not show this trend. They gained their maximum size during the Meshel term. Still, while defensive wage strikes in the early days were typically very small, they ceased to be so at the end of the period. Problems of solvency spread to larger enterprises and were no longer typical only of smaller, more peripheral, organizations.

An interesting cause for strike action is the case of union recognition. What image comes to mind in this case? I would not be surprised if most readers were to see a bitter fight by an organizing team against a stubborn, anti-union employer, as typified in the movie *Norma Rae*. The history of the trade union movement is crammed with strikes of this type and some of the most honored heroes of the movement gained their reputation in such campaigns. If so, it may surprise us to find recognition strikes in Israel. The real organizational campaigns were won in Israel prior to the establishment of the state. About 90 percent of Israeli employees are Histadrut members, or at least affiliated through related unions. Yet we see 32 recognition strikes during the Becker, 54 in the Ben-Aharon, 27 in the Meshel/Labor, 16 in the Meshel /Likud, and 13 in the Kessar periods.

Do all these strikes share this unionist flavor? When we relate the sector of ownership information to the recognition issue we face a clear puzzle. About half of all recognition strikes take place in non-privately owned sites. While it is still marginally possible to discover private employers who oppose unionization and serve as the frontier for such expansion, the public sector is totally covered by collective agreements. The Histadrut-owned sector is even more extreme. The labor movement *owns* it. Yet even in this sector we find some, though not many, recognition strikes. The answer is therefore that recognition strikes in Israel are often not conflicts between a union and a reluctant employer at all. They are disputes between collectivities of workers and the legally representative union.

STRIKE APPROVAL

Histadrut bylaws stipulate that no one can call a strike without gaining the approval of an appropriate Histadrut authority. This provision expresses the centralistic ideology of the Histadrut. A strike is not only a local event, a means for promoting the interests of a represented body of workers, but has much wider implications. Therefore, only if the social balance of pros and cons is positive should it be invoked. If it serves the social good, it should be supported both politically and economically. If it does not, it should be avoided, not sanctioned, or even be disciplined.

Table 5.14: Summary strike pattern features for strike approval and period.

Period	Strike Approval	F^1	Size^2	D^3	MDI^4
Becker	Approved	203	322	1.95	127,165
Ben-Aharon	Approved	130	1,135	2.21	327,257
Meshel-Labor	Approved	84	1,785	1.70	254,601
Meshel-Likud	Approved	91	6,655	1.83	1,111,470
Kessar-Likud	Approved	163	11,270	2.37	4,365,133
Kessar-Unity	Approved	175	5,847	1.12	1,148,757
Becker	Unapproved	286	321	2.22	203,234
Ben-Aharon	Unapproved	216	454	2.48	242,624
Meshel-Labor	Unapproved	181	915	2.25	370,809
Meshel-Likud	Unapproved	137	1,009	2.91	401,343
Kessar-Likud	Unapproved	173	789	1.54	210,500
Kessar-Unity	Unapproved	119	1,270	2.12	319,284

1. No. of strikes per 1,000 days   2. Average no. of strikers per strike
3. Average duration per striker   4. Sum man-days idle by strikes

Various means were established to enforce conformity. The most explicit is the judicial apparatus of the Histadrut. The most effective is centralized control of the Strike Fund. However, strike statistics supply clear evidence that conformity to this approach has never been very high. Unapproved strikes are the norm and not the exception. Still, strike data show a clear trend of relaxation of control. The Histadrut acts as though it prefers the "if you cannot beat them, join them" approach to the disciplinary option. Table 5.14 shows the strike approval for the six periods under study.

Approved strikes follow the usual **U**-trend. They reach their minimum during the Meshel terms. The unapproved strikes, however, show a downward trend. Per 1,000 days, the numbers of unapproved strikes called were, 286—Becker, 216—Ben-Aharon, 181—Meshel/Labor, 137—Meshel/Likud and only 119 during the Kessar/National Unity period. Since an act of approval is a binomial phenomenon—a strike can either be approved or not—the trend of unapproved strikes tells us a story of increased leniency on the part of the Histadrut leadership. This change of policy led to the approval of 59.6 percent of the strikes during the Kessar/Unity period as compared to between 31.7 and 40.1 in the periods preceding it. The first to obtain approval were powerful groups. The comparison of average strike size with its approval status shows this process. While in Becker's days approved and unapproved strikes had the same size (322 and 321 respectively), an average approved strike was larger than unapproved thereafter. The Histadrut allowed larger collectivities of workers to initiate their campaigns without efforts to constrain them. Smaller, possibly weaker, groups, on the other hand, called strikes without Histadrut blessing.

LABOR RELATIONS OFFICER INVOLVEMENT

The legislature designed the position of the Labor Relations Officer as a major preventive mechanism. For the earliest reported period it did have a significant level of involvement. The administrators of four out of ten strikes notified the Officer. The law stipulates precisely who is required to make notification and under what time schedule. Although this was not always adhered to, it was still an impressive figure. In time, however, the percentage of notification decreased. Excluding lockouts, the Labor Relations Officer was notified of 42.6 percent of the strikes in the Ben-Aharon, 27.9 percent in the Meshel/Labor, 28.7 percent in the Meshel/Likud, and 22.8 percent during the Kessar/National Unity periods.

The notified strikes are mostly longer than the unnotified stoppages. This feature may reveal that the Labor Relations Officer is called in for a specialized type of strike. Short term strikes, called mostly to raise attention to union demands, take place without notification. Strikes for which a lengthy process of negotiation are seen as more suited to this option. Still, considering the fact that the "short" unnotified strikes continue on the average for a day or two, and the "long" notified strikes, for two or three days, this explanation requires more in-depth analysis, than is made possible by the presently available data.

Another perspective on the status of the Labor Relations Officer relates to a report on the involvement of external factors in Israeli strikes (Table 5.15). Most reported strikes precipitate external intervention and this involvement is on the increase. External factors assisted in only 54.8 of the strikes during the Meshel/Labor period. This figure rose to 59.7 percent in the Meshel/Likud and to 75.7 percent in the Kessar/National Unity periods. The most active of all is the Histadrut. An external Histadrut organ intervened in one out of five strikes in the Meshel/Labor term. This figure increased steadily and reached a record of 69.8 percent in the most recent period. Taking into consideration the fact that that non-Histadrut affiliated unions have their share in Israeli strikes, this involvement is almost as high as it can be.

The Labor Relations Officer is second in ranking of involvement. Excluding Ben-Aharon's days, when the Officer assisted in more strikes than the Histadrut,[17] he dealt with between a sixth and a third of the number of strikes handled by the Histadrut. A major difference between these two third-parties is the size of strikes with which they are involved. The Labor Relations Officer serves smaller units on the average than does the Histadrut.

Table 5.15: Summary strike pattern features for collapsed[1] external involvement and period.

Period	External Involvement	F[2]	Size[3]	D[4]	MD[5]
Ben-Aharon	IR Dept.	32	367	9.68	113,980
Meshel-Labor	"	20	308	4.20	25,894
Meshel-Likud	"	22	2,928	5.62	362,130
Kessar-Unity	"	35	631	6.22	137,389
Ben-Aharon	Histadrut	22	468	2.23	23,240
Meshel-Labor	"	119	1,848	2.09	460,089
Meshel-Likud	"	66	1,567	4.63	479,185
Kessar-Unity	"	93	3,003	1.29	361,284
Meshel-Labor	Labor Court	4	463	1.01	1,832
Meshel-Likud	"	2	3,586	1.00	7,101
Kessar-Unity	"	8	3,928	4.66	145,667
Ben-Aharon	Mediator	10	2,426	1.67	39,654
Meshel-Labor	"	9	3,194	1.03	31,038
Meshel-Likud	"	6	4,439	1.00	28,150
Kessar-Unity	"	28	4,735	1.49	195,900
Ben-Aharon	No preinvolvement	53	601	1.86	59,348
Meshel-Labor	"	118	552	1.80	117,473
Meshel-Likud	"	34	1,654	1.81	103,038
Kessar-Unity	"	49	2,583	.48	60,125
Meshel-Labor	Other	6	2,726	1.51	24,859
Meshel-Likud	"	6	2,558	5.76	88,413

1. A given strike may involve more than one external agent
2. No. of strikes per 1,000 days   3. Average no. of strikers per strike
4. Average duration per striker   5. Sum man-days idle by strikes

Table 5.15 shows that during most periods (excluding Meshel/Likud) the average size of a strike handled by the Officer was in the hundreds, while that of the Histadrut was in the thousands (the Ben-Aharon term is an exception). A complementary state-operated mechanism for larger disputes is the Labor Court. The number of strikes in which the court intervened has always been small, but their size is big, at least since the 1977 political upheaval. Since the Labor Relations Officer has the authority to initiate an intervention in a dispute, while the Labor Court must be called in by one (or both) of the parties, the smaller frequency of stoppage handled by the court is self-explanatory. In a surprisingly high number of disputes, and even more, in surprisingly large strikes, mediators and other factors intervened. With no exception, the average size of a strike dealt by a mediator or another functionary has never been lower than 2,400. In Israeli terms, an average figure like this is very high.

THE RESULTS OF STRIKES

If strikes are a typical case of social action, then their initiators are interested in their results no less than in their mere existence. Therefore, the outcomes of all these disputes are highly relevant.

To what degree do they serve the objectives of the striking workers? The phrasing of the measure of success in the official strike statistics does not give us a straightforward answer on the effectivity of strikes. The official strike form asks a neutral question: "How did the strike end?" The close ended responses elicited are ambivalent. First, a set of evaluative effectivity measures are offered: "All/Part/No workers' demands were fulfilled." Then, a set of descriptive options are given: "Plant closed," "Court orders," "Meetings, warning strikes, solidarity or demonstration." Isn't the fact that a plant has closed for good, while the main objective of the workers was to keep it running, a proof of failure?! Isn't a court order, which sends workers back to work without solving those issues which were raised by them, a sound indicator for lack of achievement?! On the other hand, isn't an accelerated process of negotiation, as a result of a workers' meeting assembled to protest against procrastination, proof of a successful strike?! All these questions are left unanswered by the phrasing of the item in the official form. Thus, the traditional programmers' expression of "garbage in, garbage out" can be demonstrated once again. Most strikes are conscious acts, selected by rational actors for a purpose. Therefore, ignoring effectivity is regrettable.

Acknowledging all these limitations in the data, it is still possible to gain some useful understanding from a statistical analysis. This can be done by dividing strikes into two types, those evaluated for their effectiveness, and others. The former type includes almost half (49.1 percent) of the standardized number of strikes for the 1965-87 period. The second group includes all lockouts (3.9 percent), strikes which ended with no immediate results—expecting disparities to be resolved by further negotiation, mediation, arbitration or court awards—and strikes with no immediate objective in mind other than expression of dissatisfaction or solidarity with other collectivities.[18]

When we analyze the changes of the level of success for the first, instrumental, type, we can easily identify a typical **U**-form. Fifty percent of the instrumental strikes of the Becker period ended with full success. This figure falls to 30 percent in the Ben-Aharon term and stays on this level for the whole Meshel era (Meshel/Labor 29.7 percent; Meshel/Likud 31.5 percent). The Kessar/National Unity period swings back to the Becker level, 46.5 percent of the instrumental strikes ending with complete success for the workers. A comparable analysis of the same data from the other pole, failure, shows the same, this time inverse **U**-shape, with the worst times for strikers in the

Ben-Aharon (38.8 percent failure) and the Meshel/Labor periods and their finest hours in the Becker (24.7 percent) and Kessar/National Unity periods (27.2 percent). The correlation between the shape of successful strikes and the frequency of strikes is a further proof of the instrumental nature of strike activity. If strikes were emotional rather than rational actions, costeffective considerations would not be concommitant with them. Gain concerns, on the other hand encourage calling strikes when their success expectancy is high and avoiding strikes when it is low.

Instrumental strikes tend to be successful. Still, the larger the strike, the less does it result in a specifiable set of outcomes. The larger the strike, the more it tends to end in further negotiations or in an intervention by a third party mediator or arbitrator. We can make this conclusion on the basis of Table 5.16.

For any period, strikes that ended with arbitration or further negotiations were larger than any of the successful, partially successful, or failure strikes. However, the non instrumental strikes were not only larger but *shorter*. This short duration indicates that even these strikes were planned in advance and not a haphazard outcome of chance alone. These "non-instrumental" strikes are also conscious efforts to promote collective interests. They are an effort to achieve similar results using different means.

Table 5.16: Summary strike pattern features for strike outcomes and period.

Period	Outcomes	F[1]	Size[2]	D[3]	MDI[4]
Becker	Success	154	170	1.84	48,058
Ben-Aharon	"	68	386	2.19	57,879
Meshel-Labor	"	41	401	3.23	52,705
Meshel-Likud	"	28	832	3.54	82,952
Kessar-Likud	"	31	29,305	1.01	908,214
Kessar-Unity	"	94	1,999	2.06	385,819
Becker	Part. success	78	209	4.52	73,907
Ben-Aharon	"	71	354	7.73	194,676
Meshel-Labor	"	47	1,211	4.72	268,712
Meshel-Likud	"	34	1,521	12.12	635,191
Kessar-Likud	"	61	14,583	3.75	3,350,000
Kessar-Unity	"	53	894	2.53	118,589
Becker	Failure	76	294	2.04	45,595
Ben-Aharon	"	88	665	2.99	174,532
Meshel-Labor	"	51	454	3.53	81,622
Meshel-Likud	"	27	1,589	2.29	97,886
Kessar-Likud	"	41	587	2.57	61,735
Kessar-Unity	"	55	3,143	2.01	346,438
Becker	Arbitration, negotiation	182	514	1.75	163,503

Table 5.16 cont'd

Period	Outcomes	F[1]	Size[2]	D[3]	MDI[4]
Meshel-Labor	"	144	1,584	1.07	243,251
Meshel-Likud	"	151	4,661	1.66	1,169,526
Kessar-Likud	"	235	1,059	1.17	290,306
Kessar-Unity	"	111	3,007	1.09	362,571
" "	Plant closed	2	123	19.94	3,886
Becker	Lockout	22	162	4.23	14,742
Ben-Aharon	"	12	521	4.63	28,606
Meshel-Labor	"	19	369	6.99	46,510
Meshel-Likud	"	15	724	23.68	251,170
Kessar-Likud	"	20	112	13.80	31,684
Kessar-Unity	Labor court	5	4,376	1.63	34,079
	Other	6	236	1.15	1,730
" "	Meeting, warning, solidarity	73	6,585	0.82	396,967

1. No. of strikes per 1,000 days   2. Average no. of strikers per strike
3. Average duration per striker   4. Sum man-days idle by strikes

CONCLUSIONS

What conclusions can we draw from the elaborate data analysis of this chapter? On first thought we may be overwhelmed by the facts. On second thoughts, however, clear structural developments may be discerned. These can be divided into two subheadings: changes in the structure of strikes and changes in the degree strikes act as reflections of factors external to the Israeli irs.

The Structure of Strikes

Israeli strikes have become a massive collective act. This aspect is indicated both by their average size and by their cross-sectoral nature. While in the late 1960s a typical strike mobilized a few hundred employees, by the late 1980s it was no longer of such a modest size. Size is not merely a technical characteristic, it has wide repercussions. A teachers' strike of 50,000 is not easy to disregard. In the short run it is a blockage of a very essential service. In somewhat cynical terms, it is a curtailment of the major babysitter of the state. (The teachers are themselves well aware of this, and use strike action at elementary school level knowing that this requires working parents to stay home or make difficult alternative arrangements.) Teachers' strikes on such a scale were non-existent until the late 1970s, the first two occuring in 1978. Three more followed in 1981. From then on, widespread teachers' strikes took place in 1983 (2), 1985 (3) and 1987 (2).

Strikes of even wider calibration are associated with state employees, local government workers, or the total public sector. These have been actions of previously unheard of scope. In 1965, 19,000 academicians applied the strike weapon. By 1970 a similar action involved 35,000. In 1977, 25,000 technical engineers and technicians twice called strikes and 20,000 humanities and social science graduates twice followed suit. In 1982, more than 250,000 public sector employees twice adopted professional action. In 1984, 87,000 local government workers struck, while at least 60,000 state employees or public sector workers abstained from work on four occasions in 1987. In a country with less than 1.5 million employed persons, this has been a significant development!

All these are but a few examples of scores of wide spread labor disputes and the turmoil is on the increase. Multi-employer strikes cross-cut the whole economy, threatening its functioning. Unions opt for broadly based strike action with less restraint than ever before.

A single segment of the Israeli economy is the major focus of this increase in the average strike—the state-owned establishments of the public service. Some 480 employees took part in the average strike in this segment in the early days of Secretary General Becker. The figure grew to 965 in the Ben-Aharon era, almost tripled (2,980) in Meshel's labor sub-period and rose to 6,310 in his Likud term. The numbers kept a similar level in the first few weeks of the Kessar/Likud sub-period (5,930), before reaching a record 10,640 in his National Unity term—a twenty-two fold increase in twenty-three years!

This expansion radiated both to other state-owned branches and to non-state-owned public services. Thus, we see a similar, albeit more moderate, trend in state-owned transportation and financial services. However, neither the Histadrut sector, nor the major productive branches of the private sectors share the same trend.

Differentiation and Autonomy of irs

A primary characteristic of the Israeli irs is its level of functional autonomy. This property increasingly characterizes the system throughout the period under study. Table 5.17 demonstrates this ongoing aspect in a straightforward manner.

Table 5.17 tests the impact of two variables on the frequency of strikes. The first, the identity of the secretary general of the Histadrut, is a major irs internal variable. The second, the dominant party in government, is a central political factor. The multiple classification analysis shows an Eta of .92 for the adjusted strike frequencies of the former and an Eta of .24 for the latter. In terms of variance explained, the internal irs variable explains 84.6 percent[19] and the external one—5.8 percent!

Table 5.17: Strike frequency[1] by secretary general of the Histadrut and ruling
party: multiple classification analysis.

Variable + Category	Number of Periods	Unadjusted		Adjusted for Independents	
		Deviation	Eta	Deviation	Eta
Sec'y-general					
1 Becker	1	47.00		40.50	
2 Ben-Aharon	1	12.00		5.50	
3 Meshel	2	-34.50		-33.50	
4 Kessar	2	5.0	.99	10.50	.92
Ruling party					
1 Labor	3	10.67			
2 Likud	2	-20.00			
3 Nat. Unity	1	8.00	.50		.24

Grand Mean = 138.00

1 Frequency of strikes per year

Over time, this attribute strengthens and by the end of the period, the
Israeli irs is no longer a unified system. It has differentiated into sector-specific systems. One may wonder if these lines of differentiation do not imply a
dominance of the political system on the irs. I would argue, however, that
division along sectoral lines is primarily a process of segmentation in terms
of ownership. Just because the state is one of the owners does not make this a
political variable.

In the more vulnerable segments of the Israeli irs we see a clear decrease in
the level of responsibility. The more powerful a group is, the higher its
propensity to strike. More and more, the strike has become the weapon of
professionals, semi-professionals, clerks and skilled workers. These groups
play a power game. Institutional norms, such as the two-week freeze stipulated by law, or reliance on the assistance of the Labor Relations Officer, are
disregarded.

The autonomous nature of the system has several indicators. As we saw,
the frequency of strikes is a function of the identity of the secretary general of
the Histadrut and not of the dominant party. Thus, internal irs, rather than
political, factors shape this aspect of the strike pattern. The downward trend
in the number of strikes called by the National Union of Government
Employees (NUGE) and the upward trend in that of the National Union of
Clerical, Administrative and Public Service employees tell the same tale.
Politically dominated unions like the NUGE leave the stage to the more craft-
oriented unions. The similarity in strike practices of the Histadrut affiliated
Israel Teachers' Union and the independent Organization of High School
Teachers conveys a similar message. The irs arena is shaped less by the politi-
cal preferences of a union's leaders than by the specific irs conditions in which
that union functions.

Strike patterns are affected by sectoral affiliations. As an employer, the government suffers from an unbalanced power structure and state management reveals an inability to run the ever-growing state bureaucracy. This inefficiency leads to parity disputes and an evolving state of industrial unrest. This description holds for all régimes, be they Labor or Likud dominated or even National Unity. The private sector, on the other hand, displays a diversity of patterns. While private sector industry is relatively tranquil, its finance segment is not significantly less turbulent than state public services. Thus, the average breadth of strikes in private sector finance increased by a factor of thirteen from the early Becker days (185) to the late Kessar period (2,480).

Last, but not least, striking behavior has deteriorated: the level of responsibility has decreased; institutionalized measures for dispute management have become ineffective; striking parties tend to avoid reporting to the Labor Relations Officer and the effects of the freeze period are therefore on the decline. The increase in average strike size may, or may not, indicate a lowering of responsibility. Becker believed that the more comprehensive the unit initiating a dispute, the more responsible and cautious would a strike call be. This view might have fitted the irs of the 1950s and 1960s, with little internal differentiation and led by a centralistic Histadrut. The wider the acting union was, the closer it was to the central Histadrut bodies and therefore it was more likely to adhere to a responsible policy than a narrower workers' committee. In the later phases, with increasing reluctance of the central bodies of the Histadrut to impose control on their affiliated unions—and the corresponding increased autonomy of unions both national and local—this view may have become obsolete. Instrumental, rather than ideological considerations are taking priority.

The Israeli irs has thus reached a problematic stage. On the one hand, it has developed a high level of differentiation, an outcome with maximal impact on effectivity. On the other, it runs high risks of endangering political and economic subsystems. In the absence of a strong political subsystem—following Luhmann, a typical characteristic of a functionally differentiated society—the main challenge is the crystallization of irs-specific norms. If these are absent, both the functioning of this system and the viability of Israel as a society are in danger.

Notes to Chapter 5

1. Strike statistics have been traditionally collected by the Institute for Economic and Social Research, which is a division of the Histadrut. The Department of Industrial Relations in the Ministry of Labor and Welfare and the Central Bureau of statistics each took a part in this venture for a number of years.

2. Let MDI be the number of man days idle, F – the number of strikes, and B –The number of strikers. Then,
   $$MDI = F * B/F * MDI/B$$

3. Reshef and Bemmels report that economic determinants are more important than political determinants in the private sector, but that political and economic determinants are equally important in the Histadrut and public sector.

4. The 5,325 figure of the Kessar/Likud sub-period should be taken with caution. An average figure for a period as short as this (98 days) can easily be the outcome of the eruption of a few, unrepresentative, large strikes.

5. Union information is only available since the Ben-Aharon period.

6. Industrial relations in the ports are not the focus of this study. A deteriorating cost-benefit ratio for the union is commonly regarded as the explanation for the decrease in strike propensity in the ports. The port of Ashdod was the focus of turmoil in this industry. The high level of industrial strife at this site led importers and exporters to divert their merchandise to the port of Haifa. The resulting cut in overtime and effort premium payments to the workers in Ashdod made them reluctant to initiate further strikes or to support militant union leaders.

7. No union data are available for Becker's term.

8. We could keep a common scale for both periods and union types. The clear disadvantage is, however, that some observation will be presented in such a small size as to become indistinguishable.

9. Usable occupational data are only available since 1981. Therefore, this variable is more or less desired but not available for the present analysis. Data for 1965-72 were coded following an older version of the occupational classification and for major categories only. Adjusting the older data to the newer scheme has failed to generate usable information.

10. Since the author of this text was personally in charge of the collection of strike statistics between 1965 and 1969, he accepts most of the blame for these deficiencies. Still, there is a Jewish saying, "if I had been as smart as my wife is today, I would. . ."

11. An average for the entire period. No significant percentage differences between the various periods are apparent.

12. The Kessar/Likud period is the minimum time of strike frequency, but is unreliable for drawing conclusions. In the analysis below,

whenever this period is found to be a reference point, it will be ignored.

13. The committees headed by David Hurovitz, Hayim Barkai and Zusmann are examples.

14. The enactment of the amendment to the Industrial Disputes Law (1972) is an example of a legislative intuitive spurred by industrial unrest.

15. Their public sector included both our present public sector and the segment I prefer to label "government sector."

16. Defensive strikes are strikes motivated by a demand to maintain existing levels of reimbursement. Offensive strikes seek improvements in working conditions. This distinction was developed and used by Michael and Barel (1977).

17. This figure is probably more a proof of deficiencies in the quality of the data than evidence of the superior status of the Labor Relations Officer.

18. Changes in coding of data during the 1965-87 period make it difficult to supply percentage figures for each of the sub-categories of the non-objective type disputes.

19. Eta squared is the measure of the percentage of explained variance. Thus 0.92 squared is 84.64% and 0.24 squared is 5.76%

6

Strikes and irs Autonomy:
A Hierarchical Multi-Level
Model and Its Demonstration
on Israeli Data

General Introduction

Reference to the concept of a system in general, and of a social system in particular, is very common. Terms like system, subsystem, entropy, feedback, hierarchy, or emergence can be found in many sociological publications. Still, in many cases these terms are used more as figures of speech than as authentic theoretical constructs.

> A system could . . . be defined as a complex unit in space and time so constituted that its component subunits, by 'systematic' cooperation, preserve its integral configuration of structure and behavior and tend to restore it after non-destructive disturbances. (Weiss, 1973, p.14)

Yet, in how many studies can we find an identification or verification of issues like continuity in time and space, identification of subunits, inter subunit relationships or structure *prior* to the application of system terminology. The idea of a system is taken for granted. This approach does not stem from a complete acceptance of system assumptions. It is more a stylistic convention.

No one would dare accuse Talcott Parsons of neglecting the essentials of system methodology. His social system conceptualization has become a landmark in sociological social theory. Nevertheless, Parsons' lead is no longer accepted. His writings have been criticized for their level of abstraction and conservatism, and have become a 'classic,' frequently quoted, but mainly evoking lip-service.

Niklas Luhmann (1979, 1982) is on the verge of becoming the major system theorist of the 1980s. Luhmann rejects Parsons' assumption that social integration is based on value consensus. He argues forcefully that modern society, with its high level of specialization and diversity, shares a bond of only a very diluted degree of value belief. As a society highly differentiated along functional lines, its integration is a precarious challenge, never to be taken for granted. A system approach, as far as Luhmann is concerned, is based on a duality, both a target system and its environment. A system is an autonomous entity, engaged in communicative interaction with its environment. A systems analyst must keep an open eye on both elements, even if his main focus of interest is internal. He should never ignore the point, though, that a research object cannot be regarded as a system unless it is endowed with a significant degree of autonomy. This stress on system autonomy and underemphasis of the importance of a central value system are tempting for the analysis of the industrial relations arena in general and industrial conflict in particular. Prior to the adoption of Luhmann's scheme,

> at least . . . one point . . . still has to be supported . . . *One has to be certain that there are social systems in reality.* For only then is a systems theory of the social justified. (Podak, 1986, pp. 58-59).

The present paper can be regarded as a test of the reality of systems theorizing. The identification of a functioning industrial relations system may support Luhmann's claim for a social system theory.

The idea that the field of industrial relations can be comprehended effectively by system conceptualization was originally introduced by Dunlop (1958). Dunlop's notion of system has since been frequently cited by researchers and practitioners, but generally as a vaguely defined idea rather than as the basis of serious theoretical consideration.

The present chapter is an effort to relate to Dunlop's work on a theoretical basis, to elaborate his model and to apply it to a concrete setting. Such an object requires a clear specification of system autonomy and a typology of systems by their level of autonomy. Here Luhmann comes to our aid. Autonomy, writes Luhmann "refers to the degree of freedom with which the selective criteria of the system can regulate the relations between system and environment" (1982, p. 142). This freedom may include various mechanisms. First, the higher the level of autonomy of a system the less sensitive will it be to changes in the environment. On a more statistical level, the higher the autonomy of a system the *lower* will be the coefficient of determination for the environmental variables on system variables. Second, Luhmann stresses,

> in order to be autonomous a system must first of all 'have time'. It cannot always be forced to react immediately to outside impulses, instead, it must face time to apply its own processes of selecting causes and effects. (p. 143)

Here, once again, the level of the coefficient of determination in a regression analysis can serve as an indicator of the level of autonomy of a given system. The supply of time for system functioning depends on the degree to which a system is institutionalized in the wider society.

> A . . . system must be more or less generally accepted in its social environment. As a system it must enjoy . . . credit, which does not rest upon its making specific promises about what its decisions will be. This credit is not created by a continued bartering, or taken back after every failure. (p. 143)

The level of institutionalization must be investigated for using qualitative methods. A description of a society, it's structure, history and dynamic functioning, may supply us with relevant information on this topic. Another facet of autonomy is the ability of a system to treat its environment in a selective way. A perfect non-autonomous system, (which is a contradiction in terms, since such a unit is not a system!) reacts in a fixed way to changes in its surroundings. The wider the range of scenarios from which a system is able to choose, the *higher* its level of autonomy. Thus, if we run a longitudinal study of a given social domain, the more we can show that under different conditions, this domain reacted selectively to various factors, the more forcibly can we argue that this domain acts as an autonomous system. This last assertion must be taken very carefully. Differentiated reaction can stem from changes of societal structure. A war period, for example, may increase societal solidarity and bring strike activity to an all time low. Such an event should not be comprehended as the autonomous action of an industrial relations system. This is a moratorium imposed by society at large.

Still, when a change can be interpreted as serving the interests of a system, it may support the argument for a system's autonomy. Snyder (1975) showed that American strikes reacted to political and organizational variables during the pre-World War II period, while they had a high correspondence with economic factors after that war. Snyder conceptualizes this change in terms of two institutional settings. I prefer to regard it as a sign that the post-war American industrial relations system had gained autonomy and had entered a stage where internal IR considerations took precedence. Political constraints ceased to interfere with the irs functioning. On the other hand, Korpi and Shalev (1979), analyze the trends of strikes in Western Europe. They come to the conclusion that it became in the best interests of the labor movement to exhibit constraint in the IR arena and to seek achievements through political action. Here, the correspondence between political action and strike measures is a sign of the consolidation of a strong irs, which selects its routes of action on the basis of internal IR consideration—a clear indication of enhanced autonomy.

Dunlop conceived

> an industrial-relations system at any time in its development ... as comprised of certain actors. certain contexts, an ideology which binds the industrial-relations system together, and a body of rules created to govern the actors at the work place and work community. (Dunlop. 1958, p. 7)

These four elements, actors, contexts, ideology and rules, can be regarded as representing four interdependent subsystems: the industrial relations system (irs), and three contextual subsystems, economic, political, and technological. Dunlop and his followers used his terminology mostly to describe a single unit of analysis (UOA) such as a nation, an economic branch, or an organization. This tradition trivialized the system approach and ignored the hierarchical nature of the industrial relations arena. The present work tries to fill this gap by portraying a hierarchical model of Dunlop's industrial relations system.

Figure 6.1: A hierarchical model of Dunlop's industrial relations system.

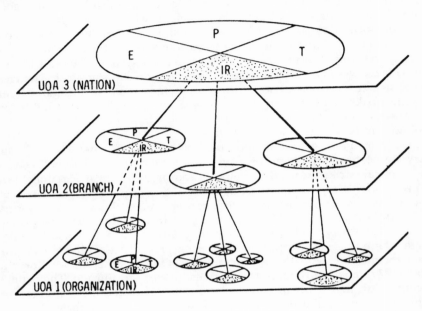

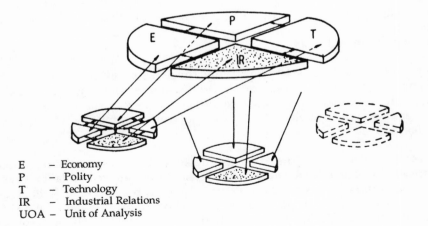

E   – Economy
P   – Polity
T   – Technology
IR   – Industrial Relations
UOA – Unit of Analysis

The model is based on the assumption that the industrial relations of a given setting are a summary outcome of the characteristics of four distinct systems that crystallize around identifiable UOAs and their intra- and inter-relations. Reality includes myriad details, and the model makes several assumptions as to their significance. First, the hierarchical nature of the model implies the predominance of relationships between contingent UOAs and the insignificance of paths between unconnected UOAs. Therefore, in Figure 6.1, all effects of UOA3 (nation) on UOA1 (organization) are assumed to be mediated through UOA2 (branch).

Second, the existence of four detectable systems—the irs, the economic, the political, and the technological—implies relative system autonomy, abundance of intra-system connections and relative scarcity of inter-system associations.

Third, the juxtaposition of these two assumptions implies the precedence of intra-system—inter-UOA effects on inter-system—intra-UOA relationships. Thus, the main impact of a superordinate on a subordinate UOA is channeled through their corresponding subsystems: national-level economic processes (e.g., inflation) affect branch-level economic developments (e.g., supply of and demand for branch products) more than they control the outcomes of collective negotiations.

A substantiated claim for an independent system theory of industrial relations (as well as economics, political science or technology) is based on these three assumptions. Figure 6.1 demonstrates this idea on a sub-part of the model, comprising two UOAs. The detailed scale of the figure allows explicit demonstration of my third assumption. The contingent UOAs are joined by four bipolar connections. Each specialized system maintains inter-system ties. The schematic form of the figure should not detract from our understanding of the meaning of these relationships. Ideological support (or repudiation), material resources, power, influence, or commitment, are all hidden behind a symbolic straight line.

The autonomy of a system has been discussed above in theoretical terms. Some ideas have been vented on methods by which the degree of system autonomy can be identified. However, a more detailed methodology is clearly desired. Since any quantitative analysis of industrial conflict entails the depiction of relationships between variables, it seems worthwhile to approach the measurement of the degree of autonomy using a model phrased in inter-variable terminology. The extreme categories of this scale are a situation where a domain is clearly *not* a system and a situation where a domain is *beyond* autonomy. The two other categories will display intermediate levels of system autonomy. The four categories are as follows:

    a. Closed system (beyond autonomy) – A self-contained set of variables, unaffected by any external variables.

    b. Highly autonomous system – A partially self-contained set of variables, affected by external variables in a self-selective way. (A statistical interaction is found between the internal and the external sets of variables).

    c. Low level autonomous system – A partially self-contained set of variables, affected by external variables in a nonselective way. (No statistical interaction exists between the internal and the external sets of variables).

    d. Non-system – A set of variables totally determined by a set of external variables. The relationships are a clear case of independent variables relationships.

These four categories can be related to conventional statistical procedures (regression, log-linear, cross-tabulation, etc.). Cases approximated by a given category can be labelled as belonging to one of the four systems.

The present work serves as a step in testing the validity of the proposed model. The testing will be carried out in two steps. First, the political and industrial relations features of both national and subordinate UOAs will be related. By cross-classifying these variables, the existence of an autonomous hierarchical model will be tested. A claim supporting this model will be raised if the data confirms it. Second, the degree of autonomy of the Israeli irs will be tested in a temporal perspective. This attribute of the irs is supposedly a variable, under permanent change. Both the degree of autonomy and its determinants will be looked for.

The Israeli Situation: Some Structural Characteristics

The Israeli labor market has at least three attributes, relevant to the present analysis:

    a. *It is highly unionized.* "About 88% of Israeli employees are unionized in trade unions which cover almost the whole range of the professional groups" (Krausz 1980,p. 14).

    b. It has a single dominant union movement.

    c. *It has a large and extensive public sector.* Approximately thirty percent of the Israeli labor force is employed in governmental, municipal or other public-owned enterprises. Another twenty percent of Israeli workers earn their living in the Histadrut sector, more than half (54 percent) as salaried workers. (Institute for Economic and Social Research, 1977, p.25)

All three of these attributes of Israeli society have far-reaching political implications. The unionization of a labor market transforms employer-employee relations from the individual to the collective mode (Flanders 1970). The process of collective negotiations "is best described as a diplomatic use of power" (Flanders, 1970, p. 219). Such negotiations are conducted by union officials and managements. In Israel, the main union, the trade union division of the Histadrut, is a political organization, led by representatives who are elected through political, party-mediated, channels. Management in governmental and municipal-owned units is constantly exposed to the pressures of central and local political organs, all of which are, once again, predominantly composed of party officials.

A large majority of the salaried workers are members of unions whose policy formulation and implementation procedures may be heavily motivated by party-line considerations. These structural features create a constant threat to the autonomy of its irs. Israel is a highly politicized society. Public-owned enterprises and the public services, are heavily integrated in the political sphere. Election periods are times when political tones are amplified to their maximum. Therefore, an analysis of strikes in Israel, a study focusing on the actions and decisions of the various actors of the irs during election periods and in the public sector, bring to a critical test the system component of Dunlop's irs concept and its autonomy. This test is the issue of the present analysis.[1] The crystallization of the autonomy of the Israeli irs is a second principal topic. Given the primary importance of the Histadrut, irs autonomy as noted in previous chapters, has been influenced sequentially by the last four secretaries general of the Histadrut, Becker, Ben-Aharon, Meshel and Kessar.[2] The usefulness of the concept of autonomy will be tested through its predictive potential for strike decision-making processes.

Israeli Strike Statistics: Some Relevant Data

The Israeli strike pattern can be typified as having medium frequency, medium size, but very short duration. The short duration of a strike is a clear indication of the political underpinnings of Israeli strikes (Shorter and Tilly, 1974). Israeli strikes are not usually wars of attrition. They are exchanges of symbolic gestures and an integral part of an institutionalized negotiation process.

Strikes are never distributed evenly in an economy. For the United Kingdom, an official document of the Department of Manpower reports that

> it is abundantly clear that Britain does not have a widespread strike problem, but rather a problem of stoppages concentrated in a small minority of manufacturing plants and in certain non-manufacturing sectors. (Smith et. al., 1978, p. 63)

Israeli strikes are therefore unusual, not for their systematic or uneven distribution, but for their economic branch and ownership sector location. As can be seen in Table 1 the propensity to strike (col. 8) is at its peak in public utilities. Workers in the electricity and water branch have a tendency to strike more than twice their share (2.3) in the salaried workers' population. A similar (1.5) tendency characterizes employees in transportation and public service units (2.1). Parallel analysis can be done along the ownership sector axis. Here the results are clear: approximately 69.7 percent of the strikers work in pub-licly-owned units, whereas these places of employment account for a mere thirty percent of the salaried workers. The propensity-to-strike of this category of workers is, therefore, 2.3!

Table 6.1: Number of strikers and the number of salaried workers by owner-ship sector and industrial branch (Israel, 1965-83).

Economic Branch	Number of Strikers				Total	AdB[1]	PSW[2]	(6) (7)
	Private	Histad.	Public	Multi-Sector				
	(1)	(2)	(3)	(4)	(5)	(6)	(7)	(8)
Agriculture	2,675	2,375	4,361	4,032	13,443	0.5	2.5	0.2
Industry	112,553	44,232	42,482	6,583	205,850	8.9	28.0	0.3
Electricity-Water	–	–	60,992	–	60,992	2.7	1.2	2.3
Construction	1,906	7,147	9,161	15	18,229	0.8	8.3	0.1
Commerce	10,893	433	2,809	150	14,285	0.7	7.7	0.1
Transport.	2,414	32,061	200,233	4,231	238,959	10.4	7.1	1.5
Finance	40,717	345	126,131	1,200	168,393	7.3	7.0	1.0
Public Services	82,001	146,897	657,544	688,223	1,574,665	68.0	32.8	2.1
Private Services	7,740	1,474	5,818	–	15,032	.7	5.4	.1
Non-classi-fiable	–	–	27,400	743,458	770,858	..	..	..
TOTAL	260,899	234,964	1,136,931	1,447,912	3,080,706	100.0	..	..

1. AdB = Adjusted percent of strikers. Non-classifiable divided among various branches by their proportional size.
2. PSW = Percent salaried workers. Total number of salaried workers equals 100%.
3. – = none.
4. ·· = irrelevant.

Methodology

Two complementary data sets will be used below, one set for a log-linear analysis and the other for regression analysis.

DATA

Log-Linear Analysis

The data files of the Institute for Economic and Social Research of the Histadrut in collaboration with the Department of Industrial Relations in the Ministry of Labor and Welfare are the main source for the present analysis. Raw strike figures are available from the year 1965.

Five Knesset (Israeli Parliament) terms existed during this period, each body passing through election, operation and dissolution. For each of the five, three subperiods were sampled: pre-election, post-election, and "normal" business.[3] Each of the three periods covered 91 days—before an election date, immediately after it, and two years later. Table 6.2 presents the basic data for the analysis, the frequency of strikes by Knesset and election-time categories.

Table 6.2: Strike frequency by Knesset and election-time category.

Election Date	Knesset	Election-Time Category			Total
		Pre	Post	Normal	
11. 2.65	6	86	76	34	196
10.28.69	7	37	32	34	103
12.31.73	8	2	10	14	26
5.17.77	9	53	23	29	105
6.30.81	10	22	11	24	57
TOTAL		200	152	135	487
%		41.1	31.2	27.7	100.0

Two main events must be considered, prior to any meaningful analysis of Table 6.2: the October 1973 Yom Kippur War and the May 17, 1977 political upheaval. The former erupted very close to an impending election campaign. The election date was postponed, but it can hardly be said that life returned to normal. As can be seen in Table 6.2, labor unrest almost disappeared. Only *two* strikes are reported for the three-month period before elections and only 10 occurred in the post-election period. The Yom Kippur War and its peculiar repercussions are not relevant for our present interest, and therefore, the data for the two pre- and post-8th Knesset periods were dropped from the current analysis.

The 1977 political upheaval, in which the Labor Party lost its 29-year majority in the Knesset is, on the one hand, of cardinal importance for our discussion. It opened the door to a situation in which the ruling party in the government and the leading party in the Histadrut were not the same. Ignoring this fact may imply a disregard for a possible major source of strain between the Israeli irs and the Israeli political system (Reshef 1986). An optimal research design for our purpose would have included six sub-categories, each appearing the same number of times: pre-election, postelection, and normal for the pre-1977 elections and three others for the post May-1977 elections. Insisting on equal cell frequencies by limiting each category to the lowest common denominator would have shaped our data to a single sub-period for each category. This is because a Likud government only once experienced a pre-election period under its rule. In order to keep a six-cell design intact while overcoming the limitations of the data, strike frequencies per 100 days[4] instead of raw strike figures were selected for the analysis. Table 6.3 shows the data in their modified form.

Table 6.3: Strike frequency and strike frequency per 100 days by election period and ruling party.

Strike Measure	Raw Strike Frequency		Strike Frequency per 100 Days	
	Ruling Party			
Period	Labor	Likud	Labor	Likud
Pre-elections	178	22	64	24
Post-elections	118	34	59	19
2 years after elections	82	53	30	29

As we can see in Table 6.3, striking styles changed dramatically after the 1977 political upheaval. Both pre- and post-election periods, which during Labor Party rule were customarily times of peak strike activity, dropped to very mild levels. Normal business periods, on the other hand, reached almost identical levels under both regimes. The changes are primarily restricted to election periods and may not show on the total trends.

REGRESSION ANALYSIS

Ashenfelter and Johnson (1969) offer a detailed economic model of strike frequency. The model is based on a three-actor image of industrial relations: management, union leadership and union rank-and-file. The model was developed and tested for the U.S. Its main features were applied by Pencavel (1970) on British data. The structure of the IR system in the U.K. is quite different to that of the U.S. The model, nevertheless, successfully managed to fit the British experience. This statistical success lends some doubt as to the validity of its theoretical foundations. It supports, however, its presumed usefulness. Ashenfelter and Johnson were predominantly interested in the economic determinants of strike activity. The present paper follows Dunlop's (1958) approach and therefore, political, as well as economic, variables are included in the database.

The present analysis is based on monthly figures for the period January 1965-December 1987. Israel Kessar took office as the new Secretary General in May 1984. The 1984 Knesset elections and the establishment of a national unity government followed. A reliable analysis of this period requires an extension of the number of variables. Incorporating the more recent period in the analysis is almost the fulfillment of a researcher's dream. It enables establishing a distinction between the time trend and the dichotomous Labor/

Likud distinction. Still, since not all information on this period is available, our present analysis is to be confined to the available data.

VARIABLES

Log-Linear analysis

Dunlop's IRS model can be perceived as a two-dimensional construct, one hierarchical and the other, nominal. The hierarchical dimension of the IRS refers to the level of the unit: the enterprise, the economic branch, the ownership sector, or the locality. Each level serves as a constraint for those below it. On each level, on the other hand, a distinction should be make between the irs itself, and its environmental constraints—the economic, political, and technological constraints.

Raw strike data refer to an irs activity performed by a specific unit. Most Israeli strikes are actions either by enterprises (plants or specific offices), or by professionals (a given occupation or profession). Therefore, strike statistics include information on items such as cause, outcome, ownership sector, economic branch, state of approval by the appropriate trade union authority, identity of the striking and the approving union, employer association, etc. An examination of the autonomy of a given UOA from its surrounding environment requires information on higher levels of organization, i.e., the national level UOA.[5]

The present analysis includes the following three striking unit level variables and two national level characteristics.

Striking unit variables

Approval of the strike by the legal representative union: (1) approval granted (2) wildcat strike. The bylaws of the Histadrut prohibit a union at a given level from making an independent strike declaration. Approval authority is granted to a superordinate level of the union echelon.

Economic branch: (1) public services or public utilities (2) other economic activities. The first category includes the following branches: (a) electricity and water, (b) transportation, and (c) public services. Strikes by nonclassifiable units were dropped from the analysis. All other branches are included in the second category.

Ownership sector: (1) public ownership (2) private ownership. The public sector includes government, municipal, national and Histdrut-owned enterprises.

National level variables

Timing of strikes: (1) pre-Knesset elections (2) post-Knesset elections (3) Normal, non-election periods. All three time categories extend for thirteen weeks (91 days). A set of complete weeks was adopted to take care of the fact that strikes do not erupt with the same frequency on every day of the week. The non-election period (category 3) is a ninety-one day period whose median is exactly two years after a given election date.

Regression Analysis

Economic variables

Level of unemployment: The monthly average number of adult males unemployed.

Level of profits: The percentage capital return by month. This figure is published on an annual basis by the Institute for Production and Incomes. This Institute was established by the Histadrut and the private sector employers' associations to enhance informed and fact-founded national level wage negotiations. A twelve month moving average of the original figure is used in the present analysis.

Real wage change: Following Ashenfelter and Johnson's lead, this variable is computed as a six-month PDL Almon variable.

Political Variables

Leading party: (1) Labor Party (2) Likud Party

Pre-elections: (1) 3 months or less preceding a Knesset elections month (0) otherwise.
Post-elections: (1) 3 months or less following a Knesset elections month (0) otherwise.

Statistical Method

Log-Linear Analysis

The first stage of data analysis was made through contingency table analysis using a log-linear method. This method allows us to describe the structural relationships among a set of categorical variables. This is the main reason for dividing three of the four above-described variables (Approval of the strike by the legal representative union, Economic branch and Ownership sector) into only two values. Dichotomization highly simplifies the log-linear analysis, and is therefore preferred. The procedure will not be described in detail here. Details of the method can be found in Fienberg (1980) and in Knoke and Burke (1980).

Regression Analysis

The second stage of data analysis was made using a Time Series Processor (TSP). This statistical package (TSP, 1980) offers an option for dealing with polynomial distributed lags—Ashenfelter and Johnson's solution for relating real wage changes to strikes.

ANALYSIS

Log linear analysis

We can imagine three alternative polar system states in the industrial relations arena:

a) strike activity is a purely industrial relations phenomena and is totally determined by the internal factors;

b) strike activity is a multi-system activity, characterized both by IR factors and by its surroundings; and

c) strike activity is totally determined by external, i.e., political, factors.

This typology corresponds in part to the listing presented above on the different degrees of system autonomy. The latter first type is parallel to the closed system, the second, to either the high or the low level autonomous system and the last, to the non-system situation. In the case of the IRS, the situation is somewhat more complicated. As we saw in Figure 6.1, the industrial relations system is hypothesized to be a multi-level construct at national, sectoral and plant level, for example. Therefore, one more dimension should be included in our current listing, that of level. For each of the three system states at least two subdivisions exist, the first limiting processes to a single given level and the other incorporating level effects.

Strikes at a given level, let us say a given plant, can be shaped solely by factors like the power balance between the local union and the local management, the number of representative unions, the ideology of management, etc. In this case, the irs is a closed system (type a) of the single level type. A more typical Israeli example will be a case where the local, plant level union is highly supported (or, sometimes, restrained) by the local workers' council, which is the extension of the Histadrut in a given locale. In this case we have two irs levels (workers' committee and workers' council) and no external (i.e., political, economic or technological) factors. This is an example of a multi-level closed system case. Similar combinations can be suggested for the two other system states, but further elaboration of this point is not needed.

The log-linear procedure allows us to test the applicability of these system-state possibilities for strike activity in Israel. By means of model selection methods and comparison of different models, an evaluation of models can be made and a limited number of parsimonious models can be chosen.

Table 6.4: Strike activity in Israel: Comparison of various models.

Model Title	Model*	df	G^2
External constraints model	[45]	42	126.69[†]
Closed system model	[123]	40	82.88[†]
Hierarchical system model I	[123][45]	35	29.04
Hierarchical system model II	[12][13][23][45]	36	29.03

*Legend	1. Approval of strike by representative union	4.	Timing of strike
	2. Ownership sector	5.	Ruling party
	3. Economic branch	†	$p < .001$

Prior to any presentation of the findings, a short technical explanation of Table 6.4 may be helpful. (Readers familiar with log-linear method are advised to skip to the next paragraph). Each model in col. 1 of the table is hierarchical. The term [123], for example, means the sum effects of variables 1, 2 and 3, the bivariate interactions of 1-2, 1-3 and 2-3, and the trivariate interaction term 123. A log-linear model is tested by comparing expected and observed figures through a quasi-chi square statistic. The critical test of a model is its ability to reconstruct a distribution *as similar as possible* to the observed distribution of the data. Therefore, *insignificant* results indicate the superiority of a model. In Table 6.4, the first two models should be rejected *because* of their *significant* results, while the last two models are supported because of their *insignificant* results.

Table 6.4 presents relevant information for the analysis. Neither the external constraints model nor the closed system model supplies a satisfactory fit for the data. Therefore, strikes in Israel can neither be regarded as a deterministic result of the political environment, nor as a purely industrial relations system affair. Hierarchical model I, the first supported model, shows that the odds of calling strikes are the composite outcome of two clusters of variables. Items 1, 2 and 3—approval by a representative union, ownership sector and economic branch—are subordinate UOA related measures. These three items covariate. This statistical relationship is an indication of the interaction of the three measured aspects. Self-contained variables were suggested to describe an autonomous system. Thus, an autonomous subordinate system for this UOA is disclosed by the analysis.

However, is it a closed, a highly autonomous or a low autonomous system? Is it of the uni-level type or of the multi-level type? The statistical salience of the two external factors, timing of the strikes along the election sequence and identity of the ruling party, show their own independent influence. These two variables act as a second cluster of factors, though once again, in an interactive fashion, shaping the odds of strike activity. The existence of these national level political factors in the selected model refutes the possibility of the closed model option. Both national level and lower UOA variables shape the odds of striking in Israel. The fact that neither external variable has interactive relationships with the subordinate measures helps us reject the possibility of a low level autonomous system.

Factors inherent in the striking UOA influence strike activity without regard to the political constraints. Most striking unit related variables are typical IR variables. If the irs were subordinated to the political system, we could expect the political upheaval—the fact that two rival parties find themselves occupying two different power bases (government and the Histadrut) to make the IR arena into a political means for inter-party skirmishes. The fact that such a phenomenon is not identified testifies in favor of a claim that the irs is an autonomous entity in the social fabric of the Israeli society.

Thus far, the issue of the level of system autonomy. But what about the differentiation of the irs to a hierarchically organized structure? A partial answer to this question can be given if we engage in a content analysis of the three subordinate UOA items. Are all three of the same kind? Do they refer to the same level constellation? Clearly not! The measure of the economic branch is an immediate characteristic of a striking unit. As a matter of fact, it is one of the major characteristics of any striking UOA. The same cannot be said of the other two variables. Approval by an authorized union depicts a two-sided relationship between a legally recognized representative union and one of its branches (in most cases, the workers' committee). A branch may exhibit some degree of autonomy, for otherwise, no case of a wildcat strike would ever occur. Nevertheless, this autonomy is limited. If not, approval of a strike would have no meaning. The same can be stated about the ownership sector variable. This item reflects a two-sided relationship, between the owners or the superordinate management, and the local management. The owners of a unit nominate their delegates to the senior managerial positions, and they can fire them, or change their terms of authority. But such management must have discretionary powers to make meaningful decisions. Management is nothing but an empty title if accorded no leeway, i.e., if it has no authority.

Both the owners of an enterprise and the superordinate unions are actors in an irs. The representative union is an actor on the sectoral, economic branch, or national level irs. The same holds true for the owners of an organization. Does the present analysis identify a level-differentiated irs in Israel? Unfortunately this question cannot be confidently answered on the basis of the present set of variables. A much wider variety of variables, measuring both higher and lower level UOAs, is needed. Expanding the analysis to a wider number of variables would make the use of the present log-linear method very problematic. An expected abundance of zero cases cells, or a very complicated set of findings, would both distract from any experimentation in this direction. Other methods may serve the testing of this point in a more promising way.

The conclusions of this analysis are not simply that the concept of an autonomous industrial relations system realistically describe the strike situation in Israel but that:

(a) Striking units exhibit an autonomous, though not independent, UOA.
(b) The irs's of the striking units are highly connected to those of their superordinate UOAs.
(c) The political system of highest superordinate UOA—the national level UOA—serves as a significant constraint on the odds of striking.

The first conclusion stems from the finding that variables 1, 2 and 3 crystallize as an interactive cluster and from the absence of four- or five-degree interaction with variables 4 and 5.

The second conclusion is derived from the fact that variables 1 and 2 describe not only features of the irs of the striking unit, but also its connections with a superordinate irs. This idea must be tested by a much wider set of variables before it can be confidently accepted.

The last conclusion finds support in the analysis from the existence of a separate interactive term of variables 4 and 5. Both variables are derived from national level political spheres. Their covariation indicates the existence of a national level political system. They seem to have their independent impact on the odds of calling a strike, in parallel to the influence of the striking unit variables 3, 4 and 5.

Conclusions (a) and (c) accord, by and large, with our theoretical model as described in Figure 6.1. The two national level political variables—the timing of a strike (before elections, after elections or during a routine business period) and the identity of the ruling party—are dissociated from the striking UOA variables *while* being kept in the log-linear model.

The national level political processes are related to the functioning of the subordinate UOAs, but the latter maintain their autonomy as well. The striking UOA exhibits its own inter-system relationships. Our data include three striking unit variables, an economic (economic branch) and two irs-related measures (approval of the strike by the legal union and ownership-sector). All three co-vary simultaneously, whether in a second- (model I) or third-order (model II) fashion.

Conclusion (b) only partially supports our model. On the one hand, the UOA connective nature of the strike approval and ownership sector variables lead us to predict that these variables will have second-order interactive relationships. On the other hand, their intermediate nature, i.e., their connection with both the striking UOA and its superordinate UOA should mitigate their relationship with the economic branch variable. The absence of purely UOA-specific irs-related measures in the present study hinders direct testing of this important feature of our model.

Regression analysis

The idea that industrial relations actions are determined both by internal IR factors and by environmental variables may seem trivial and almost self-evident. Many studies, both empirical and theoretical, have sought the relationships between such variables as union density, union membership stability, union elections and strike activity. Many analyses have been conducted relating the level of economic activity, the ideologies of governments, or the technological characteristics of industries, with industrial action. Most past and contemporary research is not, however, interested in the systemic character of industrial relations activities. What are the relationships between inter-IR and intra-IR forces? Is there a process of specialization whereby internal system variables come to the fore? Are there times when the irs ceases to assure an acceptable level of IR functioning, leading to an increased importance of environmental factors, be they political or economic? All these questions stem from a systems logic, and answering them requires a systems approach.

Recent Israeli history can serve as a setting for demonstrating processes of societal specialization. From the 1930s on, Israeli society was led by a single dominant elite which formed a dominant party holding a majority in both the pre-independent semi-governmental bodies of the Yishuv (Zionist Jewish community) and the General Federation of Labor. With control of ideological, political and economic centers, all major policy issues were considered simultaneously. Under such circumstances no meaningful subsystem can function. It can be expected that in an undifferentiated society like this, political, economic and IR variables will co-vary.

Such a monolithic model does not fit Israel nowadays. The country has undergone a significant process of change. Although a political upheaval[6] brought Menachem Begin's Likud Party to government in 1977, another major round of elections left the Histadrut as the stronghold of the Labor Party. The private employers, who had avoided national level involvement in the past, established their own employers' associations and coordinating bodies.[7] Package and framework agreements between government, labor and private employers became quite common. These developments changed both the patterns of strike activity in Israel, and what is more relevant to our present discussion, its determinants. Table 6.5 compares the strike pattern characteristics of three periods, distinguished by the identity of the secretary general of the Histadrut.

Table 6.5: Israeli strike pattern characteristics by the identity of the secretary general of the Histadrut.

Strike Pattern Dimension	Histadrut Secretary General		
	Becker 1.65-12.69	Ben-Aharon 1.70-3.73	Meshel 4.73-4.84
Strikes per month (F)	15.5	12.8	8.5
Strikers per strike (Bbar)	315	576	2,340
Duration per striker (Dbar)	2.03	2.46	2.62

Following Stern (1978), strike volume can be conceived as a three-dimensional construct—frequency, breadth, and duration. The three dimensions of strike activity are expressions of three different aspects of the strike phenomenon.

> *Frequency* represents the decision to take or call a strike, and is most responsive to current environmental conditions. The *breadth* of participation measures the mobilization of workers for strike activity. This dimension is primarily related to the nature of the organization of the work force and the stricture of bargaining . . . *Duration* represents the time it takes to settle after the 'rational' calculations to take or call a strike have been made. This dimension responds primarily to specific local conditions . . . type of strike . . . and secondarily to organization and economic characteristics. (Stern, 1978, p. 39)

An increase in system autonomy decreases its vulnerability to external uncertainties. Under this condition rational decision makers would be more sensitive to internal system considerations and less perceptive to environmental developments. Therefore, fluctuations of strike frequencies should become a) less sensitive to political and economic variables and b) more related to intra-irs factors. Table 6.6 does not allow us a test of hypothesis (b). It does, however, supply us with some indicators for testing hypothesis (a), although a comparison of coefficients of determination across samples is problematic. Therefore, the forthcoming discussion should not be taken as conclusive.

The coming to power of a Likud dominated government and the defeat of the Labor Party in 1977 was a landmark in Israeli political history. The implications of this change for the Israeli irs are straightforward—it led to a significant increase in autonomy. This trend I have described above.

The irs developed from an undifferentiated, still subordinated domain in the Becker term, to a contested autonomous system in that of Ben-Aharon. The defeat of the Labor Party gave the Histadrut a unique status. From the standpoint of the government it was a disdained entity, acknowledged, but unappreciated. From the perspective of the Labor Party, it was the only stronghold left, treasured but hard to control. The Labor and the Likud dominated terms are, therefore, two interesting periods for comparison. The third period, starting in 1984, brought the hybrid type of government, the National Unity coalition. This period deserves separate treatment. The Histadrut fought its way back to the central decision-making setting. While the government acknowledged its importance, the Labor Party failed to resume its control over it. This combination produces complicated effects on the system behavior. Therefore, I will devote a special section to the later years.

Table 6.6: The frequency of strikes and its prediction: economic,[1] political[2] and industrial relations[3] variables as predictors by the dominant party and the secretary general of the Histadrut.

| | | PERIOD | | | | | | |
| | | Dominant Party | | | | Secretary General | | |
Measure	Total	Labor	Likkud	Nat'l Unity	Becker	Ben-Aharon	Meshel	Kessar
R^2	.3036	.3280	.1830	.2566	.7395	.4602	.1708	.3430
Adj. R^2	.2518	.2474	.0219	-.1682	.6504	.2475	.0662	.0023
D-W[4]	1.241	1.202	1.796	1.764	1.393	1.966	1.858	1.957
No. of months	261	141	86	34	52	47	126	42

1. Economic variables included are: Level of unemployment, level of return on capital, Almon-lag measure of change in real wages.
2. Political variables included are: dominant party (Likud, National Unity), elections (3 months before, 3 months after).
3. Industrial relations related variables included are: periods of Ben-Aharon, Meshel and Kessar as secretary generals of the Histadrut.
4. Durbin-Watson adjusted for 0 gaps

The Labor and Likud Years (1965-1984)

Of the strike pattern components, frequency, size and duration, only the first variable shows any systematic trend. The frequency of strikes exhibits a clear trend of decrease in the level of the coefficient of determination (R squared). Of all dimensions of strike activity, this is the variable most expected to reflect the degree of irs autonomy. This trend starts with the Becker, continues during the Ben-Aharon and terminates in the Meshel, terms. (It increases again, although not to the Becker level, in Kessar's first years.) The correlation between the number of strikes and the economic factors displays a secular trend of decrease. Starting with an R^2 of 0.57 for the

Becker period, and continuing with coefficient of 0.31 and 0.05 for Ben-Aharon and Meshel respectively. Similar trends can be seen when the political factors are added to the set of independent variables. Seventy-four percent of the variance in strike frequency is explained by environmental factors during the Becker period as compared to a meager seventeen percent for the Meshel years.

This clear difference between the Becker and Meshel periods is quite surprising since Meshel was the first secretary general of the Histadrut to encounter a non-Labor dominated government. While the only items available for regression analysis for the first period were election period related variables, both these items *and* the ruling party variable were available for the last period. The level of the correlation coefficient at the start of the period is similar to that reported by Pencavel (1970). It falls massively at its end.

As indicated by Table 6.5, both strike breadth (B) and strike duration (D) have changed during these years. Nevertheless, these dimensions of the Israeli strike pattern show no consistent sensitivity to political and/or economic fluctuations, a fact lending support to Stern's ideas .

The trends of change in the Israeli IRS can be depicted on the political axis, by distinguishing between the determinants of strike activity during the Labor and the Likud regimes. This way, the data can be divided into three sub-periods, January 1965 to May 17,1977, May 18, 1977 to July 23, 1984, and July 24, 1984 to December 31, 1986. The first period was ruled by Labor Party led coalitions. The second, by Likud-led coalitions and the third, by a National Unity coalition. Table 6.7 will show the detailed results of three regression analyses, relating economic, political and IR related variables to strike frequency for the three periods.

On the whole, the average number of strikes per year of rule decreased from 90 during the Labor period to 59 in the Likud period. It returned to 86 in the National Unity goverment years. The Likud era decrease came as a surprise to many politicians, who expected that the IR arena would be used by the main opposition party as a lever against the government. The Histadrut, on the other hand, adopted a policy of restraint. The desire not to be accused of politicizing union affairs created quite a cooperative labor movement. The relationships between Finance Ministers and the Secretary General of the Histadrut were on the whole collaborative, with tensions created mostly by frequent switching of the Finance Minister. When we compare the coefficients of determination for the two periods, a decrease from 0.3280 to 0.1830 is discerned, as mentioned above. The figures of Table 6.7 can tell us a more elaborate story, one of a disappearance of any significant relationship between any of the independent variables and strike frequency.

The Labor period model includes four significant regression coefficients, three meaningful ones and one of a more technical nature. First, the constant term is highly significant, conveying the fact that even when all independent variables are set to zero, the expected number of strikes is greater than nil. The other significant results are substantively more interesting. Two economic variables, the level of unemployment and the level of capital return have negative relationships with strike frequency.

The relationships between unemployment and strikes were studied intensively. Most studies show this same relationship, the higher the level of unemployment the lower the number of strikes. This finding is taken to indicate the rationality of strike activity. The availability of job seekers stiffens the stand of the employers and weakens that of the unions. This explanation may not be as appropriate to the Israeli situation as it is elsewhere, because security of employment has been a cornerstone of Israeli employment relations.

Table 6.7: A comparison between the determinants of strike frequency during the Labor (1965-77), Likud (1977-84), and National Unity administrations[1] (1984-87).

Summary Statistics

Statistic	PERIOD		
	Labor	Likud	Nat'l Unity
Sum of squared residuals	4740	1150	684
Standard error of regression	6.1581	4.0242	5.7083
Mean of dependent variable	12.3475	8.2791	12.5000
Standard deviation	7.0983	4.0690	5.2815
R^2	.3280	.1830	.2566
Adjusted R^2	.2474	.0219	−.1682
Durbin-Watson statistic	1.1847	1.7957	1.7642
Number of observations	141	86	34
F-statistic	4.0675	1.1357	.6041
F-statistic—DF	(15,125)	(14,71)	(12,21)
Log of likelihood function	−447.884	−233.528	−99.278

Table 6.7 cont'd
Period-Specific Statistics
Labor Party Period

Variable	Estimated Coefficient	Standard Error	T-Statistic
C[1]	28.06943	3.027769	9.270663
Q1	2.539526	1.624531	1.563236
Q2	−.1025093	1.558762	−.6576332D–01
Q3	.9340795	1.575029	.5930553
UNEMP	−.9644719D–03	.2887263D–03	−3.340436
CAPRET	−1.253002	.2155521	−5.812992
DRWP1	.2083702D–05	.3916224D–05	.5320691
DRWP2	.2045199D–05	.4807413D–05	.4254261
DRWP3	−.3317139D–05	.6606995D–05	−.5020647
DRWP4	−.1647611D–05	.7632187D–05	−.2158767
DRWP5	.1042345D–04	.9499266D–05	1.097290
DRWP6	−.7757373D–05	.1171291D–04	−.6622925
BELEC	.4148999	2.131962	.1946094
AELEC	−1.225991	2.215032	−.5534870
Ben-Aharon	4.143380	2.036669	2.034391
Meshel	−.9798423	2.332529	−.4200772

Distributed lag interpretation for: DRWP Mean lag = 1.2970 Standard error = 14.945
Sum of lag coefficients = .46920d-05 Standard error = .10385D-04 T Statistic = .4518

Likud Party Period

Variable	Estimated Coefficient	Standard Error	T-Statistic
C	11.87675	2.748103	4.321798
Q1	1.467202	1.361552	1.077595
Q2	−1.819509	1.375169	−1.32311
Q3	−2.427983	1.309675	−1.853883
UNEMP	.2077710D–03	.1866490D–03	1.113164
CAPRET	−.3622129	.2585558	−1.400908
DRWP1	.3347321D–10	.2627428D–10	1.273992
DRWP2	−.4790402D–10	.2286751D–10	−2.094851
DRWP3	.1288482D–10	.2190598D–10	.5881875
DRWP4	.1887671D–10	.2217623D–10	.8512135
DRWP5	.2163934D–11	.2494602D–10	.8674464D–01
DRWP6	−.4255056D–10	.3808550D–10	−1.117238
BELEC	.1920726	2.547580	.7539414D–01
AELEC	.9541145D–01	2.124797	.4490379D–01
Kessar	7.124754	5.050979	1.410569

Distributed lag interpretation for: DRWP Mean lag = .0 Standard error = .0
Sum of lag coefficients = −.32627d-10 Standard error = .42926d-10 T Statistic −.7601

Table 6.7 cont'd

National Unity Period

Variable	Estimated Coefficient	Standard Error	T-Statistic
C	25.40028	7.420913	3.422797
Q1	7.686716	3.919907	1.960944
Q2	2.969213	3.382898	.8777127
Q3	1.342620	3.315733	.4049240
UNEMP	−.2492203D−02	.1568126D−02	−1.589287
CAPRET	1.200645	1.481433	.8104619
AELEC	−5.531308	6.670214	−.8292549
DRWP1	.1491329D−11	.1584130D−11	.9414181
DRWP2	.1448556D−12	.1268071D−11	.1142330
DRWP3	−.1440518D−11	.1396120D−11	−1.031801
DRWP4	.8696726D−12	.1685160D−11	.5160771
DRWP5	−.1102195D−11	.2325892D−11	−.4738805
DRWP6	.1658510D−11	.2750822D−11	.6029142

Distributed lag interpretation for: DRWP   Mean lag = 1.2939   Standard error = 7.2383
Sum of lag coefficients = .13604d−11   Standard error = .22825D−11   T Statistic = .5960

1. Method of estimation – ordinary least squares.
2. Legend: C = Constant; Q1,Q2,Q3 = 1st/2nd/3rd quarter;
   UNEMP = Average daily #; CAPRET = Return on capital of male unemployed;
   DRWP1–6 = 1–6 months Almon lag changes in real wages;
   BELEC/AELEC = 3 months before/after elections;
   BEN–AHARON/MESHEL/KESSAR = secretary generals of Histadrut

Most Israeli strikes take place in the most secure sector, the public services. This sector has never been able to secure any significant rationalization, not to say decrease in employment, during a recession period. This ideology still characterizes Israeli IR at present (1989), but it was much stronger during the 1965-77 period covered by the present analysis. Nevertheless, this relationship significantly holds during the Labor era. The second economic variable having a significant relationship with strike frequency during the first period is the measure of capital return. The negative coefficient indicates a constant pressure for increasing labor remuneration. Under stressful economic conditions, when employers were facing a decrease in their profits, they had to wrestle with uncooperative unions that disregarded the economic constraints. Thus, secretary general Ben-Aharon was an ardent initiator of industrial strife. A variable identifying his period reached a significant positive figure. As we can see, of the economic variables, only the real wage change measure (DRWP) became insignificant.

The Likud period is reflected by a different set of indicators. The constant term continues to be significant, but adds little to our understanding of the strike situation. Another significant, but meaningless coefficient is the seasonal measure of the third quartile of the year. One of the real wage change components, the item measuring two months lag is significant, but the real wage change set is insignificant. This single ambiguous finding can easily be disregarded. The total impression is of a phenomenon losing any meaningful relationships with its external constraints. If the frequency of strike can be regarded as an indicator of irs functioning, and if the set of variables incorporated in the present analysis is accepted as representative of the economic and the political arenas, then, the irs of Israel's Likud Party period can be typified as an autonomous social system, its degree of autonomy being significantly higher than that of its predecessor.

The transfer from a Likud dominated administration to a bi-party government had some impact on the coefficient of determination. Still, no one single variable of substantive meaning reaches statistical significance. The autonomy consolidated at the Likud years stays intact.

Conclusion

Three statistical analyses of Israeli strike data for the period starting in 1965 tested the degree of autonomy of the Israeli industrial relations system. My interest in studying this topic was raised by a set of findings indicating that Israeli strike activity has a unique, somewhat puzzling, pattern. This uncertainty stemmed from findings such as the following: strikes tended to act as safety-valves, extending their level of mobilization in times of political dissatisfaction and decreasing when government support was extant (Chermesh, 1977). Strikes were common when they were regarded as harmless, and were avoided in work places which involved a threat to crucial national interests (Chermesh, 1979). There was hardly any correspondence between the intensity of strike activity and the image it had in national newspapers (Chermesh, 1982a). The propensity to strike depended on factors internal to the irs of the target enterprise and not on its economic, political or technological characteristics (Chermesh, 1982b). Last but not least, strikes were not a social problem for their primary actors, management and local unions. They did have a threatening impact on the General Federation of Labor and on the Israeli macro system (Chermesh, 1985). All these finding put the Israeli irs in a unique position, requiring explanation. Luhmann's neofunctionalistic approach is a promising means for answering these puzzling findings.

Luhmann (1982, pp. 232-8), treats societal differentiation as a three phase process. The first, 'segmentation' divides society into *equal* subsystems, the second, 'stratification', divides it into *unequal* hierarchical subsystems and the third, which he regards as the most advanced, is 'functional differentiation', which "organizes communication processes around special functions to be fulfilled at the level of the society." While lower and middle level societies, those differentiated along segmentation or stratification, are dependent on a core of values embodied in a system of beliefs for their integration, this mechanism is no longer necessary in functionally differentiated societies.

Indeed, Luhmann argues, such systems of belief lessen its coping potential with environmental uncertainties. This pure model of functional differentiation may fit the Israeli case to a much lesser degree than Luhmann may imply. Israeli society is young, and its stratification is much less mature (in Luhmann's meaning) than its European counterparts. Still, one major characteristic of stratified societies is very much characteristic of Israel. It is a society which was shaped by an ideology. While this was not the ideology of the bourgeois, it defined the good and the bad, the sacred and the profane. In ideological Israeli terms, an ethos of work was sanctified. This placed work-related organizations at the center of society. The economy, the main context of work, acquired its meaning from the world of work. Productivity became an ultimate value. Profitability was pushed aside. The Histadrut gained its supreme status by being viewed through this prism. During the last decades, processes of deideologization have changed many spheres of action in the economic, as well as in the political realms.

Still, the domain of industrial relations has maintained its distinct status. The sanctity of the strike was shared by all IR actors, management as well as union. The supremacy of collective bargaining on legal consideration was a well established norm. So, both on the basis of its resources and on societal ideology, actors in the irs gained autonomy, an autonomy that could not be tested so long as environmental processes coincided with IR subsystemic ones. The political upheaval unwrapped it from its societal shield and made it into an interesting feature of Israel. It created a situation for its crystallization and consolidation. Says Luhmann,

> In the social dimension the most important condition for autonomy is that the . . . system not see itself faced with a solid power in the environment, but instead depend on several relevant environments.

This condition may explain the paradoxical finding that the Israeli irs gained its highest degree of autonomy during the Likud regime. The sympathetic Labor Party administration confronted the Histadrut leadership with a monolithic environment. The political upheaval of 1977 confronted the Histadrut leadership with two opposing political counterparts, the Likud government and the defeated Labor party apparatus. This political split contributed to the consolidation of an autonomous Israeli irs.

Nevertheless,

> the risk increases dramatically when a . . . system that is becoming autonomous demands that it be given sufficient time to act and total authority on decision making. Such authority can make almost anything possible since there are no longer powerful external controls that can keep decisions within the bounds of the desirable (p. 157).

The findings of this study show a potentially risky situation. It can supply us with few clues, if any, as to the probability of a colossal impending disaster. A reflexive irs can develop autonomous procedures for minimizing risk. It is not clear at all that such mechanisms have evolved in the Israeli case.

Notes to Chapter 6

1. For a former step in the same direction see Chermesh (1984). The present secretary general of the Histadrut, Kessar, is excluded from the present analysis for lack of data.
2. The current secretary general of the Histadrut, Kessar, is excluded from the present analysis for lack of data.
3. No assumption is being made on the "normality" of these periods for any reason other than the one relevant for the present analysis—maximum subjective distance from both past and forthcoming elections. The term subjective is added so as to take care of the fact that the highest probability for a maximum time distance both from the last and from the forthcoming elections occurs two years after a given election takes place. Even if ex post factum a Knesset is terminated after less than its four years term, this cannot be assumed in advance.
4. The choice of 100 days as a unit of standardized is only for clarity of report. Any other basis for standardization would have brought identical results in the log-linear analysis. The present paper does not deal with a second form of autonomy, the degree of independence of a given irs from its environmental constraints. For a detailed treatment of this issue see Chermesh(1982). I would like to thank Moshe Hartman for introducing me to the log-linear approach.
5. The present analysis does not deal with a second form of autonomy, the degree of independence of a given irs from its environmental constraints. For a detailed treatment of this issue see Chermesh (1982).
6. The term "political upheaval" is reserved in Israeli political and journalistic slang for the May 1977 Knesset elections. The elections results were traumatic enough to deserve this unique term!
7. The Manufacturers' Association of Israel was actually established as early as 1920. The Coordinating Bureau of Economic Associations, the framework which serves as a representative body for the private sector employers, was set up in 1967. However, neither of these bodies managed to acquire a significant posture until the 1970s.

7

Strikes as Social Problems: A Social Problem Matrix Approach

Introduction

Labor unrest is commonly regarded as a cause for social concern (de Boer, 1977; Chermesh, 1982; Estey, 1976, p. 113; Royal Commission, 1968 Shorter and Tilly, 1974). In order to clarify the issue of social concern at least three key questions must be asked:

(1) Who are concerned about labor unrest? Who are unconcerned?

(2) Why are some concerned and others unconcerned?

(3) How, if at all, can such concern be mitigated?

A tentative response to all three questions will be presented below, based on a social problem matrix approach that derives from the treatment of social problems by Merton and Nisbet (1971, 1976). The diagnosis and the prognosis will be limited to a specific period of time (the years between the Yom Kippur War, 1973, and the establishment of a Likud government, 1977). This particular choice stems in part from the availability of relevant data. The approach, however, is proposed as a general method for analyzing the range of issues identified as social problems by Merton and Nisbet.

> A social problem is a perceived discrepancy between what is and what people think ought to be—between actual conditions and social values and norms—which is regarded as remediable. (1976, p. 40)

This approach identifies "an objective aspect of a social problem; this is the way of behavior itself" and "also a subjective aspect" (Merton and Nisbet, 1971, p. 1). Subjective analysis of social problems (Spector and Kitsuse, 1973; Kitsuse and Spector, 1975; Becker, 1967) explain which solutions are apt to be selected and the degree to which resources are mobilized for this purpose.

A social problem may be treated as a potential social dysfunction, i.e., "a designated set of consequences of a designated pattern of behavior, belief, or organization that interferes with a designated functional requirement of a designated social system" (Merton and Nisbet, 1976, p. 37). Dysfunctional consequences can be researched and identified at both the overall and the sectorial levels. Specific subgroups may be affected differently by a given issue. Frequently, "one group's problem [is] another group's solution" (p. 9).

A macro-social diagnosis should be included in this matrix. The total social system can be treated, as Parsons has suggested, by confronting values with the objective realities. A more restricted approach can be used by treating the government as the system's specialized organ of goal attainment, i.e., as the body charged with the responsibility of establishing priorities among system goals and mobilizing system resources for their attainment on behalf of society at large.

The inclusion of both sectorial and comprehensive units of reference can be regarded as a means of linking the *two faces of society* approaches, the consensus and conflict perspectives, into a single body of analysis. This procedure tests the utility of each perspective.

THE SOCIAL PROBLEM MATRIX

A complete matrix should include a set of five columns, and a limited number of rows. The columns should present (1) a set of principal values or norms (2) a relevant description of reality (relevant in terms of the desired (value) or expected (norm) set of standards), (3) some indication of the existence or absence of a significant discrepancy between reality and its advocated qualities, (4) a statement on the degree to which a solution to an extant gap is available to the relevant party, and (5) a claim for the existence or nonexistence of a social problem for each of the relevant actors (given in the rows of the matrix).

The rows of the social problem matrix present a list of the major social units which are either active producers of a specific cultural item of interest or are exposed to its effects. A theory, if available, can facilitate the choice of relevant units and simplify the construction of the matrix.

The item of interest for the present analysis is, of course, the strike. The relevant units for inclusion in the matrix are derived from Dunlop's (1958) theory of industrial relations systems, discussed in previous chapters. We recall that,

> The actors in a system. . .are (1) a hierarchy of managers and their representatives in supervision, (2) a hierarchy of workers (non-managerial) and any of their spokesmen, and (3) specialized governmental agencies (and specialized private agencies created by the first two actors) concerned with workers, enterprises, and their relationships. (p. 7)

A strike may be declared, negotiated and ended on *at least* two levels of the industrial relations arena, the national and the local. Therefore, at least six[1] relevant actors should be included in the matrix, three for the local level and three for the national level. Both suppliers and consumers, whether in direct or indirect relationships with a struck unit (Chamberlain and Schilling, 1954, p. 39) can be added to the list, so as to arrive at a more comprehensive list of actors. Finally, the macro-social, or governmental level should not be omitted.

This chapter is structured as follows: the second section offers a schematic presentation of the Israeli industrial relations system; the third section describes the strike phenomena in Israel, while the fourth provides a sequential analysis of the implications of strikes on the national and local level actors within this irs. Section five is a macro-social analysis of strikes as social problems, focusing on the effects of strikes on the functioning of Israeli society. The final section sums up the analysis in the condensed format of a social problem matrix.

The Israeli irs

Chapter 2 described in detail the national level of the Israeli irs. Therefore, even though I will discuss national level implications of strikes, there is little room for further elaboration at this point. The situation on the local level, that of the actual sites of work, does require a more detailed description.

THE LOCAL LEVEL

Two main actors take part in the industrial relations process at the local level—management and the workers' committee. They are assisted sporadically, and mostly on their own initiative, by various third parties, such as the Regional branches of the labor court, the Regional Commissioners of Industrial Relations and the upper echelon functionaries of the Histadrut.

Local management

The local management group is the least studied actor in the Israeli industrial relations system. Scattered evidence (Vardi et al., 1980) indicates their resemblance to western type managers. Living in an environment as unstable and unpredictable as Israel encourages the notion that management is, above all, creative improvisation (Zald, 1978, p. 38). This being so, management has need of wide authority. Such authority may be vertically restricted in two ways, in relation to the owners and higher level management, and to worker representation. Column (1) of Table 7.1 presents local management's perceptions of the degree of authority bestowed on it during contract negotiations.

More than half of the managers (56.1 per cent) consider that they wield authority (i.e., they see themselves as limited only by general policy or guidelines), while a quarter (24.4 per cent) state that they lack decision taking powers, and a fifth (19.5 per cent) acknowledge very limited negotiation leeway. Table 7.2, on the other hand, shows that the local union has a much lower evaluation of managerial authority.

Table 7.1: Degree of authority granted to local managements and local unions (self-descriptions).[*]

	ACTORS	
Degree of Authority	Management	Union
	(1)	(2)
Discretion limited by general policy	24.4	15.6
Discretion limited by general guidelines	31.7	20.0
Discretion limited by specific guidelines	19.5	20.0
No final discretion	24.4	44.4
Total	100.0	100.0
n	(41)	(45)

*All interviews were done before, during or following strikes or strike threats.
For details see Chermesh (1982).

Table 7.2: Degree of authority imputed to local managements and local unions (counterpart descriptions).[*]

	Authority Imputed	
Degree of Authority	by Management to Union	by Union to Management
	(1)	(2)
Discretion limited by general policy	7.7	22.5
Discretion limited by general guidelines	28.2	17.5
Discretion limited by specific guidelines	17.9	17.5
No final discretion	46.2	42.5
Total	100.0	100.0
n	(40)	(39)

*All interviews were done before, during or following strikes or strike threats.
For details see Chermesh (1982).

In almost half the cases (46.2 per cent), the local union believes that management requires prior approval for any offer it tries to make. The gap between the self descriptions of managerial authority and the image imputed to it by labor, differs by ownership sector. For example, the percentage difference between the 'no final discretion' categories is the widest in the Histadrut owned (67 per cent) sector, second in public ownership enterprises (34 per cent), and practically nonexistent in private sector firms (8 percent).[2]

While some issues (e.g., changes of basic rates of pay) are traditionally negotiated in Israel on the national level, and others (e.g., the appointment of senior managers) are decided outside of a given local organization, most managers interviewed reported that a very high percentage of administrative, remunerative and policy-related issues are decided internally. The accord between management and local union on this topic is significant ($r = .71$). But here, once again, the situation differs by ownership sector. While managers in private and Histadrut owned enterprises profess that a very high percentage (87.6 and 91.2 per cent respectively) of the managerial subjects are determined under their auspices, public sector managers report a lower figure (71.4 per cent).[3]

The local union's involvement in management can be gauged on two levels of intensity. On one hand, the union can take part in organizational decisions and adopt a de-facto participative managerial style. Labor representation may, on another level, not be required to share in decision-making, but at least serve as an instrument for disseminating information. In the first mode we find that between 22 per cent (according to management responses) and 26 per cent (according to labor responses) of the issues mentioned above are co-decided by management and the union. At the less intensive level a greater degree of involvement in decisions is observed. Workers' committees are found to share in the decision making process, participate in discussions, voice their views or receive information on two thirds of a wide ranging list of topics.[4]

There is additional evidence of the sensitivity of managers to union involvement in managerial activity. Managers of private and public industrial enterprises were interviewed by Aharoni and Lachman (1982) and were asked about the influence exerted by certain environmental elements on their freedom to make decisions, and about the desired level of influence of these elements. Local unions and the Histadrut were not highly graded on either list (pp. 41-42). However, when the gap between desired and expected levels of influence of the various elements is measured, workers' committees are regarded as having the highest level of influence on the public owned organizations and the Histadrut is ranked third by private sector managers.

Thus, if a generalization can be drawn from our sources, it is that Israeli local management has a relatively high level of autonomy *vis-à-vis* external agencies, while sharing managerial responsibilities with its counterpart, the local workers' committee. This sharing is regarded by management as usurpation of its authority.

The local union

Workers' representation on the enterprise level in Israel is accomplished through workers' committees. An organization may have only a single committee, representing all its employees, or as many as several dozen speaking for specialized segments of a large and diversified place of work. The workers' committee has a unique status in the Histadrut hierarchy. It is the only unit that can claim direct representation as its source of legitimacy. All other Histadrut functionaries are either elected through party line channels or appointed as salaried workers in the union's bureaucracy. The local union is the absolute exemplification of the direct representation principle. All salaried employees, whether Histadrut members or not, are eligible to vote and to be elected to any committee positions. Thus, the fact that the committee serves as the extension of the Histadrut on the local level may sometimes interfere with the representation of constituency interests.

This contradiction between a committee's loyalty to the union organization and to its own rank-and-file led Friedman to treat workers' committees as a prototype of an economic union. An economic union, according to Friedman, is oriented to the short range and is interested primarily in gaining more for its members, restricting its perspective to its own particular membership. Referring ahead to column 1 of Table 7.6, we find that local union leadership is the actor least inclined to treat the issue of harmony in labor relations as a value in itself. The norms of the industrial relations process are regarded by the stewards as a convenient means for enhancing their members' interests. Expediency, rather than ideology, explains their support of the system.

The workers' local leaders do not perceive themselves as independent and authoritative. Forty-four per cent of our union respondents admitted having no discretion during contract negotiations (Table 7.1, Column 2). This view of their authority is shared by management (Table 7.2, Column 2). Workers' committee members succeeded nonetheless in translating the burden of high accountability into an asset. Through conceding that they had no mandate, they were able to promote their demands.

Appropriation of managerial prerogatives is a common phenomenon in Israeli organizations. We have seen above that local unions share decision making privileges on 22 to 26 per cent of the major issues and on a much higher proportion of topics are at least kept informed. They are thus effectively powerful agents of local interests though lacking formal constitutional authority to fulfill such a role.

Strikes in Israel

The description of both national and local level industrial relations system actors in the preceding sections was deliberately selective. The data presented so far are intended to serve as background information enabling us to answer a single question: are strikes a social problem for these actors?

Table 7.3 shows the ranking of sixteen industrialized countries along five measures commonly used in the analysis of strikes. This list was selected by the Israeli Institute for the advancement of Labor Relations for their

International Comparisons between 16 Industrialized Developed Countries (Gilday, 1980).

> The choice of countries was made on the assumption that Israel is an industrialized developed country, having an industrial relations system comparable to those of other developed countries. (p. 9)

International Labor Office (ILO) data were used for all but Israeli statistics. Data for Israel were provided by official Israelis sources.

The raw figures for the years 1974-76 were transformed into five standardized strike measures. Columns 1, 2 and 3 of Table 7.3 present the three elementary dimensions of the strike patterns of the various countries. (Shorter and Tilly, 1974; Britt and Galle, 1974). The Israeli strike pattern in comparison with that of other countries, displays relatively moderate frequency, large size and short duration. However, if we scrutinize the raw figures, we find that rank-ordering of countries overemphasizes the relative broadness of Israeli strikes, and understates their relatively short duration.

Italy is ranked immediately above Israel in size of strikes, even though the average number of participants in an Italian strike is more than three fold that of its Israeli counterpart (2,947 vs. 805). Denmark on the other hand ranks eighth to Israel's fourteenth even though it is similar in size (599). Strike duration exhibits distortion in the opposite direction. There is almost no difference between the first ranking country (Switzerland—1.70 days) and Israel (fifth—2.09 days). Thus, the Israeli strike pattern can be typified as having medium frequency, medium size and short duration. The extensivity (column 4) and cost measures (column 5) place Israel in the middle rank of the international order.

Settlement of Labor Disputes (1958) and the Histadrut bylaws, only the Histadrut's Trade Union Division, its National Unions, or its Local Workers' Councils have the authority to approve a strike. Unapproved, (i.e., wildcat) strikes are therefore mostly organized and led by local workers' committees.

Almost half (48 per cent) of Israeli strikes are not aimed directly at immediate fulfillment of specific demands. Indeed, such strikes mostly take the form of 'workers' meetings', held during working hours. They may be regarded as part of an accepted protocol (Reder and Neumann, 1980), signalling the local union's dissatisfaction with the effectiveness and efficiency of the negotiation process.[5]

The effectiveness of strikes can be measured by the degree to which they result in employer acceptance of the strikers' demands.

As can be inferred from Table 7.4, all demands were accepted in more than a quarter of Israeli strikes (28.7 per cent), and partially accepted in another third (33.7 per cent). In more than a third of the stoppages (37.6 per cent) all the demands were turned down.

Table 7.3: Strike activity levels rank order of 16 countries (Averages
for 1974-76).

Rank	F/SW (1) (few)	Bbar (2) (small)	Dbar (3) (short)	B/SW (4) (narrow)	MDI/SW (5) (low costs)
1	Switzerland	Switzerland	France	Switzerland	Switzerland
2	Norway	Finland	Denmark	Sweden	W. Germany
3	Sweden	Sweden	Finland	W. Germany	Sweden
4	U.S.A.	N. Zealand	Italy	Norway	Denmark
5	Belgium	Belgium	**ISRAEL**	Belgium	Norway
6	Denmark	U.S.A.	Australia	U.S.A.	Japan
7	Japan	U.K.	N. Zealand	Denmark	Belgium
8	U.K.	Denmark	Japan	U.K.	**ISRAEL**
9	**ISRAEL**	France	W. Germany	Japan	France
10	Canada	Japan	U.K.	**ISRAEL**	N. Zealand
11	France	Norway	Switzerland	Canada	Finland
12	Italy	Australia	Belgium	N. Zealand	U.K.
13	N. Zealand	Canada	Sweden	France	U.S.A.
14	Australia	**ISRAEL**	Norway	Finland	Australia
15	Finland	Italy	Canada	Australia	Canada
16	a (many)	a (large)	U.S.A. (long)	Italy (broad)	Italy (costly)

Legend
F   – The number of strikes;   B – The number of strikers;
MDI   – The number of man-days idle;   SW – The number of salaried workers in 199,000s;
F/SW – The number of strikes per 100,000 salaried workers;
Bbar   – The average strike size (B/F);   Dbar – The average strike duration (MDI/B);
B/SW – The number of strikers per 100,000 salaried workers;
MDI/SW – The number of man-days idle per 100,000 salaried workers.
a   – Frequency of strikes figures for West Germany are unavailable.

Table 7.4 presents the detailed strike pattern figures for Israeli strikes of
various degrees of success by their approval status. Approved strikes are more
successful than non-approved strikes. Similar results are reported for the
years 1960-69 by Michael and Bar-El (1977, p. 226). The Histadrut's power and
authority are clearly a possible explanation for this finding.

Strikes which ended in partial satisfaction of unions' demands were larger
than both completely successful and completely unsuccessful strikes.
Histadrut backing, though, was instrumental in cutting the length of partially
successful strikes. When approved, they lasted on average 3.8 days, while the
length of partially successful, wildcat strikes, was 5.5 days.

Table 7.4: Strikes in Israel by approval status and the degree of success
(Average for 1974-77).

Degree of Success	Frequency – %		Average Strike Size		Average Duration	
	Official	Wildcat	Official	Wildcat	Official	Wildcat
All demands accepted	44.1	21.0	206	619	6.0	2.3
Demands partially accepted	35.6	32.8	1,959	835	3.8	5.5
Demands not accepted	20.3	46.2	112	510	8.1	3.5
Total demand-related strikes	100.0	100.0	810	635	4.2	4.1
Total non-demand related strikes	49.1[1]	47.3[2]	2,652	1,378	0.7	1.2
Total Israeli strikes	33.9[3]	66.1[4]	1,715	987	1.6	2.2

1 – % of total official strikes   2 – % of total non-official strikes
3 – % of total strikes   4 – % of total strikes

Local unions, on the other hand, are more skillful in assessing the prospects of complete success or complete defeat, and they do so much faster than the leaders of official strikes. Thus, the duration of approved-successful strikes is 6.0 days, while that of unapproved-successful strikes is 2.3 days; approved-defeated strikes are longer (8.1 days) than unapproved-defeated strikes (3.5). We may conclude, therefore, that leaders of wildcat strikes are effective both in maximizing benefits and in minimizing costs. They are less effective, though, in mixed outcome situations. On the other hand, the Histadrut is at its best with large strikes involving complicated negotiations.

Two clear clusters of industrial strike patterns can be distinguished, one pertaining to public utilities (water and electricity, transportation and public services) and the other to market related industries (manufacture, commerce and personal services). The public utilities sector displays a moderately high, broad, and short strike pattern, while the market-related industries exhibit a medium frequency, medium breadth, medium duration pattern. This distinction will be referred to below in our discussion of the social problem matrix of strikes.

Table 7.5 presents further information regarding the propensity to strike of wage earners in various industrial categories.

Table 7.5: Strike activity by economic branch (Average for 1974-77).[1]

Economic Branch	F/SW (1)	Bbar (2)	Dbar (3)	B/SW (4)	MDI/SW (5)
Agriculture	5.5	53	2.8	291	809
Manufacture	12.2	241	5.2	2,929	15,300
Electricity & Water	11.5	1,354	1.2	15,603	18,053
Construction	1.9	435	2.4	806	1,957
Commerce	5.6	214	3.1	1,198	3,679
Transporta- tion	50.7	569	1.8	28,844	53,165
Finance	11.3	2,539	2.0	28,739	58,348
Public Services	11.2	1,687	2.0	18,825	36,991
Private Services	8.6	142	2.7	1,214	3,289
Total	12.7	922	2.2	11,676	25,481

[1] For legend see Table 7.3.

A final note is due with reference to the damage caused by strikes in Israel. Michael and Bar-El's (1977) cost estimation, cited earlier, refers to the objective aspect of strike damage, and to a specific part of it. Subjective evaluations are of no less importance. Chermesh (1979) sums up the views of managers and labor representatives in organizations which have experienced strikes or strike threats in these words:

> The damage incurred by strikes to various social categories is regarded by union and management both as small and in a decreasing trend. Nowhere was a category [including owners, management workers' representation, strike involved workers, uninvolved workers, clients, suppliers, and the public] labelled as very vulnerable to a given strike's harm. In cases of some damage, time perspective [meaning response immediately after the strike was over or three months later] indicates less need for responsibility (p. 344).

The behavioral implications of this finding become more explicit when strike-prone organizations are compared with units exhibiting low propensity to strike (Chermesh, 1982). There it was found that "an organization with a low propensity to strike can be identified by...[the fact that]...the damage incurred by a strike [in the reference unit] is perceived to be high" (p. 427). This conviction is shared by both management and labor representative in the enterprises under study.

Strikes in Israel—A Social Problem Matrix Analysis

LOCAL MANAGEMENT

Three main normative considerations can be pinpointed for a discussion of local management. Although not be the only values, they seem the most relevant ones for the current analysis. Local management treats harmony of industrial relations as an important value, and it is keen to promote authority, certainty and predictability. The research of Galin-Goldfarb (1972, p. 180) has led to some interesting findings regarding the differential attitudes of local managers and employees' committee members toward labor relations. Attitudes toward labor relations were measured by Galin-Goldfarb in terms of answers to the following question:

> An important issue which you raised during negotiations was blocked by the other side. If you use pressure you may win your demand. But, the mere initiation of pressure will bring about a significant deterioration in labor relations. When would you favor the initiation of pressure? (1) We would initiate pressure if the probability of gaining our entire set of demands was 100, 90, 75, 50, 25, or 10 per cent. (2) In principle, we would never initiate pressure if this might jeopardize labor relations.

Table 7.6 shows the distribution of responses by level and actor. As can be seen, fifty-six per cent of the local managers, as compared with twenty-three per cent of the shop stewards, attach principled importance to labor relations. The value related meaning of this belief must be emphasized.

On their own testimony, at least, non-expedient factors motivate the majority of local managers to withdraw their demands only because of their undesired implications for labor relations. Calculative considerations may lead another group of managers (30 per cent) to avoid increasing pressure.

Strikes create an unfavorable challenge to the local managerial group, disrupting the harmony of industrial relations. They also have a complex impact on management's authority value. On the one hand, they raise the importance of negotiation principles above norms of compliance, thereby impinging on the value of authority. On the other hand, in a situation of usurped authority they establish a clear distinction between the two parties. While workers' committees are a quasi-latent partner in day-to-day management, a strike endows managers with an ultimate managerial capacity.

Table 7.6: Attitude toward industrial relations by level and actor.

Level/ Actor	Harmony of Labor Relations[1]				
	Principled Importance (1)	High Importance (2)	Medium Importance (3)	Low Importance (4)	% (5)
LOCAL Management	56	30	10	4	100
Labor	23	47	25	5	100
NATIONAL Management	72	18	10	0	100
Labor	29	50	21	0	100

Source: Galin-Goldfarb, 1972, p. 180.

[1] Legend: Probability of winning: high – 90-100; medium – 50- 75; low – 10- 25.

Local managements may be expected to be eager to prevent external involvement during strikes. Such boundary defense can be motivated by considerations of all three basic values. If the harmony of internal industrial relations is a meaningful concept for the management, then it has to be reconciled with the need for managerial authority. External interference, whether in terms of government action or Histadrut mediation, implies a lessening of managerial authority and hence becomes a threat to the freedom of managerial action. Requests by senior managers for assistance from outside the organization are an admission of failure. Finally, organizations prefer to deal with uncertainty through boundary specialization rather than through border evasion methods. Any external intervention, particularly if it is augmented by official legal authority, carries the threat of disrupting the internal power structure of local management. Informal and tactful assistance may be welcome, however. If so, this may explain the inclination of industrial relations commissioners to display a low profile as well as to avoid any reference to their compulsory privileges as specified by law.[6]

Thus, the social problem matrix for local management indicates that strikes create a significant gap between the three values of harmony of industrial relations, authority, and predictability on the one hand, and the reality they encounter on the other. It is doubtful, however, if this situation can be remedied, given local management's own normative considerations, which impede any initiative for change. No unilateral change can be initiated in a conflictual situation without a readiness to take risks. As will be shown in the next section, the labor counterparts of local management show no inclination to initiate change, and the managers' concern with harmony of industrial relations leads them to perceive the situation as non-remediable. Therefore, management is satisfied with its perception that the costs of strikes is negligible. If strikes are almost damageless, then they do not justify a normatively costly remedy. Strikes are therefore not regarded as a social problem by local management in Israel.

LOCAL LABOR REPRESENTATION—THE WORKERS' COMMITTEE

As noted above, workers' committees, as economic unions (Friedman, A. (1972), advocate a *more and now* ideology. Their leaders see themselves as promoting the particular interests of their rank-and-file. Of the various categories of actors they display the least belief in the importance of industrial relations (Table 6, column 1). Only twenty-three per cent of the local representatives of labor, as compared with fifty-six percent of the local managers, believe in harmony of industrial relations *per se*. Almost half of them (47 per cent) express readiness to disrupt industrial relations whenever a high probability of success can be anticipated.

Thus, the standard criterion by which strikes are evaluated by workers' committee members is their balance between costs and benefits. They do not perceive this balance as discouraging. In almost half of Israeli strikes, concessions by management are not directly demanded. Most of these strikes are symbolic gestures aimed at facilitating collective negotiations. No direct measure of their effectiveness is available, but whether successful or not, their costs are low, as indicated by their very short duration. These non-demand related strikes may be regarded by shop stewards as an unwelcome symptom of an ailing and ineffective industrial relations system. They are not, however, deemed negative in themselves.

On the other hand, instrumental strikes can be evaluated not only by their costs, but by their results as well. More than three-quarters of the official strikes have results beneficial to the employees. Therefore, workers' committee leaders can be expected to support almost any stoppage approved by the Histadrut. They may be more hesitant in initiating an unofficial strike. Still, while failures are always deplored, they can hardly be regarded as costly for labor representatives on the local level. When they are the losers in official strikes, they have a respectable partner—the Histadrut—with whom to share the blame and when unapproved strikes fail they can console their rank-and-file by emphasizing their own high level of strike management skill. After all, unsuccessful non-approved strikes last, on the average, only three and a half days while unsuccessful approved strikes last more than eight days! Strikes are not, therefore, a social problem as far as the workers' committee members are concerned, since they do not impinge on any of their primary value tenets.

NATIONAL LABOR REPRESENTATION—THE HISTADRUT

The Histadrut, following Friedman's (1972) typology, is a political union "concerned with the needs of the state and the economy more than it is concerned with the needs of the workers" (p. XVI). Its official title indicates its ideology. It is the General Federation of Labor, and general, rather than particular interests take precedence. Responsibility is a major principle. As a nationwide federation, encompassing a wide range of occupations and activities, the Histadrut highly values stability. The fact that it is independent of governmental regulation is also highly valued. Stability and responsibility are regarded as the best guarantees for the preservation of its autonomy.

The Histadrut's non-particularistic ideology can be discerned indirectly from the study by Aharoni and his associates, *'Performance and Autonomy in Organizations: Determining Dominant Environmental Components'* (1978). These researchers found that

> while increase in export increases dependence on the employees and the plant union, the opposite is true for the other two bodies of workers' representatives [The General Federation of Labor and the Local Council of the Histadrut].

They explain this finding by saying

> this is probably so because the latter are much more sensitive to macro-level considerations than the former, and export is a highly valuable national goal in Israel' (p. 955).

The Histadrut's reluctance to approve strikes is also an indicator of its interest in generality, responsibility and stability. The Histadrut has a particular stake in the preservation of industrial harmony. Most strikes represent sectoral interests. Some of these interests are in line with the policy of the Federation, for example, equality of rights for male and female workers, and the improvement of work conditions of production workers. The majority of these claims, however, threaten the internal balance of the trade union movement by disrupting institutionalized wage and work conditions, differentials and relativities.

The Histadrut is a master employer as well as a trade union. Almost twenty per cent of the Israeli civilian labor force is employed in Histadrut-owned concerns. Thus, it has an added interest in stability and self-restraint.

The aspirations of the Histadrut leadership can be expected to be frustrated by the state of the industrial relations arena. The majority of the stoppages in Israel are wildcat strikes (66.1 per cent). Most of these unapproved strikes are concentrated in those Israeli industries which are the most exposed to public criticism, e.g. public services, and in the most sensitive part of it, the publicly owned sector.

The Histadrut's sense of responsibility can be gauged by examination of its policy toward the alternative to the conventional strike—the use of work sanctions. Such actions take many forms, the most popular of which are refusal to work overtime, nights or weekends, slowdowns, refusal to perform assignments and the like. These sanctions occur mostly at the plant level, thus bypassing formal union channels. Wilkinson and Cohen (1982) explain the Histadrut's reluctance to approve such work protests as resulting from its "awareness that sanctions strongly destabilize labor relations" (p. 232).

There is an evident gap between industrial reality and Histadrut's values. The question is whether it can be bridged? Paradoxically, the Histadrut's major status in Israel both limits the available options for ameliorating the situation and opens up the path to possible solutions. None of the Federation's core values can be maintained in a situation where the Histadrut forfeits its almost monopolistic authority in the labor relations arena. Thus, legal reforms that intensify the involvement of the government and of the judicial organs in labor disputes are significant threats to the Histadrut. Such strike remedies may throw the baby out with the bath water as far as the national level of labor representation is concerned. Therefore, the leadership of the Histadrut had continuously opposed and successfully blocked any efforts to establish compulsory arbitration in Israel.

However, the Histadrut has supported the issuing of temporary back-to-work orders by the government in cases of national emergencies, as well as the establishment of a strike insurance fund by the private employers' associations. Strange as it may seem, such support has been aimed at establishing a power balance between local employers and local workers' committees. Such a balance deters local workers' representation from initiating wildcat strikes and enhances the need for the intervention of a national level union in local disputes.

Remedies for the strike situation can be sought through the increased participation of local labor leaders in the Histadrut, a policy that has been adopted, albeit reluctantly, by the Histadrut's political leadership in recent years. A complete upheaval could destroy the generality of the Histadrut, while total evasion of pressure from below might render it ineffectual and vulnerable to eventual disintegration.

Strikes are therefore a social problem as far as the Histadrut is concerned. A gap exists between its ideology and the reality it faces. This gap is remediable, but the means must be selected carefully

NATIONAL MANAGEMENT REPRESENTATION—EMPLOYERS' ASSOCIATIONS

Little can be said regarding the values and norms of management representatives at the national level as only minimal research has been done in this field.

As can be seen in Table 7.6, national management functionaries are the group with the highest concern for the principle of harmony. Almost three quarters of the respondents in Galin-Goldfarb's (1972) study identify with the principle of avoiding actions that would jeopardize labor. This indicates a significant sensitivity to strikes in general, and to wildcat strikes in particular. Officials of employers' associations in the private sector do not face the pressures exerted on Histadrut leaders to represent general interests. They represent a particularistic interest set and as such are not exposed to rank-and-file opposition. They may not be as sensitive as local management to organizational autonomy, but nevertheless, they may lack motivation to oppose the ideologies of their local members. Therefore, their dilemma may be insoluble.[7]

THIRD PARTIES

Three actors serve as third parties in the Israeli irs: the Labor Court, The Department of Labor Relations in the Labor and Welfare Ministry, and various Histadrut units. Since the status of the Histadrut has already been discussed at length, the present section will deal only with the two specialized agencies.

The Labor Court and the Department of Labor Relations share the basic value of the Israeli irs autonomy. Industrial relations are regarded by both agencies as primarily the concern of management and labor. This belief was only half-heartedly shared by the politicians who designed these two organs

THE DEPARTMENT OF LABOR RELATIONS

The Department of Labor Relations is a unit in the Ministry of Labor and Welfare. Its code of ethics can be described on the basis of two partially supportive sources, the law and the belief of its officials. The legal source of its authority is the Settlement of Labor Disputes Law (1957). The law reflects the intentions and normative conceptions of the legislative and the executive branches. The Labor Relations Officer was granted significant, albeit restricted, authority. A required fifteen days advance notice of an intention to strike is stipulated, so as to ensure the Department's awareness of approaching labor disputes. During this fifteen-day period, the official is empowered to compel the parties to attend meetings he convenes. He may request relevant evidence, interrogate the parties, direct them to supply information, and even fine them for failing to comply with his directives. This authority is restricted in time and is not complemented by the power to enforce his rulings. Thus, a value of state supremacy can be inferred from the letter of the law.

The values of the Department's staff are more significant for the present discussion than those of the politicians. A fully conformist Department would adopt the ideas of state supremacy and would try to put them into practice. When faced with an uncooperative counterpart, whether management or labor, it might serve as an agent for changing the industrial relations system. A nonconformist Department of Labor Relations, on the other hand, would act differently.

As described above, the staff of the Department is empowered to impose compulsory mediation services on the parties in conflict. But "none of the mediators interviewed could recall an instance in which a party had been forced to participate" (Galin, 1979, p. 491). This 'soft' approach can be seen in the annual reports of the Department. Three main methods were used, mediation, arbitration and encouragement of direct negotiations. Most reported activities of the Department, are recorded as either mediation (between 43 and 70 per cent of the collective labor disputes dealt with in any given year between 1974 and 1978), or assistance in, or conducting of, direct negotiations between the parties involved in a dispute (between 10 and 28 percent). Between six and thirteen per cent of the reported cases were dealt with by arbitration on a voluntary basis.

Voluntarism and a conception of their task as facilitation of agreement are espoused by the mediators. In such a context, gaining the cooperation of the parties takes precedence over the economic, political or social effects of strike activity. The reputation of the Department as a discrete helper, ready to serve but reluctant to impose itself, enhances the willingness to cooperate. The Labor Relations Officer is regarded by both management and union as a congenial partner, available when needed, but secondary in importance. Thus, there seem to be no gap between what is and what the Department thinks its role ought to be. Strikes and strike threats are its bread and butter. The endurance of strikes ensures its functionality. A radical modification of their pattern would require a fundamental revision of the Department's ideology and conception of reality. Such a development is unlikely given the present analysis.

THE LABOR COURT

The Labor Court Law (1969) defines the functions and the authority of the Labor Court. As elaborated in Ben-Israel (1978, p. 225), the Labor Court was established in Israel for the purpose of: (1) centralizing the processes of employment related legal claims; (2) enhancing the expertise of a specialized legal staff; (3) increasing the efficiency of this specialized legal service; and (4) encouraging recourse of management and unions to courts instead of to strikes. These four objectives are directed toward external, Labor Court related and internal, industrial relations.

Both centralization and claims to expertise imply a claim to a specialized domain. The legal establishment can easily accept specialization based on technical considerations. Criminal, civil, real estate, tax, corporate or individual legal activities have all become formally codified professions. Each treats legal rights in a specialized context. Labor law, and particularly collective labor law, deals with a reality which is dominated by power considerations. The consent of the parties, rather than the authority of the state, is its ultimate source of order. Thus, the external front of the Labor Court is the legal profession. The issue under debate is the Court's claim to autonomy.

This same situation is inverted in the internal arena. The Court cannot expect to be the dominant factor in the search for accord. It must adopt a subsidiary position. The Labor Court Law (1969) envisions this situation. The nomination procedure for a Labor Court judge is very similar to that for all other judges. A candidate for a judicial position in the Court must be qualified for nomination as a judge according to the criteria stipulated in the Judges Law (1953). This provision, which is needed to ensure the status of the Labor Court in the legal community, opens the way for a claim of particularity. A team of three people serve on the bench of the Court, a judge and two public delegates, one representing management and the other representing the union. This composition symbolizes the dualistic ideology of the court— responsiveness and autonomy. The three members of the judicial team bring to the court both legal expertise and work-related experience. These qualities are deemed essential for achieving accord with the disputed parties.

> The legislature believed that the establishment of the labor courts would serve as an impetus for improving labor relations by bringing about a change in the attitude of the employees' organizations toward the judicial process. (Ben-Israel, 1978, p. 226)

This message was adopted by the court which acknowledged that "injunctions cannot replace negotiations. The appearance of the parties in court opened the way for the return to the bargaining table" (Ben-Israel, 1978, p. 237). Therefore, the law gave the Court no right to initiate an action before, during, or after a dispute. The only actors who are allowed to take such an initiative are the representative organizations who signed a given agreement, i.e., the Histadrut and the related management. Even when an approved single actor demands court action, the Court was found to be reluctant to act. "Of the 137 requests for injunctions, the court agreed to issue only 31" (Ben-Israel, 1978, p. 237).

Thus, the Labor Court claims a very specific territory—the domain of disputes which are willingly remanded to it by the representative organizations of labor and management. In the context of this abridged domain, the court can claim significant success. Twenty-eight of the thirty-one injunctions issued were complied with by the affected side. Therefore, a specific segment of Israeli industrial strife was appropriated by the Court as its domain. As far as this part is concerned, none of the values of particularity, responsiveness or autonomy were threatened. In the absence of a significant discrepancy between reality and ideology, strikes are not a social problem for the Labor Court.

Strikes in Israel—A Macro Social Analysis

The macro-social characteristics of Israeli strikes are presented in Tables 7.3, 7.4 and 7.5. Their impact on Israeli society and the probability of their being selected and defined as macro-social problems require further discussion. A macrsocial problem matrix analysis poses formidable problems. In order to ascertain whether strikes are a macro-social problem, we require specific information on each and every cell of the matrix. Particular data for a case study like the present, should preferably be gathered and analyzed within a comparative research design. Such data are not available to the present author. A more or less opposite approach, use of the most generalized frame of reference such as Parsons' generalized media of exchange[8] is tempting. This option, however, does not attain the specificity that is desired. Nevertheless, it may be useful as a frame of reference for future research.

The Parsonian scheme depicts a four cell functional structure including, on the social system level, the following four subsystems: the economy (A); the polity (G); the normative-integrative system (I); and the legitimating social order (L). Parsons identifies four separate value principles, one for each subsystem: utility for the economy; effectiveness for the polity; solidarity for the integrative; and integrity for the legitimation. If we treat the maximization of all four principles as the ultimate values of society, we can explore the impact of a given social act (e.g., strikes), on the accomplishment of the various goals.

Beginning with the value of utility for the subsystem of the economy, the disutility of strikes can be measured by the degree to which they hinder the production of societal products. If we treat Michael and Bar-El's figure of 0.046 per cent of the value of the local product lost because of strikes as a rough approximation of the costs, then strikes are not a real economic problem.

The evaluation of the impact of strikes on the level of effectiveness of the Israeli system is more complicated. Strikes may be regarded as an institutionalized channel for conflict behavior. As such they are a legitimate social activity, to be regarded as a given factor in the context of a particular society. Not all strikes are, however, institutionalized action. Wildcat strikes come the closest to the uninstitutionalized type. The preponderance of unofficial strikes (66.1 per cent) is an indication of authority evasion, i.e. ineffectiveness.

Are all strikes equally meaningful as far as social goal attainment is concerned? The distinction between the center and the periphery of a social system may help us answer this question.

Whether we define the center of a society in terms of values or organizations, in Israel the idea of collectivity and the public sector are of ultimate importance. Therefore, they may be regarded as the center of the system. Thus, public utilities are more central than marketable goods, and publicly owned are less peripheral than privately owned enterprises. A temporary cessation in the supply of public services and/or of publicly owned firms will tend to be regarded as clearer indications of political failures than stoppages in privately owned or supplied economic channels.

As can be seen from columns 4 and 5 of Table 7.5, workers in transportation, electricity and water, and in public services tend more to take part in strikes and to incur more idle man-days than employees in primary production industries. The coverage of strike activity by the mass media is determined predominantly by their frequency (Chermesh, 1982a). Almost two thirds of the strikes (63.9 per cent) occurring from 1974 to 1977 were in public utilities, and only a quarter (27.7 per cent) took place in the manufacturing or agricultural industries. A similar indication of the countereffective impact of strikes stems from their ownership sector distribution. More than two thirds of the strikes (70.5 per cent) of that period were called in public or Histadrut owned units, while less than a quarter (23.6 per cent) were called in privately owned enterprises. Employees of public utilities and public sector enterprises are thus not only more strike prone than workers in market or private sector organizations, they also account for the majority of the stoppages.

The public probably takes a worse view of the situation when strike duration and breadth are both taken into consideration. Strikes in public utilities are both shorter and larger (involving more workers) than strikes in the productive branches. The counter-effective impact of wider strikes is obvious, but what about their shorter duration? Institutionalized social processes, whether social fact-finding, mediation, control or change, are all time consuming interactions. Short strikes, like terrorist activities, are therefore almost immune from social restraint. Longer strikes, on the other hand, allow the institutionalized channels, the collective negotiation process or the courts, sufficient time to wield their power and influence. From this point of view, Israeli strikes are therefore a real and perceived obstacle to anticipated effectiveness.

The value of solidarity pertains to the search for harmonious balance among the subgroups of a society. In the context of a structural-functional approach, a strike is always regarded as a hindrance to societal solidarity, given the fact that it expresses conflict between at least two subgroups. But as an institutionalized means of industrial action, it may well be taken for granted in a Western-like developed country, and thus not be too divisive. This is not true of inter-union rivalry. The competition among groups of workers for relative prestige may be regarded as a disruption of solidarity. In the Israeli industrial relations system, the determination of relative ranking is traditionally delegated to the Histadrut and is dealt with in the demands selection and formulation phase. Therefore, wildcat strikes can be regarded as protests against the integrative norms of the society no less than as a claim directed at the employer. Israeli strikes are, therefore, a threat to the solidarity values of society and thus a possible candidate for the status of a social problem.

The value of maximizing integrity in the above-cited Parsonian theory is highly related to the content of the legitimization principles of society. As such, it was discussed above in reference to the norms of strike initiation (official vs. wildcat strikes) and demand selection (national vs. local levels). The prevalence of wildcat strikes, declared at the level of the organization, indicates a gap between the desired and the observed levels of integrity.

If we accept the terms of the analysis, there is a significant discrepancy between three of the four suggested value criteria and Israeli reality. Is this gap remediable without radical change in the national normative system?

Can strike behavior be modified in such a way that macro social value criteria will be adequately met or reaffirmed without changing the basic value assumptions of the society?

Corrective action can be taken through two channels, direct and indirect. Direct action takes place on the macro social level. It would aim at the immediate improvement in the level of any of the three value criteria or all three. The legislation of strike regulation or legal prohibitions, the structuring of a new, updated, prestige hierarchy, and the inculcation of moral values (national, personal or work related) would be expected to bring about a greater willingness to engage in conformist, socially acceptable behavior in the industrial relations arena (e.g., higher proportion of official strikes, willingness to accept central parity decisions). Research indicates that the degree of the trust in and support given to the center of society is highly correlated with the levels of strike activity (Chermesh, 1977). The identification of cause and effect relationships seems hardly feasible.[9] Therefore, it is most improbable that direct changes at the macro-social level, could have a meaningful impact on the described gap between central rules and industrial action.

Indirect action, is taken here to refer to the revitalization of the ailing Israeli industrial relations system. Such a policy would require an increase in the susceptibility of the system to pressures stemming from below. It would require a reform in the structure of labor representation and a reactivated Histadrut. It also implies a reorganization of management and decision making processes in the public service. The implementation of such reforms would be possible only through the cooperation of government and Histadrut leadership. Such cooperation cannot be envisaged without the existence of trust relationships between the two elites. A situation in which the Likud Party holds government and the Labor Party has the majority in the Histadrut, is particularly unpromising.

Intermediate Conclusions: Strikes in Israel in the Labor Dominated Period— The Social Problem Matrix

By way of summary, Table 7.7 presents the condensed form of a social problem matrix, and can serve as a source of reference for answering the three key questions raised at the beginning of this chapter.

(1) Who are the concerned regarding labor unrest? Who are the unconcerned? Three categories of people may be expected to be concerned about strikes in Israel. First, managers in local and national level positions, second, Histadrut officials, and third, the public-at-large and the country's leadership in particular. All three categories can be identified by a 'yes' response in column 4 of Table 7.7. The local union leadership and the staff of the two third party agencies, the Labor Court and the Department of Labor Relations, can be expected to be less bothered by the Israeli labor dispute pattern. The last three sets of people are expected to encounter no significant gap between their values or norms and reality, and were, thus, coded as 'no's' in column 4.[10]

Table 7.7: The social problem matrix strikes in Israel, 1965-77.

Actor	Values-Norms	Reality	Gap	Remedi- ability	Social State
(1)	(2)	(3)	(4)	(5)	(6)
LOCAL INDUSTRIAL RELATIONS SYSTEM					
Management	Authority Predictability Harmony	Strikes are a challenge to Authority, an unpredictable situation, indi- cating malfunct- ioning interaction.	Yes	Expensive in norma- tive terms. unworthy in terms of dam- age incurred.	Concern
Workers' Committees	'MORE' Effectiveness	High level of demand attain- ment. Low costs of failure.	No	Irrelevant	None
NATIONAL INDUSTRIAL RELATIONS SYSTEM					
Histadrut	Generality Responsibility Stability	Strikes threa- ten generality of representa- tion, contradict claim for responsibility, and destabilize the system.	Yes	Feasible only if autonomy is kept unharmed. Requires strengthening of management and participation of local labor representatives.	Problem
Employers' Associations	Harmony	Strikes indicate and cause deterio- ration of indu- strial relations.	Yes	Powerlessness. Role conflict.	Concern
THIRD PARTIES					
Department of Labor Relations	Autonomy Voluntarism	Cooperation.	No	Irrelevant	None
Labor Court	Autonomy Particularity Responsiveness	Cooperation and compliance.	No	Irrelevant	None

Table 7.7 cont'd

Actor	Values-Norms	Reality	Gap	Remedi-ability	Social State
(1)	(2)	(3)	(4)	(5)	(6)
MACRO-SOCIAL SYSTEM					
	Utility	0.046% of local national produce lost.	No	Irrelevant	None
	Effectiveness	Strikes in public utilities and in public owned units. Wildcat strikes. Short strikes.	Yes	Irremediable through macro social routes.	Problem
	Solidarity	Wildcat strikes.	Yes	Require a change in the political arena for increased feasibility of industrial-relations mediated remedies.	Problem
	Integrity	Wildcat strikes. Local demands.	Yes		

(2) Why are some concerned about labor unrest, and others unconcerned?

When people "cherish values but feel them to be threatened, they experience a crisis—either as a personal trouble or as a public issue" (Mills, 1959, p. 11). Managers on both local and national levels find their harmony of industrial relations value threatened, whereas local managers also worry that their own authority and their desire for predictability are being jeopardized. For the functionaries of the Histadrut, short unauthorized strikes in the public sector imperil their claims for the generality, responsibility, and stability of their institution. Macro social level inadequacies may cause anxiety to every member of a society, given his or her status as a citizen. Concern about low levels of effectiveness, solidarity and integrity has, therefore, been expressed in many public opinion polls.

It is, nevertheless, the role of societal leadership in general, and that of government and parliament members in particular, to cope with such objectionable phenomena. No wonder, then, that such critical responses are prevalent in public speeches, parliament discussions, and legislation. In their capacity as employees in a particular enterprise, workers tend to deny that strikes in their place of work are a subject for concern. They dwell on their relative deprivations more than on their aversion to strikes. This perspective crystallizes into a strike related pro status-quo attitude for the local leadership of workers representatives. Third party specialists may be concerned at the inefficiency of the Labor Court or about the Department of Labor Relations not being informed long enough in advance about approaching strikes, but they can hardly be labelled as concerned by strike occurrences as such.

(3) How, if at all, is this concern going to be mitigated?

People can become accustomed to their concerns, accepting them as facts of life. They may, on the other hand, take steps to change reality and eradicate the causes of their concerns. Column 6 of Table 7.7 makes the distinction between three action dispositions, a state of concern, a problem oriented conception and a state of "well being" (Mills, 1959, p. 11). A state of concern exists whenever an actor identifies a discrepancy between reality and his normative criteria for judging and evaluating it. This state of concern can be transformed into a social problem if and when this gap is regarded as remediable. A social problem can be identified for the Histadrut leadership and for society-at-large. Therefore, initiation of remedial action can be expected from two sources, the national union movement and the government.

The government's actions will be supported by the public, so long as they do not interfere with the particularistic interests of too many or too powerful groups of workers. National and local level management can be expected, following the present analysis, to be sympathetic, albeit reluctant, partners to any proposed change. They will prefer to keep things intact rather than involve themselves in an 'aimless' adventure. Local union leaders and third party specialists are identified by the present discussion as unconcerned. Therefore, this last key question does not apply to them.

Like many other sociological studies, and perhaps even more than most, the present research can be criticized for its unrepresentativeness of both actors, values or reality, and for its biased conclusions. The issue of representativeness can be addressed quite easily. Any additions to the table are welcome, and may be useful. The number of actors, the variety of values, or the selection of reality related data could be increased. Political parties, suppliers, consumers and unorganized workers, are possible candidates for such an extended list. In a model like the one presented here, actors and levels of analysis are presented sequentially, comparisons between the various components of the model are made, but the results are not summed as "a net balance of an aggregate of consequences" (Merton, 1968, p. 105). Therefore, additional data would not refute the core findings. They might, however, supply us with further sources for discussion of a given social problem's perception and treatment.

The values listed may also prove to be inconclusive. I suspect, though, that no one will deny the primary importance of most cited normative criteria. A similar case can be brought for the description of reality. It is not complete, but it is based on available data.

Should we regard the actor-related conclusions as final? The answer depends on our general world outlook. If we adopt a consensus related conception of social life and if, as we should, we phrase the hypotheses we are willing to reject as null hypotheses, then a yes answer in column 6 of Table

7.7 should serve as an orientation guide. If we prefer a conflict *weltanschauung*, then a no answer is a more significant result. One way or another, the matrix presented here can serve as a useful tool for social diagnosis.

Strikes in Israel in the Post Labor Dominated Period—A Quasi-Social Problem Matrix Analysis

The social problem matrix analysis is a protocol for analyzing social situations. It is a framework for a straightforward method given availability of information. When all relevant information is available, all we need to do is to organize the data in a structured way and to use it for diagnosis. Seldom do we live in a world of sufficient information. For most cells of the first period covered by this work, data are available. They can always be expanded, verified or modified, but nevertheless they were basically available. When we reach more recent years, those following the political upheaval of May 1977, research findings become scarce. All we are left with are official statistics and public knowledge. Fortunately, these data allow us proceed, albeit with reservations and hesitation.

Strike data are collected with several aims in mind, first, for the purpose of measuring the intensity of industrial labor unrest. For this aim we use strike pattern figures. By counting the strikes, we learn about the number of *decisions* to go on strike or to call lockouts. By summing the number of strikers, we get to know the *number of times workers were involved in strikes.* By aggregating the number of man-days idle as a result of strikes, we acquire a notion of the *economic impact of strikes.* By producing the figures for the average size of a strike and the average duration per striker, we gain an understanding of *strikes patterns.*

Strike data, though, include much more. We learn *who* took part in strikes, in which *settings* they took place (economic branch or sector), *how* the strike was announced, *by whom,* and *for what* declared purpose. All these features of strike activity enable us to reach some conclusions on the normative criteria of the actors, on the gap between these norms and values and reality, and sometimes even on the availability of solutions. In short, they help us in our effort to understand whether strikes were social problems and for what actors.

SOME ASSUMPTIONS ON STRIKE FEATURES AND SOCIAL PROBLEMS

Any formal use of data for testing ideas must include an explicit formulation of variables and criteria for their meaning. I am going to manipulate some essential aspects of strikes hoping to elicit their implications for the traditional set of IR actors and for the government. In order to do so, I divide the discussion into three. First, I will describe the variables and their impact on specific actors. Second, I will show the trends of these variables during the

Labor, Likud and National Unity governments periods. Finally, I will sum up the results and derive a quasi-social problem matrix for the two later periods. The last step will allow us to understand whether strikes were a social problem, a source of concern, or a creator of well-being for Israeli society and its IR affiliates.

The variables

Ten variables will be incorporated in the present analysis: the economic branch; the ownership sector; the validity of the contract; the cause of the strike; the outcomes of the dispute; its endorsement by a legally representative union; whether it was a strike or a lockout; whether the IR Commissioner was prenotified; the type of strike; and the follow up intervention it involved. These variables are supposedly indicative of strike implications for different actors. While specifying the variables, I will describe how they were manipulated and their assumed implications for the actors.

Economic branch

National statistics rely on a very detailed scheme of classification for the economic branch. On its most general level, this classification includes nine primary branches: agriculture, forestry and fishing; industry; electricity and water; construction; commerce, restaurants and hotels; transportation, storage and communication; financing and business services; public and community services; and personal and other services. Such a blueprint is very useful for econometric purposes. It is over-detailed for our present objectives. I would like to suggest that government, the Histadrut, and the private sector employers' association, have each a different ranking of branch clusters when they relate to strikes. The *government* and the *Histadrut* are attuned first to the public utilities and the public services.

Any malfunctioning in these branches is immediately translated into public concern and criticism. Second in rank come the financing and the business services. In a modern society, a strike in a privately owned bank may be more seriously disapproved by the public than by a procrastinating government office. Industry and agriculture, the primary branches, are of the least concern to the public. Their products can be stored for longer periods and their structure is in many cases more competitive than that of the services. Therefore, as an indicator of a gap between government and Histadrut norms and values and reality, branches will be ranked in the following order: agriculture, industry, construction and personal services having the *lowest* ranking, financing and business services having an *intermediate* ranking, and electricity and water, transportation, storage and communication, and public and community services having the *highest* ranking. *The higher the intensity of strike frequency, size or duration in the higher-ranked branches, the higher the assumed gap between reality and social standards.*

Ownership sector

Ownership privileges are of exclusive nature. They denote a claim for exclusive rights to authority and control. As such, no actor can be expected to care for any other actor's prerogatives as much as he cares for his own. Given this approach, it is more than natural to expect government, Histadrut and the private sector employers' associations to have distinct rankings on the ownership sector criterion. Still, one point may be shared by both government and the Histadrut. They may be expected to be less apprehensive about turbulence in private sector sites than in unrest of the publicly owned segment of the economy. Both parity issues and economic interests relate the latter to one another more than either relates to the private sector. Therefore, while private sector employers' associations probably hold a dichotomous conception of the labor market, both the government and Histadrut hold a three-tiered vision.

My assumptions on the different rankings held by various actors are therefore as follows: a) the government cares most about strikes in the government sector, second, in all other public sectors and third, in the private sector. b) The Histadrut cares most about strikes in the Histadrut sector, second, in all other public sectors, and third, in the private sector. c) The private sector employers' associations care first about strikes in the private sector, second, for strikes in the other parts of the economy. *The higher the intensity of strike frequency, size or duration in the higher ranked sectors, the higher the assumed gap between reality and social standards.*

Lockout or strike

In most cases, calling a strike or initiating a lockout is not a preferred way of action. Actors start a conflict since all other options are deemed less favorable. Still, if worst comes to worst, keeping the initiative has its merits. When management closes the gates, it holds more control of the situation than when a strike is imposed on it. The same logic holds for unions. In most cases, when a union starts a strike, it is in a better condition than when it finds that the gates of its members' place of work are closed. Given this approach, *the higher the intensity of strikes as compared with lockouts, the higher the assumed gap between reality and social standards for management and for the employers' associations. And vice-versa, the higher the intensity of lockouts as compared with strikes, the higher is the assumed gap between reality and social standards for the Histadrut and for the workers committees.*

Approval of a strike by a representative union

The established normative system stipulates that strikes must gain the approval of a representative union prior to their announcement and implementation. This approach is one of the most basic items on the Histadrut bylaws. It was almost taken for granted by labor law. Otherwise, prohibiting the Labor Relations Officer from intervening in unapproved strikes would have never been incorporated in the legal code. As such, *the higher the intensity of unapproved strikes, the higher the assumed gap between reality and social standards for the Histadrut, the Labor Relations Officer, and the governments.* The same approach may also hold for the employers, even though employers' associations probably adhere more to this view than do local managements.

Workers' committees do not cherish strike approval for its own sake. They do not, however, value its opposite, unapproved state. Therefore, in this case, the statement that the problem for one is another's solution does not hold here.

Existence of a valid contract at time of strike

Most labor contracts limit the use of strikes during the period the contract is in force. Some include a no-strike clause. Others limit the signatories to issues not covered by the contract, or impose further restrictions. Whoever treats strikes in the framework of an institutionalized IR setting regards respect for the contract as a primary expectation from a responsible actor. It is taken for granted, regarded as one of these pre contractual considerations seldom to be explicitly demanded. The sanctity of the contract is, however, a major value for the more established actors. The Histadrut, the Employers' associations, the Labor Court and the Labor Relations Officer, are probably its most dedicated supporters. Workers' committees, on the other hand, approach IR more instrumentally. For them, contracts are more a means to be used or a constraint to try and avoid, than a major normative consideration. Given these preferences, for the actors mentioned above and for government, *the higher the intensity of strikes prior to the expiration of a contract, the higher the assumed gap between reality and social standards.*

Strike causes

Although unions call strikes for a multitude of reasons, not all issues are of the same order of importance. While levels of remuneration are the most common declared causes of strikes, they are not the most agonizing issue. Wage demands, whether for raises or cuts, center on a known pivot, the current rate. Layoffs and pay delays are, on the other hand, signs of challenge to the more primary value—job security. Manpower cuts are in themselves the embodiment of infringement of job security. Payment delays, on the other hand, are signs of impending collapse. Therefore, *the higher the intensity of strikes caused by layoffs and wage delays, the higher the assumed gap between reality and social standards for both the Histadrut and the workers committees.*

Followup treatment after strike has ended

While in some strikes their end announces a complete agreement on all disputed issues, in many others it is only a partial agreement that brings the strike to an end. The strike is over, but a dispute remains. Quite frequently, the parties agree on a major procedural topic—the method of handling the unsettled issues. This procedure has normative implications. In an irs where autonomy is a primary criterion, external intervention by state authorities is less attractive than irs internal involvement. In a system where the Histadrut is the major actor, any relegation of authority to non Histadrut bodies is an unwelcome threat to Histadrut status. The assumed order of threat depends on the identity of the involved parties. It is my assumption that the order from the less severe to the more severe is the following: all issues were settled; the Histadrut takes care of remaining issues; other parties are selected to take care of problems; the labor court is the forum for settling open controversies. *The higher the intensity of strike frequency, size or duration in the less preferred methods, the higher the assumed gap between reality and social standards for the Histadrut.*

Type of dispute

Labor disputes may take many forms. They may be strikes or lockouts, and if the former, they can be workers' meetings during work hours, warning strikes, or conventional strikes. Both parties on the local level most probably prefer milder rather than more aggressive forms of conflict and action initiated by themselves, rather than commenced by the other party. If so, local managements and workers committees hold a shared preference for calling a meeting to a warning strike, and prefer the latter to a full-scale strike or lockout. Of course, workers' committees, prefer the outbreak of a strike to the imposition of a lockout, while management prefers it the other way round. *The higher the intensity of strike frequency, size or duration in the higher ranked types, the higher the assumed gap between reality and social standards.*

Labor Relations Officer notification

The Law of Dispute Resolution stipulates that unions or managements must notify the Labor Relations Officer of any forthcoming strike or lockout two weeks in advance. While conformity to any law is the bread and butter of any established society, this specific norm is of special interest for the Officer. Prenotification is the most important condition for his viable functioning. *The higher the intensity of strike frequency, size or duration in prenotification, the higher the assumed gap between reality and social standards for the Labor Relations Officer.*

Strike outcome

Most modern strikes are instrumental actions and their value is determined by their outcomes. Strikes are conflict situations. In most cases the achievement of one party is a defeat for the other. Strike data do not allow us to obtain a comprehensive gauge of strike effectivity. Some strikes are coded by their form (meeting, warning, etc.), procedure of continued negotiation, or the status of employment relations (closure of a plant). Nevertheless, for a large percentage of strikes, a generic measure of instrumentality does exist. For these strikes *the higher the intensity of strike frequency, size or duration in successful strikes, The higher the assumed gap between reality and social standards for management. the higher the intensity of strike frequency, size or duration in unsuccessful strikes, the higher the assumed gap between reality and social standards for workers committees.*

The variables for analysis—summary and conclusion

The data offer us ten variables for evaluating the level of the gap various actors may encounter between their normative expectations and reality. Not all variables apply to all actors, nor are all assumptions irrefutable to the same degree. Still, the availability of this information allows us to make some comments on strikes as social problems in the post Labor period. To ignore the explanatory potential of the data because of their deficiencies seems to be the least preferred option.

Method of analysis

I have presented above a list of variables for diagnosing the impact of strikes on a set of actors. This list can be used in many ways, not always leading to identical results. It is important, therefore, first to present the alternative methods and then to see the implications of their use. There are two major options in using these data, an absolute and a relative method. In the absolute method we compare units of reference by absolute frequencies of specified variables. An example is the comparison of two (or more) periods by their number of strikes, or by their number of approved versus unapproved strikes. In the relative method, the comparison uses the *proportion* (or percentage) of selected categories, rather then their absolute numbers.

When it comes to the measuring of implications of a given change on an actor, the absolute and the relative methods carry different messages. Let us say that we are interested in finding out whether the gap between the normative and the real-life setting has changed for the Histadrut. Table 7.10 supplies us with the relevant information. The average *number* of approved strikes per year was almost the same in the Labor and the National Unity periods. Sixty-six strikes were approved in a typical Labor year, as compared to sixty-seven in an average Unity year. The *proportion* of approved strikes, however, changed substantively—45.8 percent of the strikes in the later period, versus 37.8 percent in the former, were approved by an authoritative union. Given these figures, was there any change in the gap between the Histadrut's norms and values and reality?

The discrepancy between these two sets of figures stems from two sources, the decrease in the total number of strikes and the decrease in the number of unapproved strikes (from 92 to 67) with almost no change in the frequency of approved strikes. An increase (or decrease) in the total number of strikes is a source of relief for most parties, since conflict has its own costs. Still, do parties find comfort or aggravation in the mere fact that their total environment has changed? Do they react exclusively to their immediate surroundings?

I have analyzed the data from both points of view. The fifty-six percent decrease in the number of strikes per year between the Labor and the Likud periods, and the forty-nine percent increase from the latter to the National Unity period make the absolute changes in specific categories almost insignificant. The frequency of strikes in all categories decreased between the first and the second periods and increased between the second and the third. The story repeats itself when we approach the absolute analysis for the average size of strikes. Strikes increased their average size by a factor of 1.0 to 5.58 between the Labor and the Likud periods. An average strike during the first period mobilized 587 workers, while a corresponding strike in the Likud years covered 3,277 employees. There was no meaningful change during the National unity phase. The average size of a strike decreased to 3,179, only a three percent change. Average strike duration was very similar in the first two terms, 2.33 days in the first and 2.67 in the second. Their span, however, changed drastically in the National Unity years. A drop to a length of 1.32 days is a 50.56 percent decrease from the Likud era and a 43.35 percent decrease from the Labor period level.

The proportional changes, however, reveal much more interesting results. The percentage comparisons reflect an 'all-other-things-being-equal' approach. Given the fact that frequency, size and duration changed throughout the economy, what unique impact did the changes have on a specific aspect, for example, the tendency to go on unapproved strikes. Table 7.7 shows that unapproved strikes exerted a similar level of stress on the values cherished by the Histadrut in both the Labor and the Likud phases. This source of anxiety, however, decreased in its severity in the National Unity government years. Therefore, I will limit the following analysis to the proportional method.

GAPS BETWEEN REALITY AND NORMATIVE CONSIDERATIONS—ACTORS RELATED ANALYSIS

The government

Four variables are available for the analysis of the problematic state of the government, the branch composition of strikes (Table 7.8), the sector composition of strikes (Table 7.9), the tendency to approve strikes (Table 7.10), and the tendency to strike prior to the expiration of a contract (Table 7.11). These variables are not one of the same. The first two are related to the government as an employer, while the relations of the government to the other two variables are more general. Society has its own normative system, and it is the responsibility of the government to serve as its patron. While strikes in government owned sites and in public utilities are of immediate concern to the government, the maintenance of the normative web of rules is one of its taken-for-granted functions.

The Likud period was the most problematic as far as the immediate functioning of the government is concerned. We can easily draw this conclusion from Tables 7.8 and 7.9. The simplest way of depicting this conclusion is through a cumulative percentage analysis performed in the following way: first we compute a cumulative percentage set for the Labor period. The first item of this set is the highest sensitive value (54.3 percent). Next we proceed with the sum of the two most sensitive values (54.3 + 2.3 = 56.6 percent) and then we make a sum of all the items, by definition always 100.0 percent. We then run the same procedure for the Likud and for the Unity periods. For the Likud term we get the values 60.4, 65.4 and 100.0 and for the Unity phase we get 58.2, 65.1 and 100.0.

We can draw an unequivocal conclusion when all values of a given set are equal or larger than those of another set. For the present example, the cumulative set of the Likud period is above both those of the Labor and National Unity periods. Therefore, during the Likud period the government was in its worst state as far as strikes by branch are concerned. The National Unity period is somewhat more favorable to the government, but it is still second to the Labor Party years, which were the least problematic of all. The halt in the deterioration in the government-owned sector, simultaneous with the deepening collapse of other parts of the public sector in the National Unity years creates this inconclusive comparison with the most recent period.

The sector criterion does not lend itself to comprehensive clear cut comparisons, since the National Unity period ranking crosscuts the other cumulative relative distributions. The only ordered comparison, between the first and the second periods, shows a trend similar to that presented above. The Likud period was more problematic for the government than the Labor phase.

The Likud government experienced, therefore, the most extreme gap between its normative criteria and the strike ridden reality. The Likud Party has an ideology that assigns to the government the responsibility for maintaining law and order in the irs. Support for obligatory arbitration, a preference for keeping a disjunction between union and economic activity and a glorification of the state and its jurisdictional extensions. All these exhibit a belief in the feasibility of gaining a high level of industrial peace. The failure to achieve this goal is an indication of the existence of a social problem.

Table 7.8: The economic branch sensitivity of strikes for government and Histadrut (by dominant party in government).

Level of Sensitivity	PARTY			TOTAL
	Labor	Likud	Nat'l Unity	
Low sensitivity	43.4 (72)	34.7 (34)	35.0 (52)	38.3 (158)
Medium sensitivity	2.3 (4)	5.0 (5)	6.9 (10)	4.6 (19)
High sensitivity	54.3 (90)	60.4 (59)	58.2 (86)	57.1 (235)
TOTAL	40.4 (166)	23.8 (98)	35.9 (148)	100.0 (412)

Table 7.9: The sector sensitivity of strikes for government.

Level of Sensitivity	PARTY			TOTAL
	Labor	Likud	Nat'l Unity	
Lowest sensitivity	57 34.0	25 25.1	35 24.0	117 28.3
Medium sensitivity	65 38.7	39 39.6	77 52.0	180 43.6
Highest sensitivity	46 27.2	35 35.3	35 24.0	116 28.0
TOTAL	40.5 (167)	23.7 (98)	35.7 (148)	100.0 (413)

Table 7.10: Strike approval by ruling party.

Strike Approval	PARTY			TOTAL
	Labor	Likud	Nat'l Unity	
Yes	37.8 (56)	39.3 (33)	45.8 (57)	40.9 (145)
No	62.2 (92)	60.7 (50)	54.2 (67)	59.1 (210)
TOTAL	41.7 (148)	23.3 (83)	35.0 (124)	100.0 (355)

Table 7.11: Strikes called prior to expiration of contract by dominant party in
            government.

Contract State	PARTY		TOTAL
	Labor	Likud	
Contract expired	20.1	25.7	22.5
	(23)	(21)	(45)
Valid Contract	79.9	74.3	77.5
	(91)	(62)	(153)
TOTAL	57.8	42.2	100.0
	(115)	(83)	(198)

A completely different situation shows up in the more normative features of government functioning. Tables 7.10 and 7.11 show a stable trend of
decrease in the propensity to call wildcat strikes and a curtailed tendency to go
on strike while contracts are still in force.[11]

The interest of government in these two issues is, however, indirect.
Strike approval decision-making is dependent upon three actors and two levels of consideration. The interest in calling a strike is mailnly centered on the
organizational level, where more and more strikes are being called. It is up to
the union representation at this level to adopt a decision to call a strike and
upon their counterparts, the local management, to let it happen. The decision
to approve a strike or deny it approval lies in the hands of higher echelons of
the Histadrut. The government has only minor influence on either the decision to initiate a strike or the willingness to approve it. Such impotence prevents contract adherence and prevents wildcat striking from becoming a
remediable issue when it is acute. These normative considerations cannot,
therefore be regarded as an ameliorating process for the government when it
has such a minor influence on their form.

The Histadrut

Seven variables let us estimate the effects of strike activity on Histadrut
well-being. The first, the branch composition of strikes, is related to macro-
economic processes. Histadrut concern resembles that of the government and
has been discussed above. The second, sector ownership, reflects Histadrut
interests, given its ownership of significant economic enterprises. Three other
variables, the propensity to strike prior to the expiration of a contract, the rate
of strike approval and the follow-up treatment after strikes, are all related to
the fact that the Histadrut is the godfather of the union movement. The last
group of variables, the causes of strikes and the propensity to call lockouts, are
all essential elementary components of union ideology and interests.

The Likud years were the worst period from the macro-economic point of
view. As I have shown in Table 7.8, 60.4 percent of the strikes of that time

took place in public utilities, the branches hypothesized to be of the highest potential sensitivity to the Histadrut. Its exclusion from the primary circle of policy-making actually helped the Histadrut to cope with the situation. Even if a significant gap did exist, there was not much the Histadrut could do about it. Therefore, even though the gap between reality and the desired was wider in the Likud years, the perception of a 'social problem' fits more the National Unity time. The involvement of the Histadrut in the formulation of the new economic policy in 1984, and its continued participation in national policy deliberations supported the prevalence of a feeling of urgency in Histadrut circles.

The Histadrut gained some significant points in its godfather role during the twenty-three years of this study. Indications of this important aspect can be drawn from Tables 7.11, and 7.12.

Since contract[12] data are available only for the Labor and Likud periods, the analysis of this aspect of IR functioning is partial. However, the figures of Table 7.11 show that strikes during the Likud regime decreased prior to contract expiration.

This aspect of conformity to established strike behavior is accompanied by a continuous increase in the percent of approved strikes. Table 7.10 shows an increase of seven percent in the proportion of approved strikes between the beginning of the period under study and its end. This change may stem from two independent sources, either the submissiveness of subordinate union echelons to central leadership, or the relaxation of central control. Since the analysis above shows more the relaxation of control than increased conformity, *we must conclude that the Histadrut did not manage to overcome a social problem. Rather, it changed its normative criteria for facing reality.*

The first impression one gains from Table 7.12 is of an inconclusive trend of Histadrut involvement in the following-up of strikes. All three cumulative percentage distributions intersect with one another seemingly preventing the emergence of any clear ranking. A more careful reading, however, shows a clear increase of Histadrut involvement after strikes ended. Both the percentages of Labor Court and other non-Histadrut agencies involvement show a secular trend of decrease. The only gaining category is that of Histadrut involvement and the gain is very impressive. While, during the Labor period, one of four strikes (27.0 percent) received Histadrut follow-up, the proportion almost one doubled (44.7 percent) in the Likud years, and rose to 61.5 percent in the most recent period. The significant decrease of noninvolvement from 44.6 percent in the Labor, to 28.9 percent in the Likud periods, explains the seeming lack of conclusive ranking. Therefore, the leading status of the Histadrut in union representation consolidated during the period under investigation.

Table 7.12: Follow-up treatment after strike (by dominant party in gov't).

Followup	P A R T Y			TOTAL
status	Labor	Likud	Nat'l Unity	
No followup needed	44.6 (33)	28.9 (26)	28.4 (23)	33.5 (82)
Histadrut followup	27.0 (20)	44.7 (40)	61.5 (49)	44.8 (110)
Other, non court	22.2 (17)	20.5 (19)	6.2 (5)	16.3 (40)
Labor Court	6.1 (5)	5.9 (5)	4.0 (3)	5.3 (13)
TOTAL	30.4 (75)	36.9 (90)	32.6 (80)	100.0 (245)

Table 7.13: The sector sensitivity of strikes for the Histadrut.

Level of	P A R T Y			TOTAL
Sensitivity	Labor 1.00	Likud 2.00	Nat'l Unity 3.00	
Lowest sensitivity	34.0 (57)	25.1 (25)	24.0 (35)	28.3 (117)
Medium sensitivity	53.5 (90)	66.2 (65)	64.0 (94)	60.3 (249)
Highest sensitivity	12.4 (21)	8.7 (8)	12.0 (18)	11.4 (47)
TOTAL	40.5 (167)	23.7 (98)	35.7 (148)	100.0 (413)

A meaningless 0.4 percent difference in the frequency of strikes in the Histadrut sector between the first and the last periods hides a clear deterioration in the quality of IR along ownership sector lines. Table 7.13 shows that the prevalence of strikes in the Histadrut sector was lowest during the Likud period. The fact of being in opposition led the Labor Party to try to improve the IR climate in its economic enterprises. This effort brought results. The percentage of strikes in the Histadrut sector decreased from 12.4 percent in the Labor, to 8.7 percent in the Likud, years—a thirty percent decrease! This achievement was, however, short lived. In the National Unity period, the figure reverted almost to its previous level (12.0 percent).

The crisis in the public sector, which reached record intensity in the Likud years (66.2 percent of the strikes!) did not level off thereafter. While the percentage of strikes in the private sector, that of the least concern to the Histadrut, fell to a minimum in the National Unity years, the crises in the public sector kept coming. From the point of view of its ownership, therefore, strikes increased their salience as a source of a 'concern' for the Histadrut, but lack of means kept it from becoming a 'social problem'.

Union-related aspects of strike activity are of cardinal importance to the Histadrut. Curtailing the initiatives of employers, preventing resort to lockouts, layoffs and pay procrastination, are always important considerations for any union. A policy of full and secure employment was almost taken for granted in the early nineteen-sixties. The recession of 1966 was short lived and hit relatively peripheral segments of the Israeli economy, while the prosperity following the Six Days War almost wiped out the memory of this recession.

Table 7.14: The propensity to call lockouts (by dominant party in gov't).

Dispute Type	P A R T Y			TOTAL
	Labor	Likud	Nat'l Unity	
Strikes	94.7 (159)	92.8 (92)	95.3 (141)	94.5 (392)
Lockouts	5.3 (9)	7.2 (7)	4.7 (7)	5.5 (23)
TOTAL	40.4 (168)	23.9 (99)	35.7 (148)	100.0 (415)

As we can see in Table 7.14, lockouts have never been a important tactic in Israeli IR. Even at its peak period, the Likud years, no more than 7.2 percent of Israeli stoppages were initiated by employers.[13] During the Likud years employers increased the frequency from 5.3 percent to 7.2 percent. Percentage-wise, it is a very significant increase (35.8 percent), but in absolute terms, the number of lockout even *decreased* from an annual average of nine in the Labor, to seven in the post Labor, periods. The proportional changes made the Likud period the worst time for the Histadrut (and workers' committees). Still, it was not a very important aspect of daily ir affairs.

A more significant union-related issue is that of the causes of strikes. It was assumed that the Histadrut had gained an almost unprecedented security through past conflicts and political campaigns. Job security was regarded as a *sine-qua-non* given the reputation of the Histadrut. Table 7.15 shows that such assurance can no longer be taken for granted. The trend of an increased percentage of strikes called for the least preferred reasons has grown from the Likud years on. Still, the really significant leap came during the National Unity years. About a quarter of the strikes were caused by layoffs and payment problems during the Labor (25.3 percent) and the Likud (28.4 percent) years.

This figure increased by almost fifty-seven percent in the National Unity period. More than forty-four percent of the strikes in this period were called to demonstrate or fight against layoffs and/or delays in wage payments. This deterioration is a very significant drawback for the status of the union movement in Israel.

Since contract[13] data are available only for the Labor and Likud periods, the analysis of this aspect of IR functioning is partial. However, the figures of Table 7.11 show that strikes during the Likud regime decreased prior to contract expiration.

This aspect of conformity to established strike behavior is accompanied by a continuous increase in the percent of approved strikes. Table 7.10 shows an increase of seven percent in the proportion of approved strikes between the beginning of the period under study and its end. This change may stem from two independent sources, either the submissiveness of subordinate union echelons to central leadership, or the relaxation of central control. Since the analysis above shows more the relaxation of control than increased conformity, *we must conclude that the Histadrut did not manage to overcome a social problem. Rather, it changed its normative criteria for facing reality.*

Private sector employers' associations

Three variables allow us to assess the impact of strikes on the welfare of the private sector employers' associations. Two of these variables are of a normative nature, while the third reflects the interests of the private sector. The first two are the propensities to call unapproved strikes and to call strikes prior to the expiration of a contract. I have had the opportunity to present them above, the first in the paragraph discussing the Histadrut, and the second both in relation to the government and to the Histadrut. The third variable is new. It is the sector affiliation of strike stricken sites ranked from the perspective of the private sector employers.

As we can see in Tables 7.10, 7.11 and 7.16, strikes had a decreasing effect over time on the employers' association.

All three variables show an increasingly positive trend *vis-à-vis* the employers as time passes.

The most dramatic changes in the private sector occured during the Likud years, the percent of strikes in the private sector changing from the thirty-four percent Labor years level to 25.1 percent. This is a 26.2 percent decrease. The changes in the National Unity period were minimal. On the wider arena, the improvements in the strike approval rate developed later, mostly in the Unity period. Both effects, however, are cumulative and display a betterment from the point of view of the employers. Contract compliance data are available for the first two periods. They show the same trend.[14]

Table 7.15: Causes of strikes (by dominant party in government).

Cause	PARTY			TOTAL
	Labor	Likud	Nat'l Unity	
No layoffs, no pay	74.7 (105)	71.6 (67)	55.5 (78)	66.7 (251)
Layoffs, no pay	25.3 (36)	28.4 (27)	44.5 (63)	33.3 (125)
TOTAL	37.6 (141)	24.9 (94)	37.5 (141)	100.0 (376)

Table 7.16: The sector sensitivity of strikes for the private sector (by dominant party in gov't).

Level of Sensitivity	PARTY			TOTAL
	Labor	Likud	Nat'l Unity	
Lowest sensitivity	66.0 (110)	74.9 (73)	76.0 (112)	71.7 (296)
Highest sensitivity	34.0 (57)	25.1 (25)	24.0 (35)	28.3 (117)
TOTAL	40.5 (167)	23.7 (98)	35.7 (148)	100.0 (413)

Still, how widely applicable are the changes to the economy as a whole? Is it a valid assumption to expect strike approval rates in the private sector to correlate with the tendencies for the total economy? The employers' associations are the representatives of the employers on the national level of the irs. If their main interest is in state-wide developments, the figures of Table 7.10 are relevant. If, however, their main concern is sector-specific, if their participation in the national arena is motivated mainly by sectoral interests, then a more detailed analysis is needed. It is my belief that the Israeli employers' associations are in the first place lobbyists for particular interests and only to a lesser degree, the promoters of wider interests. Therefore, analysis of data following statistical control of the sector variable is an approach more suited to the present discussion.

Table 7.17 supplies us with clear indication of a disparity between the developments in the total economy and those in the private sector. There is a *decreasing* trend in the percentage of approved strikes in the private sector, those having the high ranking in Table 7.17. While 46.3 percent of strikes in the private sector obtained Histadrut approval in the Labor period, in the Likud period this figure dropped to 38.7 percent, to be followed by a similar percentage of 38.0 in the National Unity years. Although the Histadrut relaxed its policy *vis-à-vis* approval of strikes in the public sector, this passivity stayed exclusively in that realm. Strikes in the private sector did not gain increased Histadrut approval. On the other hand, this lack of approval was not a critical factor for their elimination.

Table 7.17: Approval of strikes by an authoritative union (by private sector ranking and dominant party in government).

Strike approval	PARTY						TOTAL
	Labor		Likud		Nat'l Unity		
	Low	High	Low	High	Low	High	
Approved	33.6 (33)	46.3 (22)	39.3 (25)	38.7 (7)	48.6 (45)	38.0 (12)	40.8 (144)
Not approved	66.4 (66)	53.7 (26)	60.7 (38)	61.3 (12)	51.4 (48)	62.0 (19)	59.2 (209)
TOTAL	28.0 (99)	13.6 (48)	17.8 (63)	5.4 (19)	26.4 (93)	8.8 (31)	100.0 (353)

Therefore, strikes do have an ambivalent impact on the Israeli employers' associations. On the national level irs they no longer create any a significant gap between the normative *weltanschauung* of the private employers and the reality of the situation.

As to the sector-specific effects, these are less favorable. The number of strikes has decreased, but so has their rate of approval. No longer can the employers rely on the Histadrut's powers of constraint. They need their own means, such as the development of a mutual anti-strike insurance fund. This method has proven itself as a very effective tool for defeating as well as preventing strikes. Its existence helps the private sector employers avoid a situation where strikes become for them a 'social problem'. Although strikes were a matter of 'concern' for the employers in the past, as far as we can draw conclusions from the present analysis, they no longer have such a status.

The Labor relations officer

The Labor Relations Officer fulfills many functions, most of which find no indication in the strike data. The only available variable for estimating the impact of strikes on this third party is the prenotification measure. It is a response to the question whether the Labor Relations Officer was notified of an imminent strike and if so, when this notification was made. Prenotification is a very important prerogative of this functionary, since it is a crucial prerequisite for his involvement and is thus, an important factor to be considered. Table 7.18 shows clear indications of the decreasing tendency to prenotify the Commissioner of impending strikes.

Table 7.18: Was labor relations officer notified about the impending strike (by dominant party in government).

Labor Officer notified?	P A R T Y			TOTAL
	Labor	Likud	Nat'l Unity	
Yes	35.4 (40)	28.5 (25)	23.6 (32)	28.9 (97)
No	64.6 (72)	71.5 (64)	76.4 (103)	71.1 (239)
TOTAL	33.3 (112)	26.5 (89)	40.2 (135)	100.0 (336)

The trend is almost linear, with a 6.9 percent decrease during the Likud years, followed by a 4.9 decrease in the National Unity period. At the end of the period under consideration, three out of four strikes took place without ever having been reported to the Commissioner. This trend faces this official with a clear gap between the reality, as presented above, and the unambiguous phrasing of the law.

The decrease in the rate of notification must, though, be considered in the context of the Labor Relations Officer's pattern of action. Taking a post-hock view, we see that the strikes for which notification was received were larger in size and longer in duration than the rest. An average prenotified strike mobilized during the Labor period 3,709 strikers, while an average unreported strike involved only 1,020 workers. The same pattern continued for the Likud and the National Unity years. (24,956 for a prenotified strike versus 2,302 in the Likud period, and 5,277 and 2,953 correspondingly for the National Unity days). As to duration, a notified strike lasted on the average 3.05 days in the Labor period, while unnotified strikes lasted only 1.77 days. The corresponding lengths for the Likud and the National Unity years are 2.94 and 1.41 for the former and 1.44 and 1.30 for the later.

Thus, even though the Labor Relations Officer was informed of a smaller *number* of strikes, he still held an important function for the more significant ones.

The decrease in Labor Relations Officer prenotification followed an important change in the more established part of industrial conflict. Since its inception, most reports delivered to the Commissioner came from approved strikes, 63.9 percent of the approved strikes following the requirements of the law in this regard. This figure dropped to 49.8 percent in the Likud and to 37.0 percent in the National Unity periods, a change serving as an important indication for this official. The non-established segments of the Israeli irs have never followed the norm of reporting. As a matter of fact, they are not even *expected* to do so. The established part did comply with the demands of the law, but tended to limit this pattern.

At this stage, it is important to mention that the Labor Relations Officer tended mostly to receive notification when the issues were union related. The causes entailing the highest report rates were always union recognition and labor contracts. Therefore, curtailment of reporting reflects the dissatisfaction of the established union movement with the activities of this third party.

Local management

Managements can be affected by strikes from more than one angle. First, they may be caught by a conflictual *initiative* by its counterpart, the union. Second, they may be hit by an act contradicting *contractual commitments* by the other party. Third, they may be confronted by the unwelcome *intensity* of a dispute. And fourth, they may be hit by the *outcomes* of such a dispute.

Our strike data hold information on all four topics. Table 7.14 reports on the tendency to call strikes as compared to the propensity to set lockouts. This same table can be analyzed from both sides of the bargaining table. Tables 7.19 and 7.20 show us the developments from the stand point of local management.

During the Likud years the management side gained both in initiative and by higher conformity to contractual obligations. The outcomes of instrumental strikes[15] in the Likud period were more favorable to management than in the following National Unity years. The Likud years seem to have been the occasion for a reverse of a historical trend of union domination in the IR arena. The National Unity period, however, does not lend reliable indications as to the persistence of this reverse. While the advantages gained by management in terms of outcome effectivity continued, the intensity of strikes began to be less favorable then before and management aggressiveness, meaning taking the initiative during conflict, decreased. These ambivalent indications do not allow us to assign to management a score on the significance of the gap between its objectives and its accomplishments in the post Labor period.

Workers' committees

Most management indicators serve as sources for diagnosing the status of workers' committees as well. Their ranking may differ, but the original data are the same. We can estimate the status of workers committees by strike objectives, by their level of initiative during conflict, by the intensity of conflict and by its outcomes. Tables 7.14, 7.15, 7.19, and 7.20 supply us with the available information.

The main drawback workers' committees experienced during the twenty-three years covered by this study are in terms of their objectives. Sacred issues, such as secure employment and prompt wage payment increasingly became the focus of conflict. The more these issues are made the stated causes of strikes, the less can the union take them for granted. The major pull-back on this point took place in the National Unity period. The proportion of these least preferred topics for striking increased from the 28.4 percent figure of the Likud days to a peak of 44.5 percent—a 56.7 percent increase (Table 7.15)! With this degree of change, the minor improvement workers committees gained in the outcomes of instrumental strikes over the Labor level is hardly a compensating factor. The most recent period is also somewhat milder in conflict intensity. Table shows this trend, marginal though it is in degree.

Table 7.19: Strikes by their outcomes (by dominant party in government, instrumental strikes only).

Strike Outcomes	P A R T Y			TOTAL
	Labor	Likud	Nat'l Unity	
No demand conceded	30.6 (28)	28.5 (9)	26.1 (18)	28.6 (55)
Some demands gained	28.6 (26)	39.5 (13)	24.8 (17)	29.0 (56)
All demands gained	40.8 (37)	32.0 (10)	49.2 (34)	42.4 (82)
TOTAL	47.7 (92)	16.5 (32)	35.9 (69)	100.0 (193)

Table 7.20: Type of strike by dominant party in government.

Type of Strike	P A R T Y			TOTAL
	Labor	Likud	Nat'l Unity	
Workers meeting	14.1 (15)	12.4 (12)	19.3 (28)	15.8 (55)
Warning strike	18.3 (20)	31.8 (31)	21.9 (32)	23.6 (82)
Lockout	7.2 (8)	7.3 (7)	4.8 (7)	6.3 (22)
Strike	60.3 (65)	48.5 (47)	53.9 (78)	54.4 (190)
TOTAL	30.9 (108)	27.8 (97)	41.3 (144)	100.0 (349)

The general trend is, therefore one of a weakening position for labor representation at the plant level. This development is a source for 'concern' for this actor. Can this concern be transformed into a 'social problem'? Do workers' committees envision means of coping with it? The local union can gain its strength either from above, from the union movement or from its power position at the local level. As we have seen, the Histadrut's major Achilles heel is in the economic sphere. The Histadrut continues to hold symbolic control over its affiliated bodies by means of ceasing to enforce a monolithic policy. Under these circumstances, workers' committees cannot expect to gain much from their superordinate union body.

At the local level, the union's position is also under attack. Managements look for alternative modes of employment. Since organized workers are an inflexible resource and since management believes that tenured workers are unmotivated, they are turning to subcontracting, temporary employment, etc. Since, the ultimate resource of both union and management is their shared site of employment and since workers' committees are reluctant to establish more flexible norms of employment, they have little choice but to acquiesce to the alternative modes. Lack of ability to raise strategies for consolidating their source of income relegates them to the status of a veto group. Moreover, acting as a veto group without having the resources to defend this status is a recipe for failure. It is the first time in many decades that workers' committees are on the verge of having a 'social problem' as far as the industrial relations are concerned.

THE SOCIAL PROBLEM MATRIX—A SUMMARY

In this chapter I have tried to analyze the problems of Israeli strikes impose on its IRS. I have adopted a social problem matrix approach and have tried to organize the available data in order to reach some conclusions about the state of the system. In comparison to the vast amount of information available for the 1965-77 years, the data for the more recent period are sparse. Nevertheless, it seems useful for a preliminary analysis.

As we saw in Table 7.7, Israeli society experienced a 'social problem' in three of its four functional subsystems, the political, integrative and pattern maintenance domains during the Labor Party regime. On the irs level, the Histadrut faced a 'social problem', while all other actors either had a 'no problem' (workers committees, Labor Relations Officer and Labor Court), or 'concern' (management, employers' associations) situation. Since the Histadrut was a pivotal element in the system and since a state of 'social problem' is an assumed prerequisite for change, this finding denotes a certain degree of promise for change.

The political upheaval of 1977 took the Histadrut out of the political center. It became an important ingredient of the structure, one to be taken into consideration, but whose participation was challenged by the government. This change in the political environment carried the Histadrut into the area of 'concern,' and removed it from the 'social problem' domain. The changes in the political arena brought into power a new party with a clear ideology. The Likud thus found itself in a state of 'social problem,' facing a challenging setting for implementing change. This change never took place. The new regime avoided establishing any meaningful part of its agenda. Its list of priorities did not assign the irs a very important place. The immediate winner of the stepping aside of the Histadrut were the employers. Their situation improved and they escaped from a condition of 'concern.'

The Histadrut sought to alleviate its state of 'concern.' Having few means to change reality, it preferred to adjust its normative framework. Instead of trying to regulate its subordinate bodies, it preferred to loosen its control. Such an approach imposes less tension on the system and allows it to reach a state of equilibrium at a lower level of performance.

The changes in the normative framework created a vacuum for other actors in the system. The Labor Relations Officer, who had enjoyed the good will and assistance of the major actors in the system in the past, was left with no support. As a result, he became detached from many events with which he had formerly tended to get involved. The employers' associations, who fulfilled only secondary functions in the system, opted for a more independent course of action. On the local level, management gained from the changes in the balance of power and workers' committees lost an important power base. The changes at plant level, however, were slow and less significant.

The National Unity period was imposed on the major parties after a 'hung' election brought the country to a standstill. The 1984 change brought the Histadrut back to the center, but the changes of the Likud period left their imprint. The Histadrut underwent a process of decentralization. Its national leadership preferred to engage in nationwide politics and not in specific IR negotiations, which were left to the Trade Union Division and its affiliated bodies. The Histadrut served as the patron and godfather of the institutional setting of the irs. It gained rewards from this activity, but found itself, facing very wide gaps in its role as an employer in the economic sector—Hevrat ha'Ovdim—and in its union affiliates. For none of these spheres did the Histadrut find solutions. It is trapped in a condition of 'concern,' waiting for solutions to be imported from an unidentified source.

At the same time, IR issues were not topics of major interest for the National Unity government. Strikes did not seem to raise significant gaps in the shallow common denominator between its partners, while other issues competed with the irs for the government's attention.

At the end of the period under review, the irs seems to be a system without a center, without a leading agent for change. Only insubstantiable speculations can indicate its course and the present setting is not the appropriate occasion for such guesswork.

Notes to Chapter 7

1. In the Israeli context the distinction between local and national level third parties is insignificant. Thus, five instead of six actors will be presented below.

2. The detailed figures for this paragraph are not reported here. They are available from the author on request.

3. The difference cannot be accounted for by the fact that the activities of organizations in the various sectors only partially overlap. The percentage is computed only for items which were declared to be relevant for the reported unit.

4. The following topics were included in the research instrument: 1. basic wage increase, 2. effort pay increase, 3. piece rates, 4. other incentive pay rates, 5. promotion, 6. overtime pay, 7. work rules, 8. changes in methods of production, 9. safety, 10. work assignments, 11. changes in shift work, 12. improvement of the physical conditions of work, 13. speedup, 14. discipline, 15. discharge, 16. appointment of junior managers, 17. appointment of senior managers, 18. marketing, 19. finance, 20. personal problems.

5. It is interesting to note that nondemand related stoppages whether approved by the Histadrut or not show a similar propensity to be wide and short. Almost half of both official (49.1 per cent) and unofficial (47.3 per cent) strikes were of this type.

6. This point will be elaborated on page 150.

7. Public and Histadrut owned national level management has not achieved an autonomous status in industrial relations issues. Therefore, their stand is not analyzed in detail here.

8. A working knowledge of Parsons' generalized media of exchange is assumed in the following discussion. A detailed explanation of the paradigm can be found in Baum (1976). The table on page 467 of Baum's book was particularly helpful.

9. The degree of trust in government was identified by Chermesh (1977) as a causal factor, which determines the deviations from the time trend of participation in strikes (B) in Israel. The present paper, however, deals with the determination of the strike pattern itself. The susceptibility of a strike pattern to policy decisions is still unexplored.

10. This state of 'well being' is labelled in Table 7.7 column 6 as 'none,' indicating the absence of concern as well as a sense of the existence of a social problem.

11. There are no data for the contract related measure for the National Unity period.

12. An interesting finding relevant to the evaluation of the importance of the expectation to abstain from striking prior to the expiration of a contract is the following finding: There is no difference what so ever between the propensity of the Histadrut to approve strikes when a valid

contract exists and when it has expired! This same tendency exists both in the Labor years (80.4 percent of the contract time strikes were approved, while 81.7 of the no contract category) and in the Likud period (77.4 versus 76.5 correspondingly).

13. Here is the place to add that all lockout figures in Table 7.14 are *maximum* values. The strike data file includes reference to strikes in many items. In accuracies in coding created stoppages which were coded as lockouts in some of these items but not in others. In order to achieve data consistency, I treat a stoppage which was coded *at least* once as lockout as one called by employers. This way, the number of lockout has been adjusted to its *highest possible value.*

14. The private sector respect for a prevailing contract were always higher than those of the other sectors. Only 69.0 percent of the strikes in the private sector happened prior to the expiration of a contract. The corresponding figures for the other sectors are: Histadrut - 92.2, Public - 96.2, Government - 82.0. During the Likud years the percentages were 69.0, 83.3, 82.7 and 71.9 correspondingly.

15. Instrumental strikes are those for which a report is available in terms of the degree to which the demands of the strikers were substantiated. For many strikes information is coded in a way that does not lend itself to easy outcome evaluation.

8

Strikes: The Issue of Social Responsibility

Introduction

. . .unions and management failed in one aspect of their relations to measure up to the social responsibility created by public expectations. That exception was the strike relationship. (Chamberlain and Schilling, 1954, p. VII.)

The rules for calling a strike demonstrate the seriousness of taking that step. (Schneider, 1969, p. 322.)

The relationships between strikes and social responsibility have been examined from a number of different perspectives. In the context of industrial relations, social responsibility can be understood as the sensitivity of unions[1] and management to the potential negative implications of their actions on all other parties. Chamberlain (1953) studied this issue from the point of view of public opinion and reached the critical conclusion presented above. He continued to investigate this point with the aim of

ascertaining the differing pattern of strike effects in the various industries of the American economy and for building a body of knowledge directly pertinent to the problem of public policy concerning strikes. (1954, p. VII)

This time the interpretations were more complicated. Not all strikes are alike in terms of damage. According to Chamberlain and Schilling, damage may be incurred in varying degrees to non-party members, consumers, producers, and suppliers, whether in direct or indirect relationship with the struck unit. Thus, the calculus of strike damage is very complicated, and the most evident way of minimizing harm is located at the source, i.e., in the activities and responses of unions and management.

The most important feature of union-management relationships is their mutual interdependence. Each side is tied to the other, even if only for the purposes of furthering its own interests. In the framework of collective agreements, management is dependent upon its workers' representation in hiring and firing, conditions of work and terms of employment.

The union, on the other hand, owes its existence to the continuation of the employment relationships. This interdependence is the power basis of the two sides. The labor union may be most conveniently studied in the context of power (Miller & Form, 1964, p. 288). The same may be argued for management in general and for bilateral union-management relationships in particular (Dubin, 1960). The study of strikes and strike threats may indicate the degree to which the parties try to avoid, or at least minimize, damage to third parties. Such minimization is needed for the establishment of an industrial relations system characterized by social responsibility. "A. . . system must be more or less generally accepted in its social environment. As a system it must enjoy. . . credit." (Luhmann, 1982, p. 143)[2] An irresponsible industrial relations system can expect neither acceptance nor credit. Responsibility is, therefore, an indispensable prerequisite for system autonomy

The Model

The analysis of the social costs of industrial conflict from the viewpoint of management and unions requires the development of a model which specifies each of these, along with parties in interaction with them, and the nature of the links between them. An inverse model, focusing at the primary beneficiaries of formal organizations, was developed by Blau and Scott (Blau and Scott, 1962).

> Four basic categories of persons can be distinguished in relation to any given formal organization: (1) the members of rank-and-file participants; (2) the owners or managers of the organization; (3) the clients or, more generally, the 'public-in-contact', which means the people who are technically outside the organization yet have regular, direct contact with it, under whatever label—patient, customer, law violator, prisoner, enemy soldier, student, and (4) the public-at-large that is the members of the society in which the organization operates. We propose to classify organizations on the basis of cum bono—who benefits? (p. 42)

Replacing the benefit with damage, we may ask: who is the victim of a given strike and to what degree? Figure 8.1 presents a model of a strike's main actors and their potential influenced parties. The model discerns eight reference categories.

In the center we find the main actors in the conflict, management and union. The activities of these two parties are the main issue of the present chapter. Surrounding the main actors, we find the owners and the workers involved in the conflict under consideration. The first have 'special relationships' with the management and the second with the union. The 'public-in-contact' with the strike include three categories: clients, suppliers, and workers uninvolved in the present conflict. The furthest category includes the public-at-large. All categories include individuals, groups, or organizations who stand the test of defining their inclusion.[3]

Figure 8.1: A concentric model of strike damage.

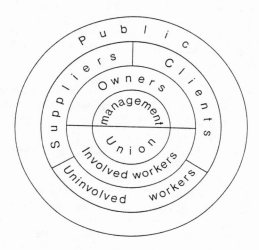

These eight categories can be related across a two-dimensional map, one relating to level and the other to functional specialization. At the struck unit level, management and union leadership act in the industrial relations system. Their autonomy is dependent upon their connections with their environment, both the economic and the political. The economic system of the enterprise level can be represented by its suppliers and by its clients. The political constraints on union action stem from the rank-and-file. Members' support, or at least members' indifference is required for union leaders' negotiation and action capacity. The same can be said regarding owners' status. So long as owners' interference in managerial decisions is restricted, management can function in its traditional capacity. At the local or state level, the public at large, through government, parliament or specialized interest groups, can call for control or substitution of any damage incurred to the supply of products or services.

Blau and Scott (pp. 45-57) elaborate the idea that the problems that an organization will face can be anticipated on the basis of its preferred relationships with a given category. The same may be argued in the case of industrial conflicts. The common, though asymmetric, problem of damage to the main actors is the issue of power. Each side may be interested in consolidating its power position at the expense of the other. In the long run, however, each side in an advanced industrial relations system is interested in cooperation with the other, an approach requiring some independence and a power base.

The problem of the next set, the actors of the enterprise level political system, i.e., the relationships between union and management with the owners and involved workers, is that of confidence and support. The burden of a strike may cause lack of confidence, promoting the possible replacement of management and/ or union leaders. The main actors and the actors of the economic system, suppliers and clients, face the problems of continuity (Katz and Kahn, 1966, pp. 14-29). Any threat to the continuation of the transactions in a unit's raw material or product market may be fatal for the unit in conflict and may endanger its future existence. Neither management nor union is interested in such a fate. The problem of the relationship between the public and the main actors is that of legitimacy (Parsons & Smelser, 1956). Both management and union need the sponsorship of the public for facilitation of their routine activities and for the perpetuation of the institution of collective bargaining.

There is a meaningful difference between the problem of power and the problems of confidence and support, continuity, and legitimacy. The problem of power is based upon and derived from the assumption of continuity, while the other problems are relevant just because continuity is not assured. Problems of the second type become irrelevant in cases where the owners are the management, uncontested union leadership, and monopoly in the product, labor, or the normative markets.

Here we will concentrate on two topics: first, the sensitivity of the main actors in industrial disputes to the damage implications of their behavior on third parties will be investigated; then, the causes of such sensitivity (or insensitivity) will be analyzed and tested.

Three characteristics of a responsible IR system will be assumed:

(a) Both of the main actors, management and union, are interested in the continuity of their relationships;

(b) Both of the main actors are interested in defending the autonomy of the domain of industrial relations from over-involvement of external factors and try, therefore, to minimize damage to third parties;

(c) Both of the main actors regards the strike (and the lockout) as a legitimate means for promoting the antagonistic goals of their counterparts.

These principles of an industrial relations system may be regarded as prerequisites for the operation of the damage model which was presented in Figure 1 and in the text above

Method

a) Data

The data for the present chapter were collected as part of a comprehensive study of strikes, strike threats and lockouts in Israel.[4] The target population of the study are all strikes, strike threats, and lockouts that covered at least seventy workers and took place (or were declared to take place) in Israel's main urban areas (Jerusalem, Tel Aviv, Haifa, and Beer Sheva) during the period April 1st, 1976 to February 28, 1977. A total of 263 questionnaires, supplying information regarding thirty-three strikes, three lockouts, and twenty-seven strike threats, were available for analysis.[5] The interviews were scheduled in three waves and two circles. For each industrial conflict, interviews were planned to take place before the start of the strike, during the strike or immediately after its end, and three months after the end of the strike. The first circle of interviewees included a senior management official and a Labor representative from the unit involved in the dispute. The second circle included key management officials and union representatives located outside the organizational unit under conflict. The interviews in the second circle were conducted only in those cases where, according to first circle reports, such extension was deemed crucial.

For the present analysis a strike unit file was arranged, and the response of the most important representative of a given side was regarded as the most reliable informant for that side.

b) The Measure of a Strike's Damage (M.S.D.)

In order to ascertain their evaluation of the expected or estimated damage of the strike in which they were involved, all interviewees, in each of the three interview waves were asked the following battery of questions:

The list below presents categories with possible relationships with any place of work. Will (have) these categories be (been) damaged, one way or another, by the strike you are being interviewed about, and to what degree?

The degree of damage was estimated on a five-point scale labelled: (1) very much, (2) much, (3) medium, (4) a little, (5) not at all. The list included the following categories:

(1) Owners of the place of work;
(2) Management of the place of work;
(3) The workers' representation;
(4) Workers involved in the dispute;
(5) Workers at the place of work who are not involved in the dispute;
(6) Direct clients of the place of work;
(7) Suppliers of the place of work;

(8) The public at large.

Results

MAIN ACTORS' SENSITIVITY TO THIRD PARTY DAMAGE

Under the assumptions presented above, the behavior of the main actors can be predicted in a responsible industrial relations system. The main characteristic of that behavior is the tendency to restrict conflict and its derived damage to the direct sides, and to minimize impact on third parties.

Strikes have differential impact on various social categories (Chamberlain and Schilling, 1954, pp. 242-45) and it may be expected that union and management officials, in a framework of a responsible industrial relation system, will try to find solutions for those highly vulnerable categories in cases under their discretion, in order to promote continuity and assure autonomy.

THE FOLLOWING PREDICTIONS CAN BE FORMULATED FOR MANAGEMENT'S EXPECTED BEHAVIOR IN THE HYPOTHESIZED CONDITIONS:

The higher the level of damage incurred by a strike to:

M(a) *management* – the more will management tend to initiate operation or maintenance plans, as alternatives to normal operations

M(b) *union and involved workers,* – the more will management tend to adopt steps intended to damage their workers (e.g., cutting extra work hours, fringe benefits, etc.)

M(c) *clients* – the more will management tend to activate stock handling provisions and arrangements with parallel producers or service suppliers

M(d) *the public* – the more will management tend to initiate the activity of mass communication organs and any other arrangements with influential public figures

Similar predictions can be formulated for workers' representation's behavior:

The higher the level of damage incurred by a strike to:

U(a) *management and owners* – the more will the union activate sanctions against management (e.g., slowdowns), or

U(b) announce their intention to go on strike not only as a threat, but also with sincere commitment to real strike action.

U(c) *the union* – the less will unions announce their intention to go on strike not only as a threat, but also with a sincere commitment to a real strike, or

U(d) take steps to strengthen their relations with other worker organizations

U(e) *involved workers* – the more will unions mobilize higher rank-and-file involvement and support through the organization of workers' meetings and secret polls.

U(f) *involved workers* – the more will unions make an effort to guarantee wages and salaries.

U(g) *the public* – the more will unions act to influence public opinion through mass communications and sympathetic public officials

The testing of these hypotheses was conducted as follows:

a) All non-missing cases were divided into high and low damage categories for each of the eight reference categories (management, union, owners, involved workers uninvolved workers, supplies, clients and the public). The median was adopted as the cutting point between the two damage categories.[6] Table 8.1 reflects the damage evaluation of management, and Table 8.2, that of union representatives.
b) The percentage of cases where a given behavioral indicator was adopted was computed separately for each damage category.
c) The difference between adoption tendencies was evaluated for direction and significance.

Table 8.1 presents the testing of predictions M(a) – M(d) regarding management's sensitivity to the damage of a strike in the place of work under their discretion.

The figures indicate a mild, statistically insignificant sensitivity of management to the negative implications of a strike on involved workers and on worker representatives, a partial sensitivity to such damage to clients and insensitivity to the repercussions on the owners and the public. High damage to the owners or management did not lead to the activating of operation or maintenance plans for the places of work under strike. High damage to the union or to the involved workers did, however, raise the probability of management-initiated steps against their workers. High damage to clients did effect the manipulation of stock, but this attentiveness did not lead to further effort as far as arrangements with clients or the opening of the market to parallel, and most probably competing, producers are concerned. The sensitivity to the public-at-large is non-existent. The trend of the results is in a direction inverse to the one expected under the assumption of a responsible industrial relations system.

The sensitivity of labor representatives to the damage of a strike to their affiliated members is presented in Table 8.2. The union's decision to adopt steps against management is not sensitive to the damage incurred by striking either on management or owners. Strike declaration is more purposeful in cases of owner vulnerability, though such a trend is not found *vis-à-vis* management and union itself. Workers' meetings are, however, convened more frequently for the discussion and the declaration of a strike in cases of high damage to the participating members than in low damage situations.

Table 8.1: Indicators regarding management officials' sensitivity to the damage of a strike in their place of work.

Indicator	Damage to Category	Degree of Damage High	Low	No.
Alternative work or mainte-	Owners	11.8	32.0	42
nance plans were activated	Management	22.2	26.7	42
Management initiated steps	Union	31.8	20.8	46
against workers	Involved			
	workers	39.3	11.1	46
Stock regulation procedures				
were activated	Clients	26.7	16.7	27
An arrangement with clients				
was realized	Clients	15.4	25.0	38
An arrangement with parallel				
places of work for market	Clients	20.0	21.4	34
regulation was used	Suppliers			
Mass communication				
media were used	Public	22.2	38.75	31
An arrangement with influen-				
tial public factors was activated	Public	38.75	60.0	41

This phenomenon finds no parallel in the use of workers' polls, but this finding can be explained by the interchangeability of these two mobilization procedures. The relative sensitivity of union leaders to the needs of the involved workers finds a further expression in their effort to find wage compensation in cases of high workers' damage. Labor representatives are sensitive to increasing damage to the public and express this tendency by extra reference to mass communications media. The same may be argued for their sensitivity to damage to their union. Their cooperation with other labor organizations is almost doubled in high damage, than in the low damage, cases. All these findings, except one, are statistically insignificant. The only significant difference is in the issue of workers' meetings convened for the purpose of strike declaration ($p(x2 = 3.7) < .05$).

Table 8.2: Indicators regarding union representatives' sensitivity to the damage of a strike in their place of work.

Indicator	Damage to Category	Degree of Damage		No.
		High	Low	
Union initiated steps against management	Owners	50.0	56.0	47
	Management	53.8	47.8	49
Strike announcement not for threat purposes only	Owners	85.7	54.5	25
	Management	72.2	77.8	27
	Union	69.2	75.0	25
Workers' meeting discussed strike declaration	Involved workers	80.6	50.0	49
Workers' meeting approved strike declaration	Involved workers	87.9	81.0	54
A secret poll approved strike declaration	Involved workers	21.9	30.0	52
Steps to guarantee wages were taken	Involved workers	25.0	8.3	32
Mass communications media were utilized	Public	53.3	40.0	35
Arrangements with other workers' organizations were made	Union	21.4	14.3	28

The total impression of the findings does not lend solid support to the existence of a responsible industrial relations system in Israel. The main actors' sensitivity to the effects of their behavior is very small, and in most cases limited to the triangle of management/union/involved workers. Such a narrow frame of reference deserves careful scrutiny. The next section is devoted to such a *post hoc* analysis.

Strike Damage: Level, Category-specific and Changes over Time

The relative insensitivity of unions and management can be explained in many ways, some of which are presented below. First, the absolute damage of the strike may be regarded as negligible. An actor's behavior cannot be expected to be sensitive to minor considerations in 'serious' events such as a strike (see the citation from Schneider at the beginning of the chapter). Secondly, third parties may be viewed as powerless, and therefore disregardable. This may be the case if they are unorganized, or if they have no other alternative sources for the products or services under the control of the striking sides. And third, striking may become a norm, instead of an exception. In such situations, striking is contagious, and no responsibility considerations are relevant.

Both main actors' estimates of the damage caused by their conflict were collected in our study and thus an analysis of the first explanation will be presented in detail. The other explanations can only be demonstratively described.

At this point it is worthwhile to remind the reader of the details of damage estimation in our study. Each interviewee was asked to evaluate the implications of the conflict in which his party was involved for the following eight social categories: owners, management, workers' representation, involved workers, workers uninvolved in the present conflict, clients, suppliers and the public. Three sets of estimations were collected during a complete interview schedule: before the strike, a few days after the end of the strike, and three months later. The evaluations were on a five-point scale ranging from (1)—very much, to (5)—not at all. For the present analysis, mean-values were computed for each actor (i.e., management and unions), interview wave (i.e., before, after and three months later), and for each category. To increase comprehensibility, each mean value was labelled according to its closest damage value label. The mean scores were computed for both strikes and strike threats.[7] Table 8.3 presents the average damage scores for management officials.

According to the figures:

a) the different categories can be arranged in the following order:

1. clients;
2. owners and management;
3. involved workers and the public;
4. workers' representation;
5. uninvolved workers and suppliers.

b) There is a clear, declining time-trend for strike damage. For all categories, excluding workers' representation which is regarded all along as suffering little damage, the highest harm score is assigned before the beginning of the strike. In those categories where damage scores differ from the score of the second and the third interview schedule, the earlier is the higher.

c) The employer side, i.e., management and owners, is more vulnerable to strike damage than the labor side. With regard to the workers, rank-and-file are more exposed to difficulties than their leadership.

Table 8.3: Average damage of strikes and strike threats on different categories by interview wave—Management officials' estimates.[1]

Category	Before the strike	After the strike	Three months after the strike
Owners	medium (2.7)	medium (3.1)	a little (3.5)
Management	medium (3.4)	medium (3.4)	a little (3.9)
Workers' representation	a little (3.7)	a little (3.9)	a little (4.0)
Involved workers	medium (3.3)	a little (3.5)	a little (3.8)
Uninvolved workers	a little (3.9)	not at all (4.5)	not at all (4.5)
Clients	much (2.0)	medium (2.9)	medium (3.0)
Suppliers	a little (3.7)	not at all (4.5	not at all (4.5
Public	medium (3.4)	a little (4.2)	a little (4.2)

[1] The numbers in parenthesis are the mean damage values for a given cell. Means were computed using the following weights:

1 - very much
2 - much
3 - medium
4 - a little
5 - not at all.

Table 8.4 presents the average damage scores for labor representatives.

According to the figures:

a) The different categories can be arranged in the following damage order:
1. owners and clients;
2. management and the public;
3. workers' representation, involved workers and suppliers;
4. uninvolved workers.

b) There is a clear, declining time-trend for strike damage. None of the categories estimated to suffer much or medium damage before the strike broke out, continued to be assigned such scores later on. Only those categories which suffered little or not at all continued to be thus regarded at the end of the strike or later.

(c) The labor side, all categories inclusive, is less vulnerable to a strike's damage than the employer side.

The comparison between Tables 8.3 and 8.4 and shows some interesting regularities:

Table 8.4: Average damage of strikes and strike threats on different categories by interview wave—Labor representatives' estimation. [1]

Category	Before the strike		After the strike		Three months after the strike	
Owners	medium	(2.4)	medium	(2.9)	medium	(2.8)
Management	medium	(3.0)	a little	(3.7)	a little	(3.8)
Workers' representation	a little	(3.8)	a little	(4.2)	a little	(4.3)
Involved workers	a little	(3.6)	a little	(3.8)	a little	(3.6)
Uninvolved workers	not at all	(4.9)	not at all	(4.7)	not at all	(4.6)
Clients	much	(2.3)	medium	(2.7)	medium	(2.9)
Suppliers	a little	(3.7)	a little	(4.0)	a little	(4.0)
Public	medium	(3.4)	a little	(3.6)	a little	(3.9)

[1]For legend see Table 8.3

a) Both sides' estimates are highly congruent. Seventeen of the twenty-four damage definitions, are identical.
b) In the pre-strike phase both management and workers' representatives agree on the level of damage for both main actors.

In this context management is more vulnerable than the union. On the other hand, the estimates of management officials of the damage to involved workers are higher than those of their representatives, and union estimates of the owners' damage are higher than those of management. The concordance between the sides is liable to encourage union aggressiveness, while the discordance may be a mitigating factor.

The patterns presented in this chapter can be related to the issue of responsibility presented above. The damage incurred by strikes to various social categories is regarded by union and management both as small and in a decreasing trend. Nowhere was a category labelled as very vulnerable to the damage caused by a given strike. In cases of some damage, time perspective indicates less need for responsibility.

This view may be defended by the use of the offset factor concept. Christenson (1953) distinguishes between current transfer, which is the transfer of orders or production from a unit under, or expecting, a strike to another source, and time-shaft offset, which is the manipulation of consumption by time regulation. The first form is of limited value in Israel because of its small size and the related monopolistic characteristics. The second version is probably very popular in Israel, and follows the short duration of most strikes (one to three days).[8]

Our argument, that strikes are regarded as causing only minor damage by their main actors, can be substantiated by one more finding. If strike damage is a function of the curtailment of the supply of products and services to the ultimate consumers, then strike threats should be regarded as harmless. In our data, almost no significant difference is found between strikes and strike threats. Thus, the absence of consumption effect can encourage unions officials and managers to dismiss the danger of damage and avoid claims for irresponsibility.

Two more explanations were suggested above for the lack of support for the responsibility model in our data. The first referred to the powerlessness of countervailing consumer organizations. This characteristic of Israel society is well known and may contribute to the lack of consideration of management and unions for the damage incurred to their clients. The second explanation mentioned the 'contagion effect' of a wave of strikes. Our data were collected during the last year of the Labor party coalition government. This was a year of disillusionment which ended with a political upheaval. Thus, in a context of distrust, social responsibility cannot flourish.

Can Israeli unions be regarded as responsible? If we judge them by the outcomes of their actions, the answer is positive. Israeli strikes of the reported period are fairly innocuous. They are very short, which makes consumer accommodation quite easy. They have virtually never been a national emergency event. Strikes of policemen, firefighters, electricity and water supply operators are almost unknown. However, it is not because of intentional responsibility that strike are harmless. The main actors of the Israeli irs do not show any effort to avoid risky and damaging conflicts. They just 'happen' not to get involved in disputes of this character. Only functional considerations are important as far as current system autonomy is concerned.

The whys and the ifs are important in the framework of future perspectives. The present chapter does not indicate the existence of that sensitivity to the needs of the external environment of the irs which can safeguard the interests of the public at large, or of any specialized sector of it. The maturation of the irs, if not accompanied by an increased concern for influential potential victims of industrial conflict, may create pressure to curtail its autonomy and to change its ideology and norms. Signs for the increased need for such a change are indicated by the intensification of industrial conflict in Israel since the political upheaval of 1977. Phenomena like a significant increase in the number of participants in an average strike, the increase in the duration of strikes, the relative prevalence of strikes in essential public services (medical services, in particular), the increase in the frequency of return to work court injunctions, and the parallel dramatic increase in evasion of court orders, all these indicate an aggravation of the industrial relations situation. An autonomous irs can be very risky.

The risk increases dramatically when a. . . system that is becoming autonomous demands that it be given sufficient time to act and total authority on decision making. Such authority can make almost anything possible since there are no longer powerful external controls that can keep decisions within the bounds of the desirable. (Luhmann, 1982, p. 157)

At the present stage we limit our discussion to the situation in the period under study. We shall have more to say on this issue in the concluding chapter.

Notes to Chapter 8

1.   The terms union, workers' representation and workers' committee will be used interchangeably in the text. In the Israeli context the first means the official representative organization of the workers—in most cases, a sub-unit of the General Federation of Labor; the second is an informal term for various negotiation levels; and the third, the direct representatives of the workers of a given place of work or employer.

2.   Luhmann refers in his discussion to the political system. Similar propositions can be raised regarding any other system, including the industrial relation system.

3.   Chamberlain and Schilling (op. cit., p. 39) present the following alternative model in their book:

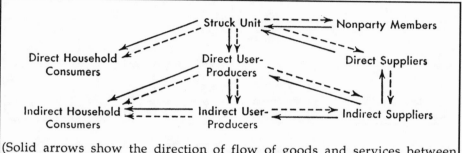

(Solid arrows show the direction of flow of goods and services between related groups, while broken arrows show the direction in which strike effects are transmitted)

<   Direction of flow of goods and services between the related groups.
<   Direction in which strike effects are transmitted.

Our model differs from theirs in the following points:
a)   The struck unit is divided into four categories: management, union, involved workers, and uninvolved workers;
b)   Family members of involved and uninvolved workers (non-party members) are not left as an independent category;
c)   No distinction is made between production and consumption clients;
d)   Only direct suppliers and clients are included in the model;
e)   The public is added as an extra category.

All these distinctions can be explained by the different aims of the two studies. Chamberlain and Schilling are interested in the estimation of the degree of total and category-specific damage of a given strike. I am interested in the actions adopted or neglected by the main actors of a

given conflict, which are aimed at the minimization of a strike's damage to a given category.
4. The work reported here was supported by grants from the Israel Academy of Sciences and Humanities, Commission for Basic Research, Chief of Labor Relations Division, in the Israeli ministry of Labor, and the Employers' Insurance Fund. I would like to thank the three organizations for their assistance. The conclusions are the sole responsibility of the author.
5. The present chapter deals only with industrial conflicts initiated by the labor side. Therefore, the three lockouts are omitted.
6. The detailed specification is as follows:

Damaged side	Responses of...			
	Management		Union	
	High Damage	Low Damage	High Damage	Low Damage
Owners	1, 2	3, 4, 5	1	2, 3, 4, 5
Management	1, 2, 3	4, 5	1, 2	3, 4, 5
Worker's representation	1, 2, 3	4, 5	1, 2, 3	4, 5
Univolved workers	Not included in present analysis			
Clients	1, 2	3, 4, 5	1	2, 3, 4, 5
Suppliers	Not included in present analysis			
Public	1, 2, 3, 4	5	1, 2, 3	4, 5

7. Specific means were computed for strikes and strike threats, but the differences between each actor-category-wave mean for the two conflict forms were negligible. Therefore, this analysis is not included in the present paper. This finding will be referenced once again at the conclusion of this article.
8. The following table represents the percentage distribution of strikes in Israel by their length for the years 1975-77.

Year	Length			Total No. of Strikes
	Less than 1 day	1 - 3 days	More than 3 days	
1975	51	18	31	118
1976	48	20	32	123
1977	41	25	34	126

The source for these figures is unpublished statistics from the files of the Ministry of Labor, Industrial Relations Unit.

9

Epilogue

> According to my lights, a last chapter should resemble a primitive orgy after harvest. The work may have come to an end, but the worker cannot let go all at once. He is still full of energy that will fester if it cannot find an outlet. Accordingly, he is allowed a time of license, when he may say all sorts of things he would think twice before saying in more sober moments, when he is no longer bound by logic and evidence but free to speculate about what he has done. (Homans, 1961, p. 378)

Homans may have picked the most appropriate term for an epilogue, an orgy. My work is done, and I keep asking myself, so what? What is its message? What did I gain from the analysis? What do I hope you, the reader, has gained?

Israeli strikes were always a mystery for me. The deeper I got into them, the more elusive they seemed. For years I looked for a key. Are they social events enacted by isolated masses, as Kerr and Siegel (1954) claimed in their classic work? If so, how is it that Israeli strikers are often the least isolated and most established employees, those working in the public sector? Are Israeli strikes explainable in political and organizational terms, as Shorter and Tilly (1974) contend for France? If so, how is it that a political upheaval as impressive as the defeat of the Labor Party, the dominant party since the 1930s, did not lead to a total disaster in the IR arena? If strikes are the cynical outcome of skilled union leaders who abuse their authority to establish a bridge between their followers' expectations and realistic possibilities (Ashenfelter and Johnson, 1969), how is it that strikes in Israel are so short? If strikes are like road accidents, caused by barriers of communication (Hicks, 1963), how is it that the most experienced leaders of the most solid unions and the professional negotiators of the public employers fall into the trap of industrial strife? And, if an institutionalized irs should be, as believes Snyder (1975), responsive primarily to rational economic factors, how is it that Israeli strikes have almost no relationship at all to macro-economic developments?

What is the rationale of Israeli strikes? Barel and Michael (1977) assumed that the syntax is economic. They intended their book on Israeli strikes in the 1960s to focus almost exclusively on the factor of economic costs. They ended up with a pioneering venture, limited by its non-theoretical view.

My understanding of Israeli strikes has developed from two seemingly unrelated sources, on the one hand a set of three correlation coefficients and on the other, my acquaintance with an impressive theoretician. Chronologically, the statistical data came first. The theory then followed.

I used to envy my American colleagues. They managed to anchor their analyses on coefficients of determination as high as ninety percent (Ashenfelter and Johnson, 1969). Mine were always close to the other extreme. These low levels of predictability were often embarrassing. I still remember when I, as a young sociologist, was summoned to the head of the Trade Union Department of those days, Yeruham Meshel. I was asked to prepare a six months forecast for the magnitude of strikes. I showed no willingness to supply the forecast. The volatile Israeli situation could not be encompassed by any reliable tools of which I was aware. Any forecast would have been no more than pure speculation and I did not see myself as an adventurous gambler. Meshel, on the other hand, was not interested in my professional scruples. He was a politician and believed that he knew *exactly* what the figures were going to be. He needed a scientific mask for his own insight. Well, I was not in a position to satisfy him. My conceptual understanding reached a turning point a few years later. At that time I found that economic and political variables showed a decreasing relationship to strike frequency. While in the Becker period the coefficient of determination reached a figure of 0.57, it decreased to 0.31 in the Ben-Aharon days and reached an almost zero level (0.05) during the years of the Meshel administration. What is the explanation of this trend? When I first saw the figures, I could only guess.

It was through the writings of Niklas Luhmann (1982) that I found a possible theoretical breakthrough in the analysis of Israeli IR. Luhmann has little to say, if at all, on industrial relations, nor has he ever written on Israel. Nevertheless, some of his innovative ideas seemed to offer promising theoretical paths to the comprehension of Israeli industrial conflict. First comes the idea of differentiation. Societies, through their evolution pass through a process of differentiation into functional domains. In his writings, Luhmann discusses domains like the economy, the polity, law, religion, science and education. I do not see why the IR domain cannot gain the same level of autonomy. Second, differentiation should not be taken for granted. Its evolvement is contingent upon situational constraints. Finally, institutional autonomy does not guarantee avoidance of risks. A differentiated social domain may be very efficient. It may, however, be very risky. Moreover, with the crystallization of a differentiated society, ideological and value laden criteria for effectivity lose their importance. An institutional domain may seek sectorial effectivity at the expense of societal functioning.

With this paradigm in mind, I found that the fog surrounding the Israeli irs began to clear away. I can think of no other instance in human history where a solid organizational basis and a comprehensive normative system of a social domain preceded its maturation, or at least its advanced functioning as a differentiated domain. The Israeli irs had reached a very developed state prior to its emergence as an autonomous social institution. The establishment of the Histadrut in 1920 set up an organizational apparatus, the major aims of which were rooted in the future. This body functioned in a vacuum brought about by a unique historical situation. The Balfour Declaration, which awarded the Jewish people an opportunity to establish a "homeland" in Palestine was not an acknowledgement of a reality. The Jewish community in the late 1910s was both small and to a large degree non-Zionistic. World Jewry was not standing in line, waiting to emigrate to Palestine. The Jewish homeland was more like a dream, shared by a few, practiced by fewer.[1] The declaration may have been more a *personal* acknowledgement to Hayim Weizman, who became thirty years later the first president of the State of Israel. The establishment of the Histadrut created an organ aimed at the facilitation of the absorption of the expected wave of *olim* (new immigrants). This history of the Histadrut is a classic example of a self-fulfilling prophecy.

Since it was a framework established by workers, it put job opportunities on its agenda. Since there were no jobs available, the founders adopted a "constructive" approached, and started creating jobs. Since work conditions were a reflection of the then current rural economy, they started campaigning for industrial frames of reference imported from the European experience and from socialist ideology. Since there was a scarcity of private capital to make their dream possible, they turned to national sources. Thus, a semi-nationalized economy was established with no need for forced acts or legislation. Since their counterparts on the employers' side were weak and fragmented, they manage to institutionalize a solid web of collective agreements and a belief in its functionality and desirability. Under these conditions, the evolving irs was in existence when both economic and technological settings were still rudimentary. The major legitimating criterion for this irs was political. Thus, the major element missing from the irs was that of interaction with the political nation-state. So long as the political domain was incomplete—before the creation of a state—the two social domains, the political and the IR could coexist in peace. The real systemic challenge for the irs appeared when Israel was established in 1948.

During the first years of the state, political processes became dominant. Israeli society of the late 1940s and the 1950s was a mobilized society. Even a strong and consolidated sphere such as as the irs could not avoid this situation. Most first line leaders switched their organizational location from the Histadrut to state political institutions and bureaucracy. Many functional units were severed from the Histadrut and attached to the state. Thus, the Histadrut became a semi-state organ. It was the rebellion from below, the crystallization of a new authentic leadership which created a critical dilemma for the Histadrut—either to be autonomous or to cease. The Histadrut managed to adopt the former course. The period covered by the present book is the time when these processes came to maturation. Becker's days are the twilight of the pioneering phase, while the Kessar period is the peak of its functional autonomy. More than one scenario exists for future developments, a topic on which I will elaborate later.

The Three Sub-Periods: Labor, Likud and National Unity Governments

Two political landmarks help us divide the period under study into three meaningful sub-periods. The first years (1965-77) show a minimal level of differentiation in the functioning of the irs. The domain developed both its strength and its deficiencies from the glorious pre-independence years and from the dominance of the Labor Party both on the state level and in the IR context. The second sub-period (1977-84) gave the irs an opportunity to benefit from the strength of the past simultaneously with the consolidation of autonomy *vis-à-vis* its external environment. The third period (1984-87) supplied a setting for gaining acknowledgement for this autonomy and started a process of internal differentiation and sub-system autonomy.

THE EARLY PERIOD—THE LABOR DOMINATED PERIOD

As previously noted, the Histadrut was, without doubt, a partner—albeit a junior partner—in the mid-1960s. Aharon Becker told me a typical anecdote illustrating this point. We met in his moderately standard apartment in Tel-Aviv. He pointed to the couch I was sitting on and recalled that in 1962, the night before a significant devaluation of the Israeli pound was announced, Levi Eshkol, the Finance Minister, sat on the same couch and informed him of the impending devaluation. From this I gleaned two important points. First, Becker, the secretary general, was a member of the inner political circle. Second, his status in this setting was secondary. He did not *make* the decision, but was consulted as to the best means to implement it. This level of involvement is reflected in Chapter 6.

Strike activity is geared to economic and political developments. Subordinating the IR domain to external considerations creates tension. Strikes become prevalent when unemployment decreases. Full employment was the credo of Labor economic policy. Over-employment creates a sellers' market, workers can improve their lot. The Histadrut, however, saw itself more on the controlling, than on the demanding, side. Wage policy was geared to productivity, an objective perpetually doomed to failure. Disciplinary actions against Ashdod Port leaders were an example of a deplorable effort to keep disobedient workers' committees in line.

Still, industrial actions—strikes, strike threats and sanctions—were self-disciplined. We saw in Chapter 8 that damage was kept to a minimum. The communication between the Histadrut and the government was based on longterm connections. Therefore, strikes were more symbolic gestures, designed to facilitate negotiations, than actions in a cut-throat war. The prevalence of strikes was problematic for the Histadrut (see Chapter 8). However, a solution was almost unreachable. For Israeli society, strikes were events of an undifferentiated nature. They reflected distrust in government and disagreements on specific status gradings, no less than specific IR related interests.

This was a period in which the irs of the organization level fought for its autonomous existence. Both approved and unapproved strikes were numerous. Faced with a patronizing Histadrut, representatives of blue collar workers tried to establish their status. Private employers tried to strengthen their position by building up their national representative associations and by supporting them with financial and organizational means. At the end of this period, the private sector employers had a powerful independent insurance fund, a counterpart to the Histadrut Strike Fund.

Strikes were handled by experienced functionaries. The source of unrest, though, stemmed from the rank-and-file and their local leaders. As we learned in Chapter 8, the immediate actors of the irs did not share the established ideological concerns of responsibility. Their actions, however, caused quite minimal damage. Night-long negotiations, back-room meetings and informal phone calls, restricted the economic harm to manageable levels.

The irs of that period was typified by an inability to "reduce the complexity of the environment" (Luhmann, 1982) in relation to which it operated. No wonder that when Becker left, a candidate promising change, Ben-Aharon, was elected. Unfortunately for him, the time was not yet ripe for change, since the Histadrut was confronted by a unified environment led by the Labor Party in government. The Knesset elections of 1977 can serve as the moment of transition between the early period and the intermediate one.

THE INTERMEDIATE PERIOD—THE LIKUD DOMINATED PERIOD

More than being a success for the Likud Party, the 1977 general elections were a defeat for the Labor Party.[2] This shock served as an impetus for irs reorganization. Two parallel developments took place. The manifest process entailed reorganization plans for the Histadrut in general and the Trade Union Division in particular. Their impact was quite minimal. The latent process, however, led to the consolidation of a differentiated irs on the national level. A terrifying ideological opponent turned to be a toothless tiger. Of all Likud's plans to control the IR arena and to disintegrate the Histadrut, nothing transpired. The new administration honored the independence of the Histadrut and respected the IR web of rules. All institutional provisions which served to detach the IR domain from its environment were kept intact. Wages continued to be linked to prices via cost-of-living increments. As a matter of fact, this linkage was even stronger than in the past. Periods of high inflation made it almost totally impractical for the new administration to adopt new arrangements. The employers' associations gained in prominence, but proved as devoted to the ideas of voluntarism and non-governmental involvement in IR affairs as did the Histadrut. As a result, strikes became an internal IR affair, political and economic factors ceasing to serve as its predictors.

The removal of a political flavor from daily IR handling made itself felt by a sense of moderation. The frequency of strikes decreased (Table 5.1). Of no lesser importance, however, was the development of strike breadth.

The increase in the average size of strikes reflects a process of differentiation *inside* the irs. National trade unions, some of which organize para-professionals and academicians, crossed enterprise borders and acted in concert. The Histadrut tried to control these acts, but despite a decrease in the propensity to approve strikes (Table 4.5), this phenomenon persisted. The Histadrut claimed to be implementing plans for increased involvement of 'authentic' workers' leaders in its executive branches. Still, in spite of few symbolic nominations, the resistance inside Histadrut establishment to such a move, nullified the accomplishments. The Histadrut tried to act as a unified setting, all functional organs, the Trade Union Division, Kupat Cholim (The Sick Fund), and Hevrat ha'Ovdim (The Economic Enterprises) being run in a centralist mode. All efforts were directed to the task of keeping the huge mammoth alive. A financial disaster in Histadrut-owned enterprises and widespread dissatisfaction with the Kupat Cholim medical services were needed for internal differentiation to be publicly acknowledged and explicitly implemented. This development awaited the election of a new secretary general and to a change in the political arena.

THE FINAL PHASE—NATIONAL UNITY GOVERNMENT—AND BEYOND

The 1984 general elections ended in a deadlock between the Likud and Labor parties. Labor got 34.9 percent of the votes and Likud, 31.9 percent. Neither could form a government without the other. This weakening of the political system was followed by a dramatic collapse in the economic sphere. Such an environment is an ideal setting for solidifying the autonomy of the irs and increasing its internal differentiation.

Chapter 3 was devoted to this topic. Political considerations confronted IR related interests. On the one hand, a Labor leader, Shimon Peres, headed the government and another Labor leader, Kessar, headed the Histadrut. Both had a strong interest in their party's recovery. On the other hand, as prime minister, Peres desperately needed all the goodwill of the world to extricate the country from political (inflation), and military (The Lebanon Campaign) disasters. The cooperation of the Histadrut was essential.

Kessar acted in a statesmanlike fashion. He was ready to mobilize his organization's resources to support the government. In return, he demanded that the state acknowledge the autonomy of the irs.

Kessar's demand was not new. Ben-Aharon had raised it sixteen years earlier. Notwithstanding the personality differences between the two secretaries general, the major distinguishing factor remains situational. Ben-Aharon acted within an irs which had hardly started the differentiation from its environment. In such a situation, the potential for handling external and internal complexity is quite small. Kessar, on the other hand, found himself leading a sphere which had gained a significant level of autonomy during the Meshel years. The differentiation of its political and economic constraints facilitated his ability to cope with the impending threats. This differentiation, however, was not enough to cope with the complexities of the organization he happened to head. For the first time, the developments in the irs held significant dangers for the Histadrut.

In Chapter 2, following a description of the main features of the Israeli irs, I said, "This structural feature of the Israeli irs assigns the Histadrut a central structural function, leaving its partners in a somewhat more peripheral status." The dominant status of the Histadrut stemmed from the fact that it used to fulfill all three functions of an irs actor, management, union, and third party. So long as the irs faced a stable environment, this multi-faceted function was an asset. It shaped the irs into a solid structure. However, the more turbulent an environment becomes, the more a system must gain autonomy in order to survive. The Israeli irs of the 1990s is going to function in a problematic habitat. Both political and economic threats are on the increase. Politically, it is almost evident that the Labor Party is not going to recoup its status of past decades. Likud Party opposed the idea of a *General* Federation of Labor. Even though no Likud government has seriously tried to disintegrate the Histadrut, this option has never been discarded. Economically, the Israeli economy faces a threatening challenge in 1992, when Israel will be exposed to free trading with the European Economic Community. This prospect can serve either as a facilitator for development or as a hazard for its existence. Under these conditions, the simplicity of a unitary Histadrut will not be able to cope with these complexities. Internal differentiation will be the key to survival.

Traditionally, the Histadrut held that its multi-functional structure was more an asset than a liability. Unless this multi-functionality undergoes significant differentiation, this property may destroy it. A differentiated Histadrut may keep all, or most current functions under the same umbrella. The legalistic issue is of minor importance. What is more important is the *logic* of its operations. Unless economic enterprises are run according to an economic rationale, unless health services follow medical principle, and unions follow IR logic, none of the Histadrut organs can survive. If, on the other hand, each of these divisions adheres to criteria relevant to its functioning, the Histadrut may reach a second golden age. Still, this development, if attained, may require a departure from the Histadrut as an *organization* and a return to the concept of the Histadrut as an *ideological movement*.

Initially, the Histadrut was an ideological movement. This allowed it to serve as the 'medina she'baderekh' (state in embryo). *In the absence of a state* it acted as a surrogate state. The need to fill this political vacuum created a multi-function organization carrying out tasks of immense importance. On the other hand, it operated in quite a simple environment. As a result, the Histadrut managed to gain dominance and kept major resources under its control.

As we reach the establishment of Israel, this vacuum was filled by the executive organs of the state. Being part of the establishment, the Histadrut managed to avoid disintegration. However avoiding an organizational disaster is no more than a minimal achievement. It had the bizarre status of being both a subordinate body and a partner, albeit minor. The government served as the godfather of the Histadrut. Once again, the external constraints of the Histadrut kept it to a low complexity level. The late 1950s and the 1960s introduced a turbulent environment, not from the outside, but from below. The Histadrut managed to control its rank-and-file which was in revolt, not so much by differentiation as through cooptation. Authentic local workers' leaders were absorbed into the Histadrut bureaucracy. Their impact on policy making, however, remained negligible.

Thus, although awareness of this wave of unrest was clearly evident, steps taken to deal with it failed, even during the post-upheaval period, following the defeat of the Labor Party in the 1977 general elections.

The Histadrut expanded its cooptation methods. It tried to use its economic enterprises as sites for rewarding powerful rank-and-file leaders. This channel was selected for two main reasons: first, all former strongholds of Labor were now held by the Likud and second, it was easier to expand a tradition than to innovate new solutions. These methods decreased the level of differentiation of the Histadrut. The nomination of grass roots leaders to senior economic positions, mainly in the personnel divisions, provided a short-term, but not an effective long term, remedy.

The combination of an economically irresponsible government, crippling inflation and short-sighted and adventurous managements in the Histadrut sector brought many enterprises to the verge of bankruptcy. The first to fall were the moshavim and the kibbutzim. These mostly agricultural enterprises were promptly followed by Solel Boneh (the major Histadrut construction concern), by Kupat Cholim (the Histadrut owned medical service), and by Koor (the major Histadrut industrial holding company).

The Histadrut faces a challenge, either to increase effectivity or to become extinct. It is the main thesis of this book that further differentiation is the most potent means for adaptation to a turbulent environment. Differentiation is not a rule of nature. The Histadrut may, or may not, embark on this route. Internal differentiation has proved to be more difficult than external differentiation and the Histadrut has thus far managed to avoid it. Yet, under the present constraints, sidestepping this option may bring about its downfall.

The Israeli irs cannot remain as described in this book without a strong Histadrut. Its structure is based on the logic of its existence. The vacuum created by the disintegration of the Histadrut may be filled both by internal and external irs elements. The major potential internal irs entrepreneurs are local managements and national unions. Both have gained more power than they previously had. Both signal a process of differentiation, increased segmentation and decreased functional specialization. In a country as small as Israel, such a process is hardly likely to continue. Therefore, from within the irs such an arrangement is only an interim possibility, and even then, not a stable one. The cardinal agent of change is the government. As a central political body, the government is a major gainer in a neocorporatist settlement. Thus, the government is interested in the existence of a dominant central actor in the irs.

Whether we envision the Histadrut undergoing a radical process of internal differentiation or envision its failure to adjust to the growing uncertainties, the Israeli irs carries a prospect of the perpetuation of a structure led by centralist organs and differentiated functionally to a very significant degree.

Notes to Chapter 9

1. Only 4% of the Jewish emigration between 1880 and 1930 went to Palestine (Eisenstadt, 1969)
2. A comparison between the results of the 1973 and the 1977 elections shows the following figures

Party	1973	1977
Labor	39.6%	24.6%
Likud	30.2	33.4
Dash	–	11.6

APPENDIX:
THREE-DIMENSIONAL
DIAGRAMS
CORRESPONDING TO
TABLES IN CHAPTER 5

Table 5.6   Summary strike pattern features for union type and period.

106[*]

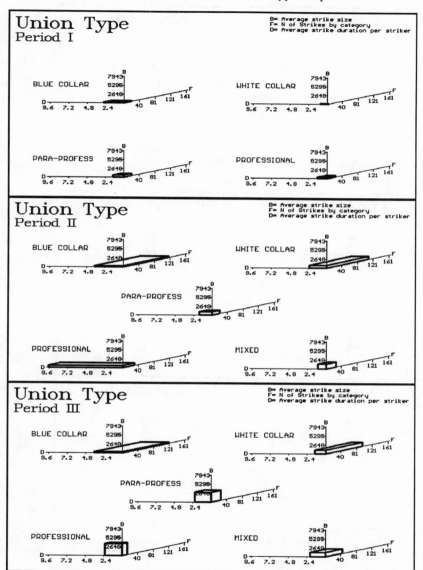

Table 5.6 cont'd.

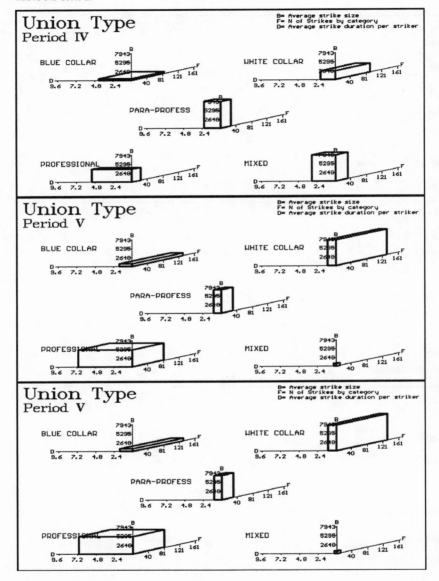

Table 5.7 Summary strike pattern features for occupation and period. 109

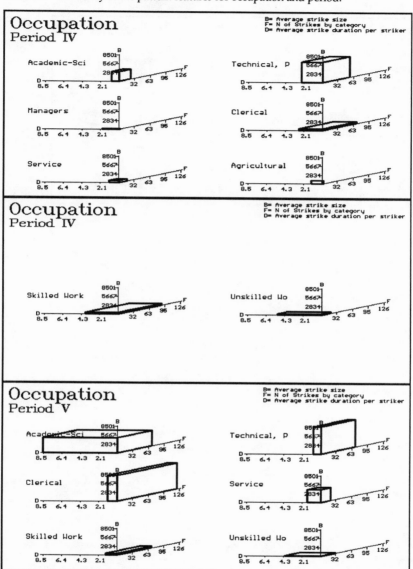

Table 5.7 cont'd.

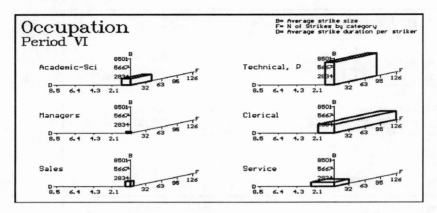

Table 5.8   Summary strike pattern features for union declaring strike and period.   112

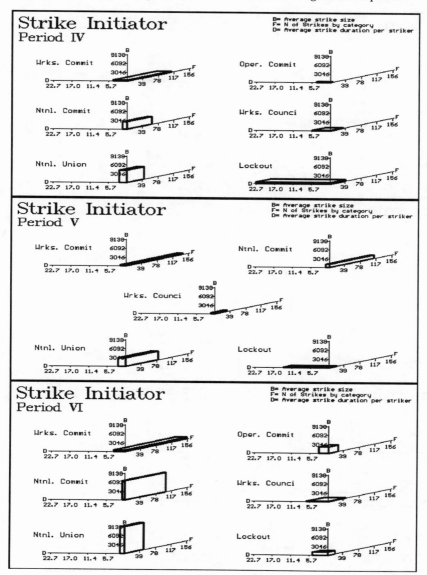

Table 5.9   Strike frequency by economic branch and period.   115

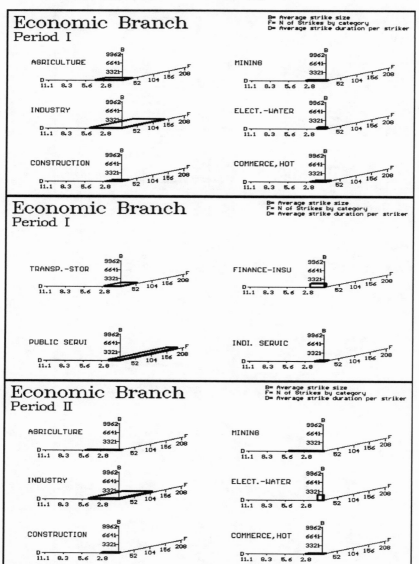

Table 5.9 cont'd.

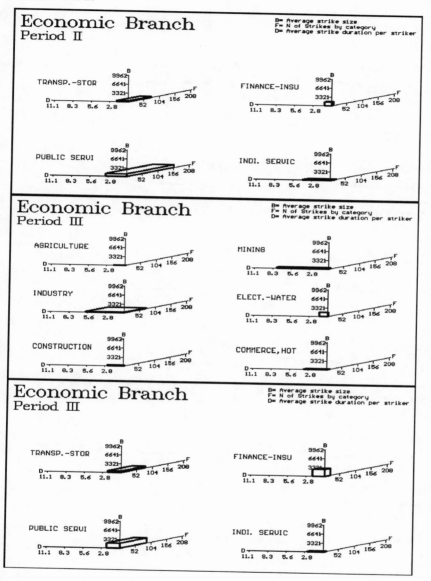

Table 5.9 cont'd.

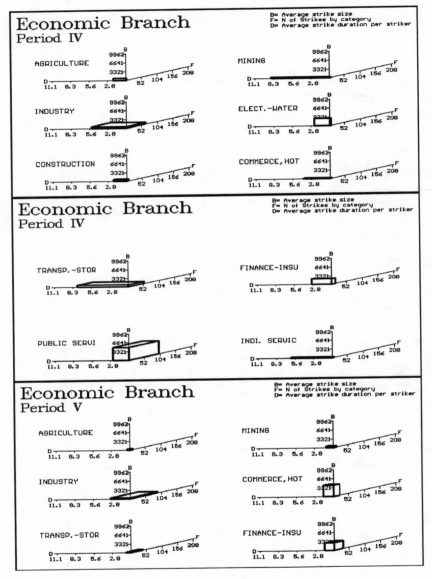

Table 5.9 cont'd.

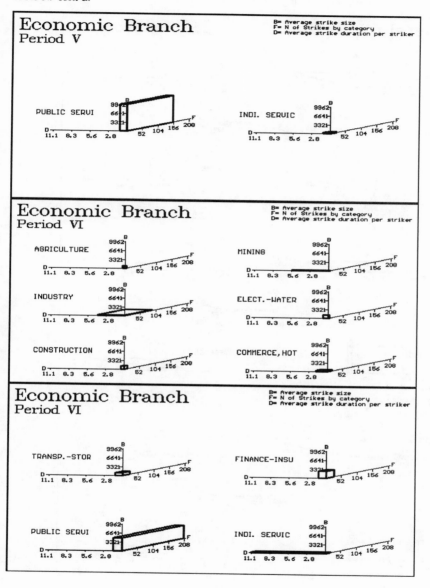

Table 5.10 Summary strike pattern features for sector and period.　　　　116

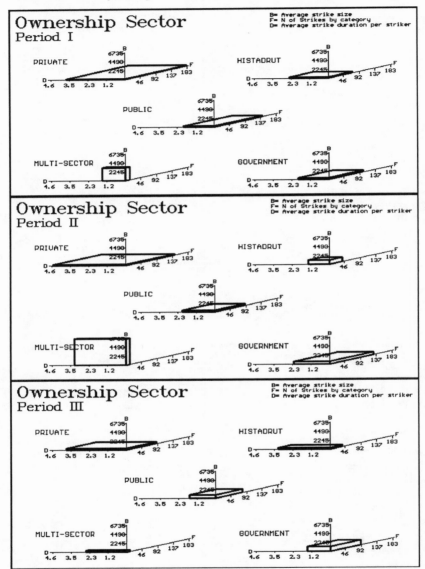

Table 5.10 cont'd.

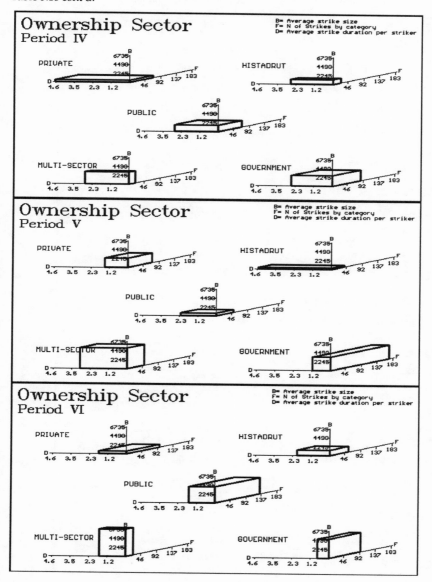

Table 5.12. Summary strike pattern features for type of strike and period.

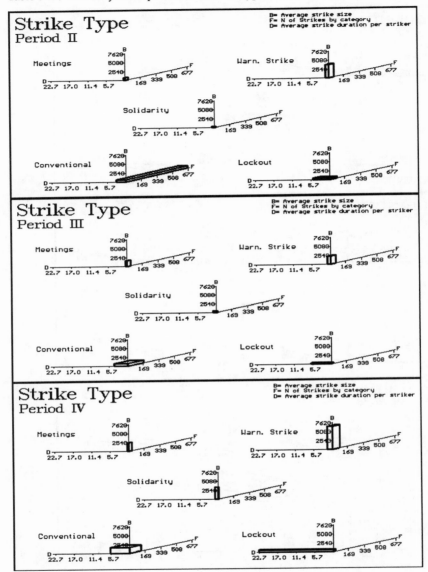

Table 5.12 cont'd.

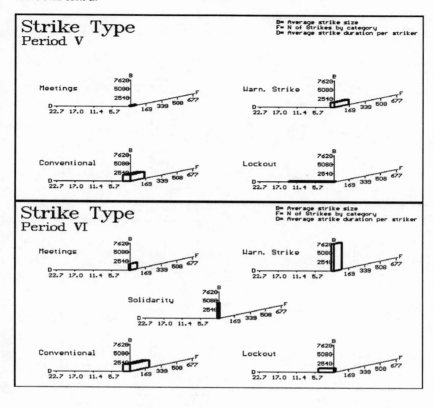

Table 5.13   Frequency of strikes by reported cause and period.   127

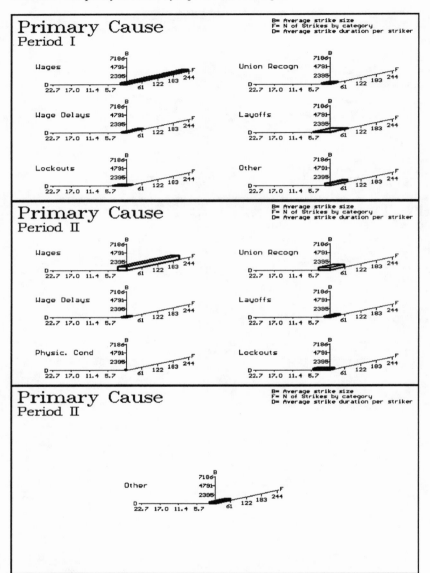

Table 5.13 cont'd.

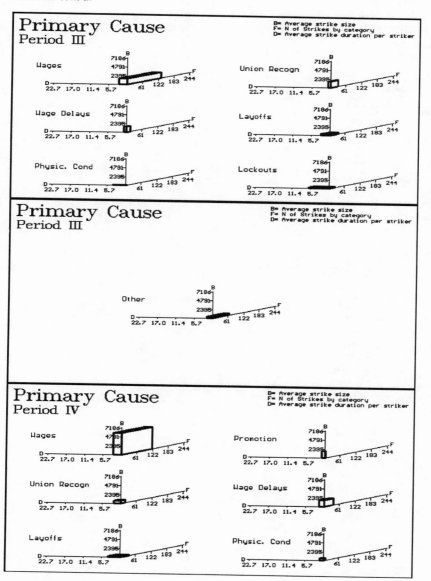

Table 5.13 cont'd.

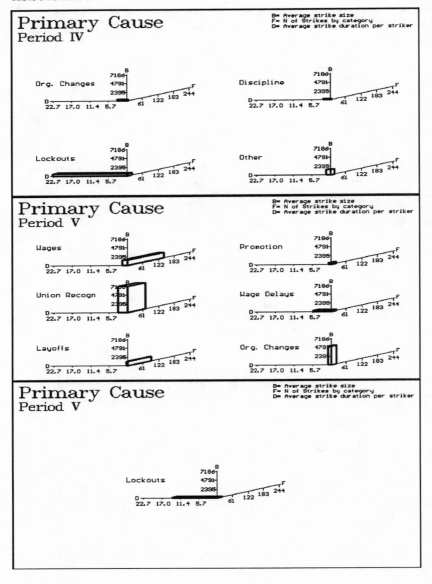

Table 5.13 cont'd.

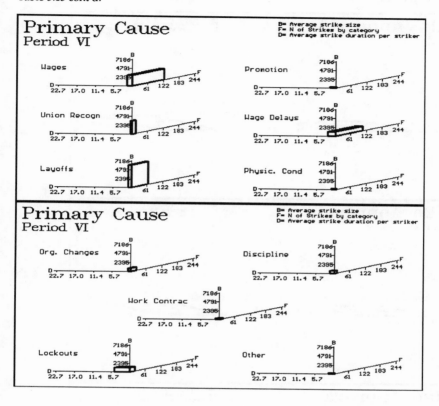

Table 5.14 Summary strike pattern features for strike approval and period.   129

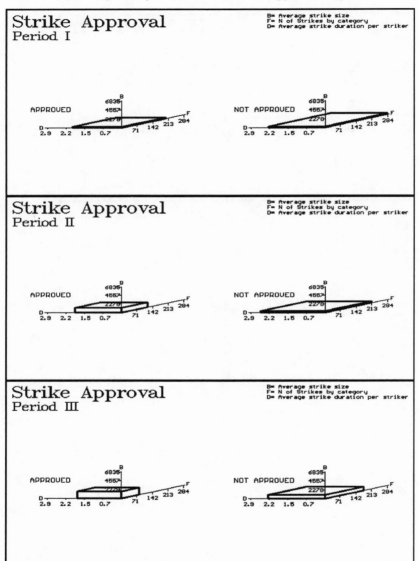

Table 5.14 cont'd.

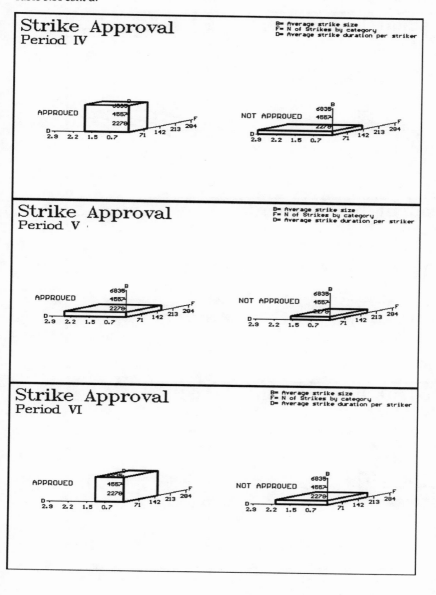

Table 5.15 Summary strike pattern features for collapsed* external involvement and period.   131

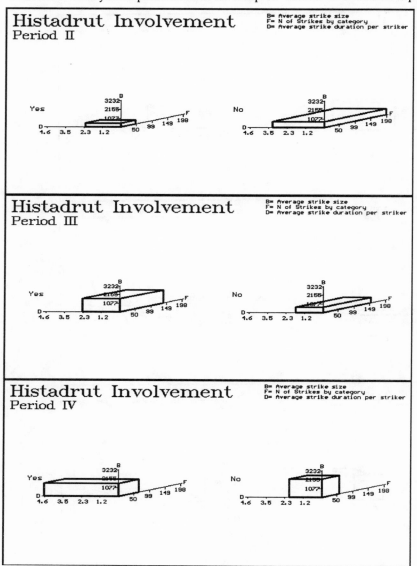

* Graphs are produced separately and presented sequentially for each party

Table 5.15 cont'd.

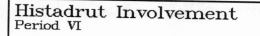

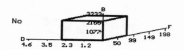

Histadrut Involvement
Period VI

B= Average strike size
F= N of Strikes by category
D= Average strike duration per striker

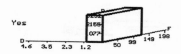

Labor Court Involvement
Period II

B= Average strike size
F= N of Strikes by category
D= Average strike duration per striker

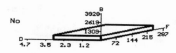

Labor Court Involvement
Period III

B= Average strike size
F= N of Strikes by category
D= Average strike duration per striker

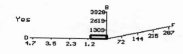

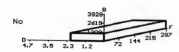

Table 5.15 cont'd.

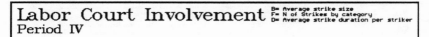

Labor Court Involvement
Period IV

B= Average strike size
F= N of Strikes by category
D= Average strike duration per striker

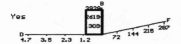

Labor Court Involvement
Period VI

B= Average strike size
F= N of Strikes by category
D= Average strike duration per striker

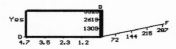

IR Dept. Involvement
Period II

B= Average strike size
F= N of Strikes by category
D= Average strike duration per striker

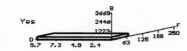
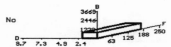

Table 5.15 cont'd.

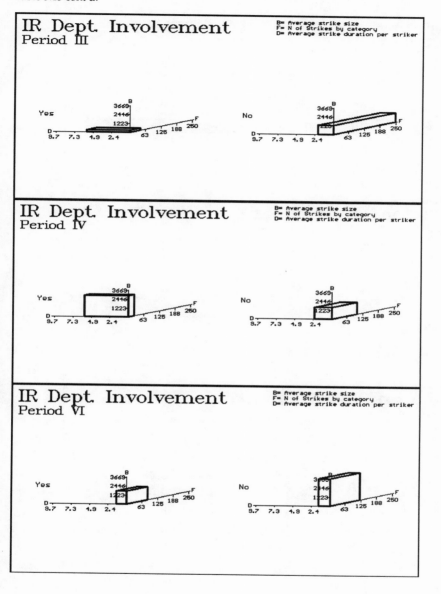

Table 5.15 cont'd.

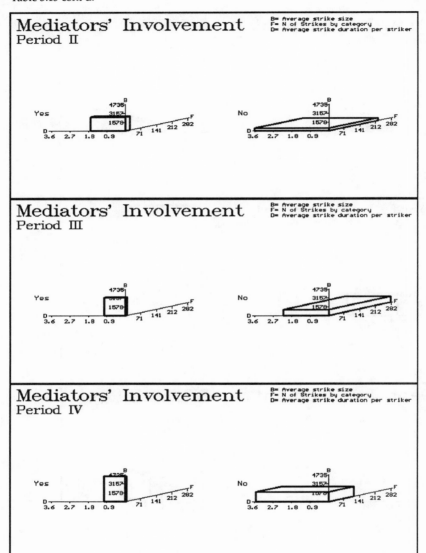

Table 5.15 cont'd.

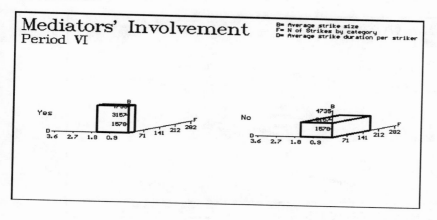

Table 5.16 Summary strike pattern features for strike outcomes and period.   133

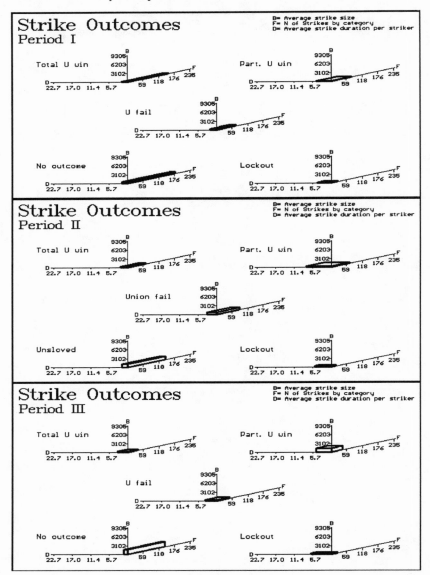

Table 5.16 cont'd.

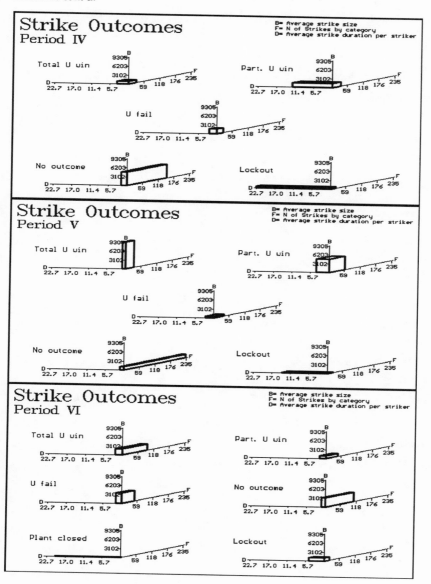

References

Aharoni, Y., & Lachman, R. (1980). Public and Private Sectors: Managerial Perspectives their Objectives. Working Paper No. 631/80. Tel Aviv: Tel Aviv University, Faculty of Management.

Aharoni, Y., Maimon, Z., & Segev, E. (1978). Performance and Autonomy in Organizations: Determining Dominant Environmental Components. *Management Science, 24,* 949-959.

Ashenfelter, A., & Johnson, G. E. (1969). Bargaining Theory, Trade Unions and Industrial Strike Activity. *American Economic Review, 59,* 35-49.

Baum, R. C. (1976). Introduction. In, *Explorations in General Theory in Social Science, Essays in Honor of Talcott Parsons* (J. L. B. R. C. E. A. A. L. Loubser, V. M., Eds) (pp. 448-469). New York: The Free Press.

Becker, A. (1982). *Im haZman uVnei haDor (With Time and Contemporaries)* (A. Shamir, Editor and consultant). Tel Aviv: Am Oved.

Becker, H. S. (Ed.). (1967). *Social Problems: A Modern Approach.* New York: Wiley.

Ben-Israel, R. (1978). Labor Court in Israel. *International Labor Review, 117,* 225-237.

Ben-Meir, D. (1978). *Ha'Histadrut (The Histadrut).* Jerusalem, Israel: Carta.

Blau, P. M., & Scott, W. R. (1962). *Formal Organizations, A Comparative Approach.* San Francisco: Chandler.

Britt, D., & Galle, O. (1974). Structural Antecedents of the Shape of Strikes: A Comparative Analysis. *American Sociological Review, 39,* 642-65.

Chamberlain, N. W. (1953). *Social Responsibility and Strikes.* New York: Harper.

Chamberlain, N. W., & Schilling, J. M. (1954). *The Impact of Strikes, Their Social and Economic Costs.* New York: Harper.

Chermesh, R. (1977). Strikes as Safety-Valve Institutions. *Industrial Relations/Relations Industrielles, 37,* 586-602.

Chermesh, R. (1979). Strikes: The Issue of Responsibility. *British Journal of Industrial Relations, 17,* 337-346.

Chermesh, R. (1982a). Press Criteria for Strike Reporting: Counting or Selective Presentation? *Social Science Research, 11,* 88-101.

Chermesh, R. (1982b). Strike Proneness and Characteristics of Industrial Relations Systems at the Organization Level: A Discriminant Analysis. *Journal of Management Studies,* 19(4), 413-435.

Chermesh, R. (1982cb). Strike Proneness and Characteristics of Industrial Relations Systems - A Discriminant Analysis. *Journal of Management Studies,* 19, 413-435.

Chermesh, R. (1984). The Autonomy of An Industrial Relations System, A Conceptual Myth or a Fact of Life. *Israel Social Science Research,* 2(1), 3-12.

Chermesh, R. (1985). Strikes as a Social Problem, A Social Problem Matrix Approach. *British Journal of Industrial Relations,* 23, 413-435.

Christenson, C. L. (1953). The Theory of the Offset Factor: The Impact of Labor Disputes upon Coal Production. *The American Economic Review,* 43, 513-547.

Dror, D., & Shirom, A. (1983). *Irgunei Ma'asikim beIsrael (Employers' Associations in Israel).* [Tel Aviv]: The Institute of Productivity; The Institute for the Advancement of Industrial Relations.

Dubin, R. (1960). A Theory of Conflict and Power in Union Management Relations. *Industrial and Labor Relations Review,* 13, 501-8.

Dunlop, J. T. (1958). *Industrial Relations Systems.* New York: Holt.

Economic and Social Research Institute. (1981). *Netunim Statistiyim, 1974-1980 (Statistical Data 1974-1980).* Tel Aviv: General Federation of Labor in Israel.

Eisenstadt, S. N. (1969). *Israeli Society.* London: Weidenfeld & Nicolson.

Estey, M. (1976). *The Unions, Structure, Development and Management.* New York: Harcourt Brace Jovanovich.

Fienberg, S. E. (1980). *The Analysis of Cross-Classified Categorical Data* (2nd ed.). Cambridge, Mass. and London, England: MIT Press.

Fischer, H. (1978). *Normative Behavior and Social Control of Labor Relations in Israel.* Doctoral dissertation, Haifa, Israel: Israel Institute of Technology.

Fischer, H., & Jacobsen, C. (1982). Unauthorized Strikes and Slowdowns in Israel: An Institutionalized Evasion of Union Rules. *British Journal of Industrial Relations,* 20, 342-7.

Flanders, A. (1970). Collective Bargaining: A Theoretical Analysis. In A. Flanders (Ed.), *Management and Unions, The Theory and Reform of Industrial Relations* (pp. 213-240). London: Faber.

Friedman, A. (1963). *Mehkar Va'adei Ovdim (Workers' Committees Study).* Tel Aviv: The Institute of Economic and Social Research.

Friedman, A. (1972). Workers' Committees and the Trade Union Department of the Histadrut - - Partners or Rivals. In A. Friedman (Ed.), *Structural*

Changes in Labor Unions (pp. 22-27). Tel Aviv: Industrial Relations Research Association of Israel.

Galin, A., & Krislov, J. (1979). Evaluating the Israeli Mediation Service. *International Labor Review, 118*, 487-497.

Galin-Goldfarb, A. (1972). *Collective Bargaining Process - Theoretical Models and Their Empirical Application* [Unpublished Doctoral Dissertation]

General Federation of Labor. (1978). *Takanon Vaadei Ovdim (Charter for Workers' Committees).* General Federation of Labor, The Executive Committee, The Trade Union Division.

Gilday, B. (Ed.). (1980). *Strikes in Israel and in the World.* Tel-Aviv: Institute for the Advancement of Labor Relations.

Hausmann, J., & Goldberg, M. (1977). *Labour Laws: Laws, Regulations, Orders, Commentaries, Precedents* (7th ed.). Tel Aviv: Sadan.

Hevrat Ha'Ovdim. (n.d.). Hevrat Ha'Ovdim 1982. The Economic Department, and Culture and Education Enterprises.

Hicks, J. R. (1963). *The Theory of Wages* (2nd ed.). New York: Macmillan.

Homans, G. C. (1961). *Social Behavior: Its Elementary Forms.* New York, Chicago, San Francisco, and Atlanta: Harcourt, Brace & World.

Institute for Economic and Social Research. (1977). *Statistical Yearbook 1968-1977* [Presented to the 13th Convention of the Histadrut]

Katz, D., & Kahn, R. L. (1966). *The Social Psychology of Organizations.* New York, Wiley.

Kerr, C., & Siegel, A. (1954). The Interindustry Propensity to Strike - An International Comparison. In *Industrial Conflict* A. W. Kornhauser, R. Dubin, & A. M. Ross (Eds) New York: McGraw-Hill.

Kitsuse, J. I., & Spector, M. (1975). Social Problems and Deviance: Some Parallel Issues. *Social Problems, 22*, 584-594.

Knoken, D., & Burke, P. J. (1980). *Log-Linear Models.* Beverly Hills, CA: Sage.

Krausz, M. (1980). Performance Appraisal Practices in a Highly Unionized Country. *Human Resources Management, 19*, 14-18.

Luhmann, N. (1979). *Trust and Power* (T. Burns & G. Poggi, Eds) (H. Davis, Raffan, John; Rooney, Kathryn) (trans., Poggi, Gianfranco). Chichester: J. Wiley.

Luhmann, N. (1982). *The Differentiation of Society* (S. Holmes & C. Larmore, Trans.). New York: Columbia University Press.

Merton, R. K. (1968). *Social Theory and Social Structure.* New York: The Free Press.

Merton, R. K., & Nisbet, R. (Eds). (1971). *Contemporary Social Problems* (3rd ed.). New York: Harcourt, Brace, Jovanovich.

Merton, R. K., & Nisbet, R. (1976). *Contemporary Social Problems* (4th ed.). New York: Harcourt, Brace, Jovanovich.

Michael, A., & Bar-El, R. (1977). *Shvitot beIsrael (Strikes in Israel).* Tel-Aviv: Bar-Ilan University and The Israel Institute of Industrial and Labor Relations.

Miller, D. C., & Form, W. H. (1964). *Industrial Sociology. The Sociology of Work Organizations* (2nd ed.). Harper.

Mills, C. W. (1959). *The Sociological Imagination.* New York: Oxford University Press.

Parsons, T. (1949). *The Structure of Social Action* (2nd ed.). Glencoe, Ill: Free Press.

Parsons, T., & Smelser, N. J. (1956). Economy and Society: *A Study in the Integration of Economic and Social Theory.* London: Routledge and Kegan Paul.

Pencavel, J. H. (1970). An Investigation into Industrial Strikes Activity in Britain. *Economica, 37,* 239-256.

Podak, K. (1986). Without Subject, Without Reason: Reflections on Niklas Luhmann's Social System. *Thesis Eleven, 13,* 54-66.

Reder, M. W., & Neumann, G. R. (1980). Conflict and Contracts: The Case of Strikes. *Journal of Political Economy, 88,* 867-886.

Reshef, Y. (1986). Political Exchange in Israel: Histadrut-State Relations. *Industrial Relations, 25,* 303-9.

Reshef, Y., & Bemmels, B. (1989). Political and Economic Determinants of Strikes in Israel: A Sectorial Comparison. *Economic and Industrial Democracy, 10,* 35-57.

Royal Commission on Trade Unions and Employers' Associations. (1968). *Report 1965-1968.* Cmnd 3623. London: Her Majesty's Stationary Office.

Schneider, E. V. (1969). *Industrial Sociology, The Social Relations of Industry and the Community* (2nd ed.). New York: McGraw-Hill.

Shirom, A. (1983). *Mavo leYahasei Avoda beIsrael (Introduction to Industrial Relations in Israel.* Tel Aviv: Am Oved.

Shirom, A. (1984). Employers' Associations in Israel J. P. Windmuller, & A. Gladstone. In *Employers Associations and Industrial Relations, A Comparative Study* (Chap. II, pp. 297-317). Oxford: Clarendon Press.

Shorter, E., & Tilly, C. (1974). *Strikes in France 1830-1968.* London: Cambridge University Press.

Smith, C. T. B., Clifton, R., Makeham, P., Creigh, S. W., & Burn, R. V. (1978). *Strikes in Britain* (Manpower Paper No. 15). London: Her Majesty's Stationary Office.

Snyder, D. (1975). Institutional Setting and Industrial Conflict: Comparative Analyses of France, Italy and the United States. *American Sociological Review*, 40(3), 259-278.

Spector, M., & Kitsuse, J. I. (1973). Social Problems: A Reformulation. *Social Problems*, 21, 145-158.

Stern, R. N. (1978). Methodological Issues in Quantitative Strike Analysis. *Industrial Relations*, 17(1), 32-42.

TSP. (1980). *Time Series Processor, User's Manual.* London, Canada: Computing Centre, The University of Western Ontario.

Vardi, Y., Shirom, A., & Jacobson, D. (1980). A Study on the Leadership Beliefs of Israeli Managers. *Academy of Management Journal*, 23, 367-374.

Weiss, P. A. (1971). *Hierarchically Organized Systems in Theory and Practice.* New York: Hafner Publishing Company.

Wolkinson, B. W., & Cohen, A. (1982). Use of Work Sanctions in Israeli Labor Disputes. *Journal of Industrial Relations*, 20, 231-246.

Zald, D. (1978). Management in Israel. *Business Horizons*, 21, 34-46.

Index

action defined, 85
agriculture, 25, 113, 114, 188, 194, 240
Aharoni, Y., 173, 182
Almogi, Yossef, 23
anthropologists, 12
anti-strike insurance fund, 208
Arab-Israeli conflict, 89
arbitration, 33, 133, 183, 185
Aridor, Yoram, 123
Ashdod Port, 23, 45, 52–53, 105, 113, 236
Ashenfelter, A., 150, 153, 233–34
Association of Industrialists, 33
Authority of State Enterprises, 13–14
autonomy: American IRS and, 143; of economic branches, 155; of Hevrat ha-Ovdim, 16; of Histadrut, 45, 55 182, 235–36; Histadrut bylaws and, 66; of industrial relations system, 34, 143; of Labor Court, 185–86; of local management, 173; Luhmann quoted on, 142, 165; of Manufacturers' Association, 38; social responsibility and, 222; systems and, 141–43, 145–46; of Teachers' Union, 41; of Trade Union Division, 41, 47; of unions, 104, 137; of workers' committee, 66. *See also* IRS autonomy

back-to-work orders, 27
Balfour Declaration, 235
banking industry, 114–15
Bank of Israel, 2, 22
Baram, U., 51
Bar-El, R., 124, 176, 178, 187, 233
Bar-Lev, Hayim, 44
Becker, Aharon: characteristics of, 42; Chermesh and, 236; decision-making process and, 236; Histadrut potency and, 16; Histadrut-state relations and, 41–42; IRS autonomy and, 147; Kessar supported by, 3; Meshel and, 46; Peretz and, 23–24, 45; ports and, 23; problem years under, 2; ranking system and, 23; strike approval and, 25; strike responsibility and, 137; Zionism and, 22, 42–43
Becker period: defensive

strikes in, 128;
Histadrut and, 235;
IRS development and,
158; lockout frequency
and, 121; multi-sector
strikes in, 119; public
sector strikes in, 119,
135; recognition
strikes in, 128; strike
approval and, 71, 129;
strike duration and,
137; strike frequency
and, 25, 107, 159; strike
success and, 132–33

Begin, Menachem, 29 n.10,
157

Ben-Aharon, Yitzhak, 2;
background of, 21;
changes by, 24; charac-
teristics of, 2, 21, 42;
cost-of-living
compensation and, 44;
election of, 2, 24, 237;
Histadrut and, 16–17,
24, 43–45; IRS auton-
omy and, 147, 238;
Kessar supported by, 3;
Peretz and, 45; Trade
Union Division and,
46; Zionism and, 42–43

Ben-Aharon period: illegal
strikes in, 65; IRS
autonomy and, 158;
Labor Relations
Officer and, 130; lock-
out frequency and,
121; multi-sector
strikes and, 118; occu-
pational comparisons
in, 107; port strikes in,
105; professional
strikes in, 110; public
sector strikes in, 119,
135; recognition
strikes in, 128; strike
approval and, 71, 129;

strike duration and,
104; strike frequency
and, 25, 104, 106, 159,
163; strike notification
and, 73, 130; strike size
and, 107; strike success
and, 132–33

Ben-Gurion, David, 15

Ben-Israel, R., 185

Ben-Meir, D., 37

Berglas, E., 50, 51

Blau, P. M., 218, 219

Britain, 87, 147, 150;
British administration, 13, 33

Britt, D., 87

Bruno, M., 50, 51

Bureau of Statistics, 121

Center of Local Government,
13–14

centralization, 16–17, 34, 38,
62, 78, 185

Chamberlain, N. W., 170,
217, 222, 231–32 n.3

Chasin Esh, 118

Chavez, Cesar, 114

Chermesh, Ran, 164, 178, 187,
189, 233–34, 236

Choushi, Aba, 23

Christenson, C. L., 228

Civil Service Code, 35

Civil Service Commission,
38

Civil Service Commissioner
(CSC), 13–14, 32, 34–35,
123

Cohen, A., 183

collective agreements: agricultural workers and,
114; employees' rights
and, 59; expiration of,
65; Israeli IRS and, 58,
59; legislation and, 11;
public sector and, 128;
status of, 59; strike declaration and, 65; strike

management norms
and, 63; strikes' goal
as, 110; Trade Union
Division and, 39; two
sides of, 58; union-
management interde-
pendence and, 217–18
Collective Agreements Law,
40
collective bargaining, 32, 35,
39, 60, 165, 220
collective negotiations, 59–
60, 146, 181, 185, 188
Commissioner of Industrial
Relations. *See* Labor
Relations Officer
Committee for Academic
Affairs, 62
Coordinating Bureau of
Economic
Associations (CBEA),
32, 33–34, 38, 53, 167
n.7
Coordinating Bureau of
Economic
Organization (CBEO),
10, 13, 14, 16, 49

Dash (Democrats for
Change), 19
Davar, 50–51
Denmark, 175
Department of Industrial
Relations, 148
Department of Labor
Relations, 39, 184–85,
189, 191–92. *See also*
Labor Relations
Officer
Department of Trade Union,
13
Diamond Manufacturers'
Association, 32
Dunlop, J. T., 5–6, 142, 143–
46, 150–51, 170

economy, Israeli: Becker
period and, 2, 24; 1984
elections and, 238;
Hevrat ha-Ovdim
and, 37; Histadrut and,
35, 212; ideology and,
165; inflation crisis in,
1 (*see also* new eco-
nomic policy); Israeli
IRS and, 54–55; multi-
employer strikes and,
135; National Unity
government and, 3,
27; nationalization of,
235; 1992 challenge to,
239; Peres and, 28;
private sector strike
approval rates and,
207; recession (1966-
67), 2, 205; Six Day
War and, 2, 205;
strikes' effect on, 187
education, 15, 37
Egypt, 92
Ehkol, Levi, 29 n.3
Ehlrich, Simha, 41
employers' associations:
defined, 31–32; emer-
gence of, 13; Hevrat ha-
Ovdim and, 36–37;
Histadrut and, 38;
ideology of, 34; Likud
period and, 237;
Manufacturers'
Association and, 38;
private sector, 32–34,
206–8; public sector and,
34–35; sector interests
and, 207; social problem
matrix and, 183–84;
strike contract and, 196.
*See also names of
specific employers'
associations*
Eretz Israel, 9
Eshkol, Levi, 236

Europe, 19, 143
European Economic
      Community, 239
extension regulations, 12–13

Farmers' Association, 32, 114
Fischer, H., 62–63, 71, 82
Flanders, A., 146
France, 60, 233
Free Education Act, 50
Friedman, Abraham, 70–71,
      123, 174, 181
functional differentiation,
      89, 164

Galin-Goldfarb, A., 39, 179,
      183, 185
Galle, O., 87
General Federation of Labor,
      16, 40, 104, 117, 239.
      See also Histadrut
Golan, Asher, 44
Gothelf, Y., 43
Government Companies
      Law, 35
Guttman, Louis, 22–23

Haaretz, 54
Haberfeld, Hayim, 28, 46–47,
      51, 53
Haifa, 23, 41, 58, 138, 221
Hevrat ha-Ovdim (HHO):
      autonomy of, 16;
      economic boost by, 37;
      employers' associa-
      tions and, 36–37;
      evolution of, 41;
      Histadrut and, 9–10,
      14, 32, 35; Likud period
      and, 238; operative
      directorate of, 35–36;
      strikes and, 37
Histadrut: administrative
      divisions of, 38; arbi-
      tration and, 183;
      authority sources for,

40; autonomy of, 45,
      55, 182, 235–36; back-
      to-work orders and,
      183; Ben-Aharon's
      election and, 237;
      concerns of, 181–82;
      Convention institu-
      tion of, 21–22, 36; cost-
      of-living allowance
      and, 53; Council
      institution of, 22, 36;
      critical dilemma for,
      235; as democratic
      organization, 90;
      differentiation level
      of, 240; disciplinary
      option and, 129;
      divisions of, 10;
      economy and, 35, 53–
      54, 212; effects of strike
      activity on, 202–6; elec-
      tions in, 1–2; employ-
      ers' associations and,
      34, 38; establishment
      of, 9, 235; establish-
      ment of Israel and,
      240; Executive
      Committee of, 22, 36,
      44; extended strikes
      and, 37; external envi-
      ronment of, 40–41,
      240; Friedman and,
      123; functions of, 10;
      godfather role by, 202,
      203, 213; Hevrat ha-
      Ovdim and, 9–10, 14,
      32 35; ideology and,
      165, 182, 239; immigra-
      tion and, 9; industrial
      reality and values of,
      183; inflation crisis
      and, 49–50; internal
      environment of, 41;
      Israeli IRS and, 15–16,
      31, 189, 239; Jewish
      national revival

movement and, 9; Labor Party and, 15, 19–20, 22, 41, 158–59; labor unrest blamed on, 17; leadership changes in, 90; Likud Party and, 27, 41, 123–24, 237; local management and, 172–73; meeting approvals by, 67–68; member voting and, 21; membership volume in, 39, 40; minimum wage act and, 34; multi-purpose conception of, 9, 239; national trade unions and, 238; new economic policy and, 53–54; organization division of, 41; Peres and, 238; Peretz and, 23, 45; power of, 23–24, 78, 176; public sector strike approval and, 207–8; public utilities sector and, 203; recognition strikes in, 128; redefinition of identity of, 3, 26; responsibility and, 137, 182; restraint policy by, 160; social differentiation and, 15; social loyalty by, 17–18; social problem analysis and, 203, 206, 212; state's commonalities with, 1–2; state's relation with, 40–41; strike approval and, 66–67, 70–71, 78, 182; strike avoidance by, 124; strike concern and, 189, 213; strike data and, 63; strike follow-up and, 203; strike frequency and, 96, 117, 119, 204; strike size and, 26, 118, 130–31, 177; strike success and, 124, 176; subsidiary relationships with, 41; survival of, 239, 240; Teachers' Union and, 41; third party role by, 40, 184; three elements of membership in, 35; trade union element of, 9, 46 (*see also* Trade Union Division); transformation of, 3–4; unemployment and, 18, 37; warning strikes and, 124; wildcat strikes and, 183; work sanctions and, 182–83; workers' committees and, 21, 22, 78, 174, 183. *See also* Becker, Aharon; Ben-Aharon, Yitzhak; Hevrat ha-Ovdim; Kessar, Israel; Meshel, Yeruham

Histadrut bylaws: dismissal authority and, 21; non-exploitative independent worker and, 48; quoted, 61–62; strike approval and, 128, 151, 175, 195; subordinate Histadrut units and, 41; workers' meetings and, 66, 69

Histadrut ha-Morim, 97

Histadrut ha-Pkidim, 97

Histadrut Ovdei ha-Medina, 97

Histadrut Poalei ha-Matechet, 97

Homans, G. C., 233

Hurowitz, David, 2

immigration, 19
industrial disputes study
    (IDS): as data source,
    62–63; methodology
    by, 63; secret balloting
    and, 70, 80; strike noti-
    fication, 75–76, 77;
    strike prohibition and,
    65; workers' commit-
    tees and, 65; workers'
    meetings and, 67
industrial relations system
    (IRS): actors in, 31 (*see
    also* employers' asso-
    ciations; third parties;
    unions); autonomy of,
    34, 143; in Britain, 150;
    as collectivistic entity,
    8; contextual con-
    straints on, 122;
    defined, 29 n.2;
    diverse forms of, 13;
    Dunlop model of, 5–8,
    143–46, 151, 170;
    elements of, 5;
    environmental
    contexts of, 6; Meshel
    and, 3; as multi-level
    construct, 153; non-
    demand related strikes
    and, 181; responsibility
    characteristic of, 220;
    social system theory
    and, 142; strike regula-
    tion and, 7–8; symbolic
    interaction and, 122;
    systems and, 4–5; two
    models of, 60; two-
    dimensional construct
    of, 151; in United
    States, 143, 150. *See
    also* Israeli IRS
Institute for Economic and
    Social Research, 63,
    120, 148
Institute for Production and

Incomes, 152;
International Labor Office
    (ILO), 175
Irgun Ha-Morim ha-Al-
    Yesodi'im, 97
IRS autonomy: Ben-Aharon
    and, 238; crystalliza-
    tion of, 147; decision
    making and, 158, 165;
    functional considera-
    tions and, 229;
    Histadrut and, 15, 239;
    indicators of, 136;
    Kessar and, 238–39;
    Labor period and, 237;
    Likud period and, 164,
    165; Luhmann and,
    234; National Unity
    period and, 236; 1984
    elections and, 238;
    political upheaval
    and, 165; political
    variables and, 135–36;
    responsibility and, 218,
    229–30; social differen-
    tiation and, 15; strike
    analysis and, 147
Israeli army, 17, 89
Israeli Institute for the
    Advancement of
    Labor Relations, 174–
    75
Israeli IRS: actors element of,
    9–10; CBEA and, 33–34;
    centralization and, 16–
    17; changes in, 18; col-
    lective agreements
    and, 58, 59; economy
    and, 24, 54–55; educa-
    tion and, 15; employer
    unity and, 31; future
    of, 238, 241; Histadrut
    and, 9, 28, 31, 240;
    ideology and, 11–13;
    industrial-sectoral-
    occupational level of,

14; Labor Party and, 9, 237; legislation and, 11; local management of, 171–73; local unions and, 173–74; Manufacturers' Association and, 33; as multi-level system, 21–22; national level of, 13–14; organizational tier of, 14–15; political nation-state interaction by, 235; pre-independence, 58; problematic stage of, 137; revitalization of, 189; rules element and, 11; sector differentiation and, 136; social loyalty and, 17–18; third parties and, 39; two-tier structure of, 78; uniqueness of, 8–9; unstated assumptions of, 16–18. *See also* IRS autonomy
Italy, 60, 175

Jerusalem, 41
Jerusalem Post, The, 51, 53
Jewish Agency, 115
Jewish homeland, 235
Jewish national revival movement, 9
job security, 161, 205
Johnson, G. E., 150, 153
Judges Law, 186

Kerr, C., 233
Kessar, Israel, 3; background of, 28; economic crisis and, 17; election campaign by, 28, 50; IRS autonomy and, 147, 238–39; new economic policy and, 51, 52–53, 54; objectives of, 47; Trade Union Division and, 46–47; umbrella policy and, 28; unemployment and, 47
Kessar period: defensive strikes in, 128; Histadrut and, 235–36; multi-sector strikes in, 119; recognition strikes in, 128; strike approval and, 71; strike duration and, 137; strike frequency in, 96, 126, 159; strike size and, 104
Kessar/Likud period, 73, 96, 118, 121, 135
Kessar/Unity period: clerical worker strikes in, 111; external strike factors and, 130; Histadrut strike frequency and, 124; lockout frequency and, 121; national committee strikes and, 112; para-professional strikes in, 110; port strikes and, 105; professional strikes in, 110; public sector strikes in, 119, 135; strike approval and, 129; strike causes and, 127; strike duration and, 104; strike frequency and, 106, 107; strike notification and, 73, 130; strike size and, 107, 118; strike success and, 132–33; technical-professional strikes in, 111; warning strikes in, 125–26
Knesset: inflation crisis and, 50; Labor Party and, 19;

labor relations debate
by, 43; National Unity
government and, 1;
new economic policy
and, 53, 54; 1977 elec-
tions of, 237; strike
frequency and, 149
Koor, 10, 240
Korpi, W., 143
Kupat Cholim, 18, 118, 238,
240

Labor Alignment, 1, 16, 82
n.8
Labor Court, 184; autonomy
of, 185–86; collective
bargaining
participation by, 39;
composition of, 186;
establishment of, 39,
185, 186; social prob-
lem matrix and, 189;
strike contract and,
196; strike follow-up
and, 203; strike pat-
terns and, 266; strike
size and, 10, 131;
success of, 186; third
party concern about,
191
Labor Court Law, 185–86
Labor Disputes Law, 72–73
Labor Party: back-to-work
orders and, 27; Ben-
Aharon and, 2, 24;
defeat of, 26, 233, 237;
dependence on, 20;
divisions and unifica-
tions of, 82 n.8;
domination by, 18–21
(*see also* Labor period);
employment and, 236;
Executive Committee
and, 44; government
functional problems
and, 200; Histadrut

and, 15, 19–20, 22, 41,
158–59; ideological
support by, 17; immi-
gration and, 19, 20;
industrialization and,
33; IRS legislation and,
11; labor representa-
tion reform and, 189;
loyalty to, 21; Meshel
and, 2; political
control by, 9; 1977
political upheaval
and, 149; strike
approval and, 71;
Trade Union Division
and, 38; workers'
committees and, 20;
Yom Kippur War and,
19. *See also* National
Unity government
Labor period: government
functional problems
and, 200; Histadrut
follow-up and, 203;
Histadrut sector
strikes in, 204; Israeli
IRS and, 236, 237;
lockouts in, 205; public
sector strikes and, 163;
private sector strikes
in, 206; strike causes
and, 205–6; strike
frequency and, 160,
198, 199, 237; strike
notification and, 209;
warning strikes in,
126; wildcat strikes in,
199; workers' commit-
tees strike causes and,
210–11. *See also*
Meshel/Labor period
Labor Relations Officer:
authority of, 184; as
congenial partner, 185;
external factors and,
130; intervention by,

195; IRS levels and, 14; national unions and, 78; political change and, 213; preventive function of, 130; social problem matrix and, 197; strike contract and, 196; strike notification and, 72–74, 76–77, 130, 208–10; strike size and, 10, 130–31; strike statistics and, 208

Lachman, R., 173

Law of Collective Agreements, 39

Law of Dispute Resolution, 97

Law of Industrial Disputes Resolution, 73–74

Lebanon War, 1, 18, 27, 50, 238

Levy, David, 123–24

Lewinson, Yaacov, 41

Likud Party: back-to-work orders and, 27; election of, 26, 158, 237; failures of, 1; General Federation of Labor and, 239; Histadrut and, 27, 41; ideology and, 90, 200; IRS autonomy and, 158, 164; labor representation reform and, 189; legislation and, 11, 27; Moslem support of, 19; negotiation intervention by, 123; reorganization plans by, 237; strike frequency and, 160. *See also* National Unity government

Likud period: contract expiration and, 203; government functional problems in, 200; Histadrut and, 124, 203, 204, 213; Israeli IRS and, 164, 165, 236; lockouts in, 205; management and, strike impact on, 210; pre-election period and, 149; private sector strikes in, 206; public sector strikes in, 204; social problem matrix and, 212; strike approval in, 71; strike causes and, 205–6; strike contracts and, 206; strike frequency in, 199, 238; strike notification and, 209; strike size in, 26, 238; warning strikes in, 27, 125; wildcat strikes in, 199. *See also* Kessar/Likud period; Meshel/Likud period

lockouts: dominant party variable and, 205; frequency of, 121; notification and, 73; prevention of, 205; social problems and, 195; strikes v., 120–21, 195–97, 210; timespan of, 112–13

Luhmann, Niklas: autonomy and, 54–55, 142, 165, 234; decision making and, 50; Israeli strike analysis and, 234; neofunctionalistic approach by, 164; political subsystem and, 137; system approach and, 88–89, 141

management: banking
strikes and, 114–15;
collective agreements
and, 11, 146; Histadrut
and, 9–10, 117, 172–73;
ideology and, 12;
interdependence with
unions by, 217–18; of
Israeli IRS, 171–73;
Labor Court and, 39;
Likud Party and, 26; as
major actor, 12;
national level IRS
and, 13–14; organiza-
tion-level, 15; owner-
ship sector variable
and, 155; political
pressure on, 147; social
problem analysis and,
164, 179–81, 192; social
responsibility analysis
and, 222, 223–24; stop-
page initiation and,
120–21; strike avoid-
ance by, 25; strike
frequency economic
model and, 150; strike
impact on, 210; strike
shaping and, 153;
union relations with,
122. *See also* strike
management norms
Manufacturers' Association
of Israel (MAI), 32, 33,
34, 38, 167 n.7
Mapai, 9, 42, 82 n.8
Mapam, 82 n.8
meetings, 68. *See also* workers' meetings
Meir, Golda, 43
Merton, R. K., 169
Meshel, Yeruham:
background of, 2, 3, 25;
Becker and, 46;
Chermesh and, 234;
government relations

and, 17; Histadrut and,
17, 25; IRS autonomy
and, 147
Meshel period: Histadrut
and, 2–3; illegal strikes
in, 65; multi-sector
strikes in, 118–19; port
strikes in, 105; profes-
sional unions and,
106; skilled-worker
strikes in, 111; strike
approval in, 129; strike
frequency in, 25, 96,
104, 159; strike notifi-
cation and, 73;
technical-professional
strikes in, 111; Trade
Union Division and,
46; wage delay strikes
in, 128
Meshel/Labor period:
external strike factors
and, 130; lockout
frequency in, 121;
para-professional
strikes in, 110; public
sector strike size and,
135; recognition
strikes in, 128; strike
approval and, 129;
strike notification and,
130; strike responsibil-
ity and, 25; strike size
and, 26, 107; strike
success and, 132–33;
warning strikes and,
122
Meshel/Likud period:
external strike factors
and, 130; lockouts in,
113, 121; national
committee strikes and,
112; para-professional
strikes in, 110; public
sector strike size and,
135; recognition

strikes in, 128; strike
approval and, 129;
strike frequency and,
117; strike notification
and, 130; strike size
and, 26–27, 107, 118;
strike success and, 132;
warning strikes and,
122, 126
Michael, A., 124, 176, 178,
187, 233
minimum wage legislation,
34
Moda'i, Y., 49, 50, 51

national committees, 10, 15,
111–12
National Insurance Institute
(NII), 50
National Union of Clerical,
Administrative and
Public Service
Employees (UCAPSE),
97, 98, 104, 136
National Union of
Government
Employees (NUGE),
97–98, 104, 136
National Union of Metal,
Electric and Electronic
Workers, 97
national unions:
contradictory strate-
gies of, 78; local
disputes and, 183;
rational unions and,
60; strike approval
and, 66, 70, 175; strike
data and, 87; strike
declarations by, 111;
strike notification and,
76; strike size and, 112
National Unity government:
economic policy by, 3;
prime ministers of, 27;
formation of, 15, 27–

28, 50; inflation and,
49
National Unity period:
government func-
tional problems and,
200; Histadrut and, 15,
203, 204, 213; IRS
autonomy and, 236;
management and,
strike impact on, 210;
private sector strikes
in, 205, 206; public
sector strikes in, 204–5;
strike approval in, 72,
206; strike causes and,
205–6, 210–11; strike
frequency in, 160, 198,
199; strike notification
and, 209; wildcat
strikes in, 199; work-
ers' committees and,
210–11. *See also*
Kessar/Unity period
new economic policy:
Haberfeld and, 51;
Histadrut and, 53–54,
203; Kessar and, 51, 52,
54; Knesset vote and,
53, 54; labor legislation
and, 28; main points
of, 49; media reports
on, 49, 50-51, 54; Peres
and, 28, 50–51; Yaacobi
and, 52
Nisbet, R., 169
Norma Rae, 128
Northrup, H.R., 122

Of Time and Men, 46
Organization of High School
Teachers, 136. *See also*
Union of High School
Teachers

Palestine, 235
Parsonian theory, 187, 188

Parsons, Talcott, 85, 141, 187
Pencavel, J. H., 150, 160
Peres, Shimon, 1, 17, 27, 28, 49, 50, 52, 238
Peretz, Yehoshua, 23–24, 45, 113
Performance and Autonomy in Organizations: Determining Dominant Environmental Components, 182
Ports Authority, 105, 113
price change, 7–8
private sector: anti-strike insurance fund and, 208; diverse strike patterns in, 137; dominant party variable and, 206; employers' associations in, 32–34, 206–8: social problem analysis and, 208; strike approval and, 207; strike frequency in, 117, 119, 187–88
public sector: collective agreements and, 128; constitution of, 34; employment cut in, 49; employment terms in, 35; Histadrut strike approval and, 207–8; Israeli social center and, 187; Likud period and, 204; local management and, 173; new economic policy and, 52, 54; ranking of, 23; size of, 146; strike causes and, 15, 119; strike frequency and, 115, 117, 119, 147–48, 163, 233; strike size and, 135; wage-

increase strikes in, 24; warning strikes and, 124–25; workers' committees' influence on, 173

Red Haifa, 58
Regional Commissioners of Industrial Relations, 171
Revisionist movement, 27

Sadat, Anwar, 1
Sapir, Pinhas, 43
Schilling, J. M., 217, 231–32 n.3
Scott, W. R., 218, 219
secret ballots, 70, 80
segmentation, 89, 164
Settlement of Labor Disputes, 39, 175, 184
Sha'ar, 51
Shalev, M., 143
Shamai, Yaacov, 52, 53
Shamir, Yitzhak, 1, 27, 50
Shorter, E., 87, 233
Sick Fund, 47, 118, 238, 240
Siegel, A., 233
Six Day War, 1, 2, 18, 19, 92, 114, 205
Snyder, D., 60, 143, 233
social evolution, 88–89
social problem defined, 169
social problem matrix, 169–70; components of, 170; criticism of, 192; dispute type variable and, 197; economic branch variable and, 194; employers' associations and, 183–84; followup treatment and, 196–97; government actions and, 192; Histadrut and, 181–83, 203, 206, 212; interna-

tional comparisons on, 175; Likud goals and, 200; local management and, 179–81; lockout-or-strike variable and, 195–96; management and, 192; method of analysis and, 198–99; ownership sector variable and, 195; private sector employers and, 208; relevant factors of, 170; strike causes and, 196; strike concern and, 192; strike contract and, 196; strike notification and, 197; strike outcome variable and, 197–98; subjective analysis of, 169; third parties and, 184–86; union and management opinion on, 178; workers' committees and, 181, 211–12

social responsibility analysis: autonomy and, 222; consumer organizations' power and, 229; damage assessment and, 226–29; distrust and, 229; IRS autonomy and, 218, 229–30; management behavior and, 222, 223–24; method for, 221; model for, 218–20; results of, 222–25; strike frequency and, 226; union behavior and, 222–23, 224–25, 229; workers' meetings and, 224

social responsibility defined, 217

social system theory, 141–42
sociologists, 12
Solel Boneh, 10, 37, 240
State Labor Court, 14
Stern, R. N., 88, 118, 158, 160
stratification, 89, 164, 165
strike approval: authority for, 175; conformity profiles and, 81; dominant party variable and, 206; economic effects and, 207; government role in, 202; Histadrut and, 66–67, 70–71, 78, 182; Histadrut bylaws and, 128, 151, 195; national unions and, 66, 70; National Unity period and, 206; party comparisons on, 129; period variable and, 262–63; political parties and, 71–72; private sector and, 207; secret balloting and, 70; secretary generals and, 71–72, 129; social balance and, 128–29; strike management norms and, 79; strike size and, 129–30; strike success and, 176; by union representative, 70–72; variables in analysis of, 71–72, 90–91; workers' committees and, 196

strike breadth. *See* strike size
strike concern, 189–92, 212–13
strike damage, 25, 97, 120, 178, 217. *See also* social responsibility analysis
strike data/statistics: compilation method

of, 63; inclusions of, 151, 193; as informational source, 62–63; Labor Relations Officer and, 208; occupational diversity and, 110–11; purpose of, 193; for social responsibility model, 221; sources of, 148, 175; strike duration and, 92; strike effectivity and, 197; study of strikes and, 86–87; technology of collecting, 87

strike declaration: collective agreement and, 65; owner vulnerability and, 224; rules for, 217; workers' committees and, 65–67, 111–12; workers' meetings and, 66

strike duration: calculation of, 193; clerical-government union comparison on, 104; collective negotiation and, 188; defined, 158; determinants of, 118; downward trend of, 95; economic branches and, 114; in Kessar/Unity period, 97; multi-sector strikes and, 118–19; non-instrumental strikes and, 133; political indication of, 147; in private sector finance, 137; public utilities and, 188; solidarity strikes and, 126; strike notification and, 209; strike opposition and,

68; strike success and, 177, 181; warning strikes and, 126; workers' councils and, 112; workers' meetings and, 126

strike frequency: blue collar unions and, 103; capital return and, 163; data on, 95–96; decision-making process and, 117–18; defined, 158; dominant party variable and, 117, 135, 160, 198–99, 237–38; economic and political variables and, 234; economic branch variable and, 113, 250–53; economic model of, 150; election periods and, 149–50; fluctuations in, 104, 158; governmental sector and, 119; Histadrut and, 117, 119, 204; independent variables and, 160–61; IRS autonomy and, 159; IRS functioning and, 164; Knesset periods and, 149; media coverage and, 187; Meshel/Likud period and, 96; occupational variable and, 105–7, 111, 147; ownership sector variable and, 147–48; private sector and, 119, 187–88; public sector and, 115, 117, 119, 163, 187–88, 233; secretary general variable and, 96, 135, 136, 159–60; social damage and, 178–79;

social responsibility and, 226; strike cause variable and, 258–61; strike success and, 133; teachers' unions and, 103–4; unemployment and, 236; union variable and, 97; warning strikes and, 126; workers' meetings and, 126

Strike Fund, 78, 129, 237

strike management norms: secret balloting and, 70, 80; strike approval and, 70–72, 79; strike notification and, 72–77; strike prohibition and, 65; workers' meetings and, 66–69

strike notification: dominant party variable and, 130, 209; industrial disputes study and, 75–76, 77; Labor Relations Officer and, 72–74, 76–77, 130, 208–10; national unions and, 76; secretary general variable, 73, 130; short-term strikes and, 130; social problem analysis and, 197; strike size and duration and, 209; timespan for, 184, 197; Trade Union Division and, 76; workers' committees and, 74, 75, 76, 77

strike patterns: banking industry and, 114–15; calculation of, 193; economic branches and, 113–15; Histadrut involvement and, 264–65; industrial rela-

tions department involvement and, 267; Labor Court involvement and, 266; market-related industries and, 177; mediator involvement and, 268–69; methodology for analyzing, 107; occupational variable and, 107, 110, 247–48; ownership sector variable and, 119, 254–55; port strikes and, 105; private sector and, 117; public utilities sector and, 177; secretary general variable and, 157–58; sectoral affiliations and, 137; strike initiator variable and, 111–13, 249; strike outcome and, 270–71; strike research and, 87–88; strike type variable and, 256–57; three dimensions of, 88; union type variable and, 245–46; variations of, 104–5. *See also* strike duration; strike frequency; strike size

strike research, 87–88

strike size: calculation of, 193; defined, 158; economic branches and, 113; Histadrut and, 130–31, 177; increase of, 95, 104; international comparisons on, 175; Labor Court and, 131; labor market structure and, 118; Labor Relations

Officer and, 130–31; Likud period and, 27, 238; mediators and, 131–32; Meshel period and, 26–27; national committees and unions and, 112; occupational variable and, 107, 111; political economic fluctuations and, 160; public sector and, 135, 188; responsibility and, 137; strike approval and, 26–27, 129–30; strike effectiveness and, 176–77; strike notification and, 209; teachers' strikes and, 134–35; unions and, 135; wage strikes and, 128

strikes: avoidance of, 25; Ben-Aharon's policy on, 25, 26; British, 147; causes of, 126–28, 153, 196, 205–6, 210–11; context of, 85–86, 113; defensive, 128, 139 n.16; effectiveness of, 132–33, 137, 175, 181 (*see also* social problem matrix); external factors and, 130; factors frequenting, 17; forms of, 121, 122, 197; grading system reform and, 2; Histadrut bylaws on, 61–62; instrumental, 181, 210, 211; Israeli scenario of, 58; late payment and, 127–28; v. lockouts, 120–21, 195–96; macrosocial analysis of, 186–89; media coverage of, 58; multi-sector, 117, 118–19; new economic policy and, 52–53; noninstrumental, 133; occupational classification of, 110–11; offensive, 139 n.16; prohibition of, 33, 65; ranking system and, 23; recognition of, 128; regulation of, 7–8; as social action, 85; social goal attainment and, 187; strikebreaking and, 59–60; unemployment and, 161; union challenge in calling, 59–60; union membership support of, 60; in United States, 57–58, 143; in Western Europe, 143. *See also* wildcat strikes

Switzerland, 175

systems, 4–5, 141–43, 145–46. *See also* industrial relations system

Teachers' Union, 41, 136. *See also* Union of Teachers

Tel-Aviv, 41, 113

third parties: actors as, 184; Histadrut role as, 40; labor courts and, 39; local IRS and, 171; main actor behavior and, 222; social problem matrix and, 184–86; social responsibility and, 226; strike concern by, 191–92; strike size and, 133. *See also* Labor Court; Labor Relations Officer

Tilly, C., 87, 233
Time Series Processor (TSP), 153
Trade Union Department, 58–59, 62, 82 n.5
Trade Union Division: autonomy of, 15–16, 41, 47; Ben-Aharon and, 24, 46; Histadrut's relationship with, 46; industrial relation negotiations by, 213; Kessar and, 46–47; labor representation by, 38; Likud reorganization plans and, 237; Meshel and, 25, 46; national level IRS and, 13, 14; officers of, 38–39; as political organization, 146–47; reform in, 18; sector nondiscrimination by, 40; status of, 38, 39; strike approval and, 175; strike notification and, 76; Teachers' Union and, 41; work conditions and, 36

unapproved strikes. *See* wildcat strikes
unemployment, 7–8, 18, 37, 47, 161, 236
Union of High School Teachers, 97, 103–4. *See also* Organization of High School Teachers
Union of Metal Workers, 103, 104
Union of Teachers, 97, 103–4. *See also* Teachers' Union
Union of the Ports Operation Workers, 105

union sanctions, 61, 82 n.3
unions: agriculture and, 114; autonomy of, 104, 137; civil service and, 97–98; economic, 174; economic activity and, 85; General Federation of Labor and, 16; interdependence with management by, 217–18; IRS ideology and, 12–13; local, 2, 173–74, 177 (*see also* workers' committees; workers' councils); member support of, 60; occupational classification of, 105; pre-Histadrut, 9; recognition strikes and, 128; social responsibility and, 222–23, 224–25; strategy of, 105; strike effectiveness and, 60; strike size and, 135; workers' meetings and, 68–69. *See also* Histadrut; national unions; *names of specific unions*
United States, 57–58, 60, 150

Va'ada Menahelet, 36

Wages Deputy, 13–14
warning strikes, 121–24
Weizman, Hayim, 235
wildcat strikes: decrease of, 202; dominant party variable and, 199; employers' associations and, 183, 206; failure of, 181; government and, 202; Histadrut and, 183; institutionalization

and, 187; private sector
and, 206; social prob-
lem matrix and, 196;
stoppages and, 182;
strike effectiveness
and, 176–77, 187;
workers' committees
and, 196
Wilkinson, B. W., 183
workers' sanctions, 182–83
workers' committees:
authority of, 174; by-
law deviation by, 67;
centralization and, 62;
disciplinary actions
toward, 236; elections
to, 174; Friedman and,
70–71, 174; Histadrut
and, 21, 22, 61–62, 78,
174, 183; Labor Party
and, 20; local
management and, 179;
member decision-
making and, 78;
national unions and,
78; new economic
policy strike and, 52–
53; political change
and, 213; power of, 65–
66; public sector influ-
ence by, 173; social

problem matrix and,
211–12; strike approval
and, 196; strike causes
and, 210–11; strike
contract and, 196;
strike declaration and,
65–67, 111–12; strike
evaluation by, 181;
strike notification and,
74, 75, 76, 77; strike v.
lockout and, 197;
union loyalty by, 174;
wildcat strikes and,
175, 196; workers'
representation by, 173–
74
workers' councils, 21, 61–62,
66–67, 111, 175
workers' meetings, 66–69,
122–26, 175, 224
World War II, 33, 143

Yaacobi, Gad, 52
Yishuv, 9, 58, 157
Yom Kippur War, 1, 18, 19,
95, 149
Young, H.A., 122

Zionism, 42–43, 114
Zionists, 9, 22, 29 n.4, 33

About the Author

RAN CHERMESH is Senior Lecturer in the Department of Behavioral Sciences, Ben-Gurion University, Beer-Sheva, Israel. His writings on industrial relations have appeared in the *Journal of Management Studies*, the *British Journal of Industrial Relations*, *Social Science Research*, and other journals in the field.